Targeting Pronunciation

Communicating Clearly in English

SECOND EDITION

Sue F. Miller

Australia Canada Mexico Singapore Spain United Kingdom United States

Targeting Pronunciation
Communicating Clearly in English
Sue F. Miller

Publisher: Patricia A. Coryell
Director of ESL Publishing: Susan Maguire
Senior Development Editor: Kathleen Sands Boehmer
Development Editor: Lida Baker
Editorial Assistant: Evangeline Bermas
Senior Project Editor: Margaret Park Bridges
Manufacturing Coordinator: Carrie Wagner
Senior Marketing Manager: Annamarie Rice

Cover image: Harold Burch

Credits: CHAPTER 2: "Getting To Know You" (Richard Rodgers and Oscar Hammerstein II). Copyright © 1951 by Richard Rodgers and Oscar Hammerstein II. Copyright Renewed. WILLIAMSON MUSIC owner of publication and allied rights throughout the World. International Copyright Secured. All Rights Reserved. Used by Permission. CHAPTER 4: "This Land Is Your Land" (Woody Guthrie) copyright © 1956 and 1958 by TRO-Ludlow Music, BMI. CHAPTER 10: "Timothy Boon," from *Fairies and Suchlike* by Ivy O. Eastwick, copyright 1946 by E.P. Dutton & Co. Inc., renewed © 1974 by Ivy Olive Eastwick. Used by permission of Dutton Children's Books, A Division of Penguin Young Readers Group, A Member of Penguin Group (USA) Inc., 345 Hudson Street, New York, NY 10014. All rights reserved. • "Oh, What a Beautiful Mornin'" by Richard Rodgers and Oscar Hammerstein II. Copyright © 1943 by WILLIAMSON MUSIC. Copyright Renewed. International Copyright Secured. All Rights Reserved. Used by Permission. CHAPTER 11: "Sneezles" by A.A. Milne, from *Now We Are Six* by A.A. Milne, illustrated by E.H. Shepard, copyright © 1927 by E.P. Dutton, renewed © 1955 by A.A. Milne. Used by permission of Dutton Children's Books, A Division of Penguin Young Readers Group, A Member of Penguin Group (USA) Inc., 345 Hudson Street, New York, NY 10014. All rights reserved. • "Leaving on a Jet Plane." Words and Music by John Denver. Copyright © 1967 Cherry Lane Music Publishing Company, Inc. (ASCAP) and DreamWorks Songs (ASCAP). Rights for DreamWorks Songs Administered by Cherry Lane Music Publishing Company, Inc. International Copyright Secured. All Rights Reserved. • "Single Slices," by Peter Kohlsaat. Copyright © 2001 Tribune Media Services. Reprinted with permission. CHAPTER 12: Text from Delta Airlines ad. Used with permission from Delta Airlines/BBDO South. Copyright © 1995 Delta Airlines, Inc. • "Pronunciation Rap" by Ellen Stein. Copyright © 1997 Ellen F. Stein/Dr. Goose Music, Inc., Closter, NJ. All rights reserved. Used by permission.

Copyright © 2007 by Thomson Heinle, part of The Thomson Corprotation. Thomson the Star logo, and Heinle are trademarks used herein under license.

All rights reserved. No part of this work covered by the copyright hereon may be reproduced or used in any form or by any means—graphic, electronic, or mechanical, including photocopying, recording, taping, Web distribution or information storage and retrieval systems—without the written permission of the publisher.

Printed in Canada.
3 4 5 6 7 8 9 10 09 08 07

For more information contact Thomson Heinle, 25 Thomson Place, Boston, MA 02210 USA, or visit our Internet site at elt.thomson.com

For permission to use material from this text or product, submit a request online at http://www.thomsonrights.com

Any additional questions about permissions can be submitted by email to thomsonrights@thomson.com

Library of Congress Control Number: 2003116183

ISBN-13: 978-0-618-44418-2
ISBN-10: 0-618-44418-1

CONTENTS

To the Student vi
To the Teacher viii
Key to Symbols xi
Acknowledgments xiv

UNIT I GETTING STARTED

Chapter 1: Improving Your Pronunciation   1

Part 1: Setting Goals 1
Pronunciation Targets 1
Goals Survey 3
Your Speech-Effectiveness Level 4

Part 2: Assessing Your Pronunciation Priorities 5
Listening to English Survey 5
Pronunciation Survey: Making a Speech Tape 9

Part 3: Making Your New Pronunciation a Habit 11
Where Do I Start? 11
  Self-Monitoring 11
  "Use It Or Lose It:" *Making Small Talk* 11
  Making the Most of the Targeting Pronunciation Audio Program 13
  Reflection Journals 14
  Overview of Your Plan of Action 14
Finishing Up 15

Chapter 2: Pronunciation Basics   16

Intonation 16
Moving Your Mouth for English 17
Thought Groups 18
Focus Words 19
Final Sounds 20
Linking 22
Finishing Consonant Clusters 24
Speech Rhythm: Stress and Unstress 25
More Practice 28
Finishing Up 31

UNIT II WORDS

Chapter 3: Stressing Syllables and Speaking Clearly — 35
- Word Stress 35
- Compound Nouns 46
- Finishing Up 51

Chapter 4: More Intonation Patterns: More Words — 56
- Predicting Stress: Which Syllable Should I Stress? 56
- Dictionaries and Pronunciation 56
- Descriptive Phrases 62
- Phrasal Verbs 64
- Names 67
- Finishing Up 72
- Unit II Progress Check 75

UNIT III PHRASES AND SENTENCES

Chapter 5: Speech Rhythm: Stress and Unstress — 76
- Sentence Rhythm: Strong Stress, Normal Stress, Unstress 76
- Predicting Stress: Chart 80
- Focus Words: The Basic Stress Pattern 83
- Changes in Focus 89
- Finishing Up 96
- Conversation Strategies 99

Chapter 6: Vowels and Speech Music — 100
- Unstress: Shortening the Vowels in Weak Syllables 100
- Reductions and Schwa Vowels 102
- Clear Vowels 108
- Moving Your Mouth for English: Contrast Three Long Vowels 110
- Moving Your Mouth for English: Contrast Three Short Vowels 112
- Moving Your Mouth for English: Contrast Two More Short Vowels 112
- More Practice 117
- Finishing Up 120

Chapter 7: Sing Along: The Melody of Speech — 123
- How Much Melody Do People Use? 123
- The Four Pitch Levels of English Speech 123
- Some Guidelines for Intonation 125
- Intonation Variations 131
- Longer Sentences 136
- Finishing Up 143
- Unit III Progress Check 145

UNIT IV SOUNDS: CONSONANTS AND VOWELS

Chapter 8: The Speech Pathway— What's Happening Where?   147
- Follow the Speech Pathway 147
- Stops: The Air Stops Along the Speech Pathway 148
- Continuants: The Air Flows Out the Pathway 155
- Are You Ready for "R" and "L"? 164
- Finishing Up 170

Chapter 9: Important Endings   173
- Part 1: "Ed" Endings 173
- Part 2: "S" Endings 180
- Finishing Up 194

Chapter 10: More about Vowels and Consonants   197
- More about Vowels 197
- More about Consonants 204
- More Practice with "R" and "L" 209
- Finishing Up 213
- Unit IV Progress Check 215

UNIT V PUTTING IT ALL TOGETHER

Chapter 11: More about Conversational Speech   216
- Reviewing Reductions and Chunks of Speech 216
- Practice with Authentic Speech 223
- Finishing Up 229

Chapter 12: More about Thought Groups   231
- Presenting New Information 236
- Thought Groups in Conversational Speech 239
- Finishing Up 243
- Unit V Progress Check 245
- What's Next? 245

Appendix A Consonants A-1

Appendix B Vowels A-12

Index of Topics A-24

Index of Activities A-27

Student and Instructor worksheets and charts are available at elt.heinle.com/targetingpron

To the Student

So you want to change your accent. Is this realistic?

You may be surprised to know that there is nothing wrong with an accent! An accent provides very little information other than where the speaker may be from. What matters is how clearly and effectively you communicate.

Pronunciation training is not meant to hide all signs of your original language and culture, nor is it likely to eliminate your accent. Few adults with noticeable accents can sound exactly like native speakers in any new language. However, you can become a confident, effective speaker, however, both at work and in your community and still have a nonnative accent.

Why do I have pronunciation problems?

We all tend to substitute the sounds and rhythm patterns of our original language when we speak a new language. The movements for speech are ingrained habits that we learn at an early age. For this reason, even people who work hard to master the vocabulary and grammar of a new language often have problems pronouncing it. Pronouncing English is particularly challenging because the written word doesn't provide a lot of clues about the pronunciation.

How do I make my accent easier to understand?

- You have to develop new speech habits. This takes time, patience, and practice, as with learning a musical instrument or perfecting an athletic skill.

- You probably need to work on your English speech rhythm and *intonation* (speech melody). Individual consonant and vowel sounds are important, but improving the intonation and rhythm is more likely to make your speech easier to understand.

- You need a plan of action that involves *self-monitoring*[1] (careful listening to your own speech). Mistakes are natural and expected. Learning to correct your own errors by self-monitoring is an important sign of progress.

- Take charge of your own learning. Although your instructor will guide you, this is a self-help program. Students willing to make mistakes, take initiative, and try out new speech skills in real-life situations make the most progress.

[1] *Self-monitoring* in relation to speech/pronunciation was first used by Joan Morley in *TESOL Quarterly* 9, no. 1 (March 1975): 83–86.

How long will it take to modify my accent?

People vary in how many changes they make and how long it takes. Here are five factors that affect progress.

- the number of differences between your native language and English
- frequency of use and conversing in English
- natural ability (How good is your ear? How well can you imitate speech sounds?)
- motivation (the key factor)
- regular attention and practice (essential!)

Here's the good news.

You really *can* improve your accent regardless of your age or your native language! Pronunciation training can help you do a number of things:

- speak clearly and effectively
- understand rapid speech more easily face-to-face, on television, and in movies
- gain confidence and increase your comfort level when speaking English
- further your career opportunities
- improve your performance at work if your job requires speaking English

This program for strengthening English speech has proven successful for students from around the globe and with diverse language backgrounds. So get started right away targeting the parts of your pronunciation that will make the biggest improvement in your speech.

To the Teacher

Welcome to the second edition of *Targeting Pronunciation,* a comprehensive program for providing intermediate and advanced ESL students with the tools they need to communicate clearly in English. Using a communicative and interactive approach, the text provides extensive listening and practice with all aspects of pronunciation. This new edition, while updated, retains all the popular features of the original text.

Targeting Pronunciation is organized around eight practical pronunciation goals, or targets. Most of these targets are *suprasegmentals* (stress, intonation, and speech rhythm). *Segmentals* (consonants and vowels) are also well covered, both in the text and in appendixes A and B. The targets presented early in the book are recycled throughout the chapters as students gain speaking experience and confidence.

Targeting Pronunciation Features

- the latest pedagogy
- assessment package for identifying individual speech needs, setting priorities, and providing student feedback
- engaging songs, poetry, chants, and dialogues
- strategies and tips for pronunciation and practice
- controlled, guided, independent speech activities
- home assignments to reinforce pronunciation changes
- communicative activities, called "Talk Times," for transferring pronunciation targets to real-life situations
- practical worksheets for classroom use, as well as additional practice with consonants and vowels

New Edition Highlights

- indexes by subject and by activity type for easy reference
- improved chapter organization into five progressive units
- increased coverage of consonants and vowels
- self-quizzes at the end of each chapter
- additional authentic speech samples including public service announcements
- updated vocabulary, activities, and pedagogy
- enhanced website activities

Text Goals

- to make pronunciation easy to teach and fun to learn for both experienced and inexperienced instructors and learners
- to promote clear, effective communication, with the understanding that nativelike speech is neither essential nor realistic for most people learning a new language
- to reach beyond the classroom by addressing what students can do on their own to make lasting changes in their pronunciation
- to build self-confidence and increase the students' comfort when speaking English

Teaching Priorities

- **Suprasegmentals.** These play a key role in speaking clearly.
- **Focused listening.** Students improve their monitoring skills by listening for specific pronunciation features.
- **Choral repetition.** Students listen and repeat phrases and sentences multiple times in unison with the whole class. Choral practice is a highly effective technique for internalizing speech rhythm. Employ it whenever possible—the more repetitions the better.
- **Multisensory approaches.** Physical movement accompanying speech is essential for shifting to English speech rhythm patterns. An emphasis on visual, auditory, and kinesthetic modalities maximizes student learning.
- **Discourse-based practice.** Activities use practical, realistic phrases and sentences applicable to the learner's conversational needs.
- **Student responsibility.** Students control their own progress by how much they practice and how many risks they take using their new pronunciation. They learn to correct their own errors and slowly incorporate what they learn into their everyday speech.

Chapter Organization

Chapter 1 offers a comprehensive package for setting goals and assessing individual speech needs. Units I–IV (Chapters 2–10) cover the eight pronunciation targets. Unit V (chapters 11–12) provides additional listening with authentic speech samples and more in-depth practice with conversational speech and the targets learned in earlier chapters.

Audio Program

The audio program provided in audiotapes and digitized CDs is integral to *Targeting Pronunciation*'s approach to teaching. Students need to listen and practice outside of class to make optimum progress. The speech models feature a neutral, American English pronunciation.

Activity Types

- *Learn By Listening*   Teaching segments that present new material to the class through explanation, listening, and repeating. Students work primarily with the instructor and the whole class.

- *Group Practice*   Teaching and practice segments using multiple repetitions in unison with the whole class. They differ from Learn By Listening in that they are usually not on tape and include teaching of individual sounds.

- *Partner Practice*   Controlled follow-ups to teaching, in which students work with each other for more speaking practice. Students are instructed to monitor their own and their partner's speech and exchange feedback and suggestions, generally for the targets recently taught.

- *Role Play* and *Communicative Activity*   Guided and free speech activities. Some are more independent than others.

- *Improve Your Monitoring*   Listening activities where students discriminate between various aspects of pronunciation. For example, students may be asked to listen for the kinds of errors they will be monitoring for in their own speech, such as missing final sounds.

- *Talk*   Oral presentations that students prepare and present to the class.

- *Join the Chorus*   Chants, poems, and limericks. Students practice specific pronunciation targets taught in the chapter.

- *Sing Along*   Recorded songs followed by exercises that relate pronunciation features to the lyrics and melody of the song. There is one song in each unit.

- *Dialogue*   Conversations using authentic language. The dialogues are carefully structured both to practice the new information in the chapter and to revisit the important characteristics of conversation.

- *Talk Times*   Communicative activities that students plan and execute in their daily lives while monitoring for specific pronunciation targets. Students self-assess and keep a record of what happened. They prepare in class with a role play.

Instructor's Website

The Instructor's Manual for *Targeting Pronunciation* provides practical suggestions and explanations for the exercises as well as teaching and correction strategies. Go to http://college.hmco.com/esl/instructors.

Student Website

This offers independent student activities, worksheets, and resources keyed to each chapter that expand the work presented in the book. Students and teachers can access an Answer Key for the exercises on the *Targeting Pronunciation* Student website. Go to http://college.hmco.com/esl/students.

Key to Symbols

The following symbols illustrate important parts of English pronunciation.

WORD STRESS

- **Stressed syllables**   Capital letters represent stressed syllables in words.

  Examples   APple   aPARTment   underSTAND

- **Longer words**   Occasionally two levels of stress are shown in the same word, such as in compound nouns. The strongly stressed syllable is indicated by large capital letters and the lightly stressed syllable by small capital letters.

  Examples   BLACKBOARD   apPREciATE

- **Unstressed syllables**   In words of more than one syllable, the unstressed syllables are left unmarked.

  Examples   PRACtical   imPROVE

SENTENCE STRESS

- **Focus words: Strong stress**   Bold type indicates the word with the strongest stress in a phrase or sentence, the *focus word*.

  Example   The desert is **BEAU**tiful.

- **Content words: Normal stress**   Capital letters that are not bolded occasionally indicate words with normal stress.

  Example   I'd LIKE the **PUR**ple one.

- **Structure words: Unstress**   Unstressed words are left unmarked.

  Example   I'd LIKE some des**SERT**.

- **Reductions**   Unstressed vowels in reduced words are sometimes indicated by a slash and schwa.

  Example   What d/ə you/ə think?

INTONATION

- Rising and falling arrows show the pitch direction of sentences.

Examples   That's not my bag. ↘

That's not your bag? ↗

- Lines showing *steps* and *glides* indicate end-of-the sentence intonation.

Examples   *Glides:*   I heard it again

Do you want to leave?

Step: I can see a rainbow.

SOUNDS

- **Consonant sounds**   Consonant sounds are shown in small gray boxes. Boxes with a squiggly underline indicate voiced consonants with vibrating vocal cords. Plain gray boxes indicate voiceless consonants.

Examples   Voiced   Voiceless

z   zoo   s   Sue

b   bill   p   pill

g   goat   k   coat

Consonant sounds are different from consonant letters. The consonant sound in the gray box may be spelled differently in different words.

Examples   Consonant Sounds   Consonant Letters

k   keep   candy   back   bake

s   sit   cent   miss   face

f   fat   phone   staff   laugh

- **Vowel sounds.**   Vowel sound symbols are shown in small gray boxes.

Examples i^y u^w o^w

Vowel sounds are different from vowel letters. The vowel sound in the gray box is often spelled differently in different English words.

Examples e^y make   pay   rain   vein

$ʌ$ cup   some   what   trouble

$ɪ$ him   busy   gym   women

OTHER MARKS

‿	This mark shows linking.
Example	My glove‿is gone.
(/)	Slashes indicate pauses in longer sentences.
Example	I'd like two fried **EGGS** / and a cup of **COF**fee. /
⟶	An arrow means sounds like.
Example	short or tall ⟶ shorter tall
∩	This symbol indicates a recorded segment.
X	X's show silent letters.
Examples	pick̶e̶d gate̶s̶
	Don'̶t̶ ask me. He found h̶is wallet.

SOUND SYMBOLS

The consonant and vowels sounds shown in the gray boxes in *Targeting Pronunciation* are a modified version of the IPA designed for the teaching of American English pronunciation. The voiced consonants are underlined with a squiggly line to show voicing.

Targeting Pronunciation Consonant Sounds			
1. pat	p	13. shoe	ʃ
2. boy	b	14. measure	ʒ
3. time	t	15. chip	tʃ
4. day	d	16. jam	dʒ
5. kite	k	17. man	m
6. go	g	18. no	n
7. fan	f	19. ring	ŋ
8. vine	v	20. lap	l
9. think	θ	21. run	r
10. the	ð	22. water	w
11. see	s	23. yes	y
12. zoo	z	24. him	h

Targeting Pronunciation Vowel Sounds	
1. see	i^y
2. it	I
3. say	e^y
4. yes	ɛ
5. fat	æ
6. bird	ɜr
7. bus	ʌ
8. stop	ɑ
9. two	u^w
10. books	ʊ
11. show	o^w
12. boss	ɔ
13. hi	a^y
14. cow	a^w
15. boy	ɔ^y

ACKNOWLEDGMENTS

I am grateful to have collaborated with the dedicated College ESL team at Houghton Mifflin Company under the skilled direction of Susan Maguire. It was my good fortune to work again with the conscientious and capable senior development editor Kathy Sands Boehmer and I appreciate her long hours of hard work and professional support for this project. My thanks go to the editorial assistant Evangeline Bermas and Nicole Parent for help with audio permissions. I am enormously grateful to Lida Baker for her outstanding editorial guidance and suggestions during the development of this revision.

I want to thank Linda Grant, Bill Acton, Olle Kjellin, and Colleen Meyers, teachers and colleagues, who have stimulated my thinking and inspired me to try new directions in my teaching, and Joan Morley and Judy Gilbert for their innovative leadership in pronunciation teaching.

My sincere appreciation to my students who taught me how they learn best and what is important to their progress. This book was created with them in mind.

Special thanks to Janet Goodwin, University of California, Los Angeles for her invaluable suggestions.

Thanks to the following reviewers for feedback about the first edition and suggestions that helped guide this revision:

    Marsha Abramovich, Tidewater Community College

    Laurie Cox, Midlands Technical Community College

    Beverly DiSalvo, Merced College

    Pamela Kennedy, Holyoke Community College

    Craig Machado, Norwalk Community College

    Donna Mendelson, SUNY, Binghamton

    Elena Moore, Pensacola Junior College

    Shirley Terrell, Colin County Community College

Finally, my deepest appreciation goes to my husband, Lee, whose life commitment to the creative process continues to be an inspiration.

Unit 1 Getting Started

Improving Your Pronunciation

PART 1. SETTING GOALS

Targeting Pronunciation takes the mystery out of improving your speech by dividing English pronunciation into eight key *targets*, or features. Although variations of English are spoken in different places around the globe, these basic features are the same. You will be learning a neutral form of spoken American English that a large number of native and nonnative speakers can easily understand.

Pronunciation Targets

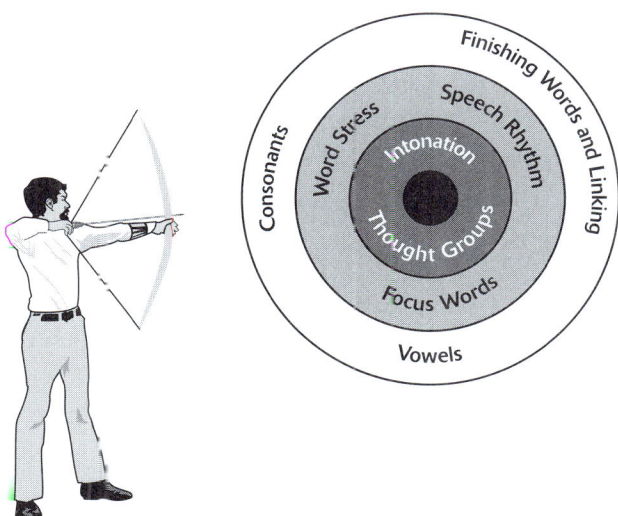

Look over the following list of features that you will gradually learn to hear in your own speech and in the speech of others. Think of these as targets or goals—as the sounds and intonation patterns to aim for as you make your English speech more effective. At first you may need help in selecting the features that will make the biggest improvement in *your* speech. When you are more familiar with your own speech patterns, you will be able to select targets on your own.

Words

Target 1 Word Stress. English speech can be hard to understand if you *stress,* or emphasize, the wrong syllable in a word or if all the syllables have equal stress. Emphasize one stressed syllable by saying it longer, louder, and higher in pitch. The unstressed syllables are short and low in pitch.

Phrases and Sentences

Target 2 Thought Groups. Pause to divide longer sentences into phrases, called *thought groups.* Each thought group has its own melody, one strongly stressed word, and a slight pause at the end. Pausing in the right place will make your speech easier to understand.

Target 3 Focus Words. In each thought group, emphasize one word, called *the focus word,* to direct attention to what is important and to highlight new information. Focus words stand out and are easier to hear than other words.

Target 4 Final Sounds and Linking. Speech can be hard to understand or distracting when final sounds or syllables are missing from a thought group. It is particularly important to pronounce grammatical endings—such as "ed" or final "s"—and small words such as "the." *Link,* or connect, the words in a thought group together so that your speech flows smoothly, and make sure that nothing needed is missing.

Target 5 Speech Rhythm: Sentence Stress and Unstress. Make your speech easier to follow by exaggerating the contrast between the stressed and unstressed words. Stress the words that contain most of the meaning—the *content words,* such as nouns and verbs. Don't leave out the small unstressed words such as *to* or *a* because they are important to grammar and speech rhythm.

Target 6 Intonation. Use *intonation,* or speech melody, to organize your speech and express meaning beyond the words themselves. For example, intonation can make a speaker sound friendly, confident, or surprised. Target specific intonation patterns for asking questions, finishing sentences, and showing contrast.

Sounds

Target 7 Consonant Sounds. Target pairs of sounds that you find challenging, such as f and v, ch and j, or r and l. Pay attention to *consonant clusters*, consonants that are grouped together without vowels.

Target 8 Vowel Sounds. Although English has approximately fifteen vowel sounds, the most important thing about pronouncing vowels is to emphasize the stressed ones. You may also want to target specific vowel sounds that you find difficult.

Goals Survey

What do you hope to accomplish regarding your pronunciation?
General Goals

- Read this list of possible goals. Find the three that are the most important to you. Write *1* next to the goal you think is the most important. Write *2* next to the second most important goal and *3* next to the third most important.

    _____ a. to eliminate my accent completely and sound like a native speaker

    _____ b. to communicate in English clearly, effectively, and naturally

    _____ c. to speak so that others can understand me much more easily than they do now

    _____ d. to gain confidence in new speaking situations

    _____ e. to understand rapid speech more easily

    _____ f. to improve my career opportunities and job performance

- Some of these goals may not be important or realistic. Write X next to any that you think are neither important nor realistic.

- Discuss these goals with the class and the instructor.

Communication Needs

- To plan a pronunciation program that fits your needs, think about times when you would like to speak more clearly and comfortably. How important is it to you to improve your pronunciation in the following situations? Write *1, 2,* or *3* next to each situation.

    1 = very important   2 = somewhat important   3 = not important

    _____ home   _____ social   _____ general community (shopping,
    _____ work/business _____ international   using government offices,
    _____ other (explain)   travel   banking, asking for
                                                    information)

- Describe three high-priority speaking situations that you find challenging. Examples: giving talks or presentations, meeting new people, making phone calls, interviewing for jobs, participating in meetings, and giving instructions.

    1. _____

    2. _____

    3. _____

- Compare your goals and needs with those of a partner or small group. Report the results to the class.

Your Speech-Effectiveness Level

1. What is clear, effective speech?

To become an effective speaker, you need to develop your pronunciation and language skills together. Good oral communication skills include clear pronunciation as well as accurate grammar and vocabulary. How clearly do you think you communicate in English? Decide which of the following six levels of speech effectiveness best fits your speech:

Level 1   People understand only a few words of my speech. Conversations in English are not possible.

Level 2   People understand less than half of what I say. I frequently need to repeat things. My vocabulary and grammar are limited. Conversations are slow and difficult.

Level 3   People understand more than half, but not nearly enough, of what I say. I need to repeat and clarify many things. There are problems with my pronunciation, sentence structure, and vocabulary. Conversations proceed in spite of interruptions.

Level 4   People understand most of what I say. My pronunciation and occasional errors in grammar or vocabulary are noticeable, and they occasionally interfere with communication. Conversations proceed with minimal interruptions.

Level 5   My speech is fully understandable. Although my accent and any isolated variations in vocabulary, grammar, or pronunciation may be noticeable, they do not interfere with communication. Conversations proceed smoothly.

Level 6   My speech is nearly native with a barely detectable accent. I use correct grammar and appropriate vocabulary. My communication is clear, fluent, and effective.

2. What is your present level? What is your target level?

Color the graph with a highlighter pen to indicate where you think your speech is now and what speech level you are aiming for. Find out whether you and your instructor agree about your current level.

Present Level	Target Level
6 - 5 - 4 - [3] - 2 - 1	6 - 5 - 4 - 3 - 2 - 1

3. How much time can you realistically spend practicing your pronunciation?

To approach my goals, I will practice _____5_____ hours per week.

_{The speech effectiveness levels were adapted by permission of Joan Morley. Joan Morley, *Extempore Speaking Practice* (Ann Arbor: University of Michigan Press, 1992), xv.}

PART 2. ASSESSING YOUR PRONUNCIATION PRIORITIES

Listening to English *Survey*

This survey will tell you how clearly you hear some features of English speech that affect pronunciation. Your instructor will provide your pronunciation listening score on the *Listening to English* Profile (please visit the Houghton Mifflin ESL website at http://college.hmco.com/esl). Listening scores improve, often dramatically, by the end of the course.

1. Syllables. Write the number of syllables you hear next to the word or phrase. [5 points]

Example   forget it. __3__

1. ____ illustrate
2. ____ crashed
3. ____ returned it
4. ____ academic
5. ____ magnification

2. Word stress. Listen to the following words. First you will hear the key word, then a sentence. Circle the stressed syllable in the word. [6 points]

Example   (pen)c i l.   a l(low)a n c e.

1. f o r g o t
2. v i s i t o r s
3. a p p l i c a t i o n
4. d e c i s i o n
5. a p p r e c i a t e
6. u n d e r s t a n d

3. Important endings. For each question, you will hear either sentence (a) or (b). Check (✓) the sentence you hear. [6 points]

Example   a. __✓__ I'll look at the letter.
              b. ____ I've looked at the letter.

1. a. ____ I'll call him every day.
   b. ____ I've called him every day.
2. a. ____ They look over all the documents.
   b. ____ They looked over all the documents.
3. a. ____ He'll decide about it after the meeting
   b. ____ He decided about it after the meeting
4. a. ____ It makes me laugh.
   b. ____ It made me laugh.
5. a. ____ They said they'd call before it started.
   b. ____ They said they called before it started.
6. a. ____ They pack up the suitcases for you.
   b. ____ They packed up the suitcases for you.

4. Missing sounds. Listen to the sentence. Check (✓) the word you hear in the sentence. It may not be the word that you expect to hear or the word that correctly completes the sentence. [4 points]

Examples My _____ is broken.   ✓ bike   ___ buy
           My _____ is broken.   ___ bike   ✓ buy

1. The _____ is ringing next door.   ___ phone   ___ foe
2. Last week he _____ a lot of money.   ___ made   ___ may
3. Please _____ your car out of the way.   ___ move   ___ moo
4. My insurance _____ went up this year.   ___ rates   ___ ray

5. Reduced speech. Write the sentence you hear. You will hear each sentence twice. [5 points]

1. _____
2. _____
3. _____
4. _____
5. _____

6. Focus words. You will hear a sentence. Listen for the word that gets the most emphasis. It affects the meaning and the response. Check (✓) the appropriate response. [3 points]

Example <u>Jane's</u> birthday is July 28th.   ___ I thought it was July <u>30th</u>.
                                               ✓ I thought <u>Marie's</u> birthday was the 28th.

1. I'd like to rent a car.   ___ What about renting a <u>jeep</u>?
                              ___ How about <u>buying</u> one instead?

2. Jim is getting married next week.   ___ Not <u>this</u> week?
                                        ___ That's <u>nice</u>.

3. I looked under the chair.   ___ Try looking <u>on</u> the chair.
                                ___ Try looking under the <u>table</u>.

CHAPTER 1 Improving Your Pronunciation

7. Focus words. Listen to the dialogue two times. Underline the **one** word in each sentence that gets the most emphasis. [8 points]

Example   A: What are you <u>doing</u>?   B: What do you <u>think</u> I'm doing?

A: What shall we do this weekend?

B: I'd like to go to a movie. What do you want to do?

A: I'd like to go to a movie. But only a funny movie.

B: We did that last weekend. I'd rather see an exciting action film. How does that sound?

8. Phrases. First, read silently the following sentences and responses. Then you will hear either sentence (a) or sentence (b) in each pair. Check (✓) the appropriate response. [4 points]

Examples   a. Look at the hot <u>dog</u>.   _✓_ Let's give him a drink.

            b. Look at the <u>hot</u> dog.   ___ I want one for lunch.

1. a. What's he doing in the darkroom?   ___ He's developing pictures.
   b. What's he doing in the dark room?   ___ He's sleeping.
2. a. Who lives in the White House?   ___ The U.S. president does.
   b. Who lives in the white house?   ___ I do.
3. a. Use "drop out" in a sentence.   ___ Don't drop out of college.
   b. Use "dropout" in a sentence.   ___ He's a college dropout.
4. a. Use "print out" in a sentence.   ___ Please print out four copies.
   b. Use "printout" in a sentence.   ___ Please give me the printout.

9. Thought groups. First read silently the pairs of sentences and responses. Then you will hear either sentence (a) or sentence (b) in each pair. Check (✓) the appropriate answer. [3 points]

Examples   "Tracy," said the teacher, "was late."   _✓_ Tracy was late.

            Tracy said, "The teacher was late."   ___ The teacher was late.

1. a. Tom bought a new car, phone, and radio.   ___ Tom bought a new car.
   b. Tom bought a new car phone and radio.   ___ Tom did <u>not</u> buy a new car.
2. a. The twenty $9 books are left.   ___ The books cost $9 each.
   b. The $29 books are left.   ___ The books cost $29 each.
3. a. Nancy said, "My brother is a doctor."   ___ Nancy's brother is a doctor.
   b. "Nancy," said my brother, "is a doctor."   ___ Nancy is a doctor.

10. Intonation. In one sentence, the speaker is finished talking. In the other sentence, the speaker is not finished and has more to say. Check (✓) the sentence you hear. [2 points]

Example I bought some milk (and some eggs) . . .   ✓ not finished

1. a. I went to the last conference.   ____ finished
   b. I went to the last conference. . .   ____ not finished
2. a. The package contains a note and a gift.   ____ finished
   b. The package contains a note and a gift. . .   ____ not finished

11. Intonation. Intonation can change the speaker's meaning. The speaker can mean what the words seem to be saying or the speaker can mean something different. Listen to the sentences and check (✓) (a) if the speaker means what the words say or (b) if the speaker means the opposite of the words. [2 points]

	(a) the same	(b) the opposite
Example I'll bet she wants to work all weekend.	____	✓
1. You must be looking forward to that job.	____	____
2. That sounds like a great idea.	____	____

12. Intonation. Intonation can change the meaning of certain questions. Listen to the question and check (✓) the appropriate answer. [2 points]

Example Do you like the red sweater or the blue one?   ____ Yes, they are beautiful.
                                                            ✓ I like the blue one.

1. Would you like ice cream or cake?   ____ Yes, please.
                                        ____ I'd like cake, please.
2. Should I call on Monday or Tuesday?   ____ Yes, that would be great.
                                          ____ Monday would be better.

Pronunciation Survey: Making a Speech Tape

Make a tape of your speech to help you and your instructor identify your personal pronunciation targets and set priorities for working on your pronunciation. Your instructor will provide feedback for you about your speech tape.[1]

Your recording will have four parts.

1. Introducing yourself
2. Reading
3. Describing pictures
4. Talking about a topic

1. Introducing Yourself

Talk briefly about yourself for one or two minutes. Speak informally using natural, unrehearsed speech. Do not practice or write out your answers.

- Tell your name, where you are from, and your educational background.
- How often and where do you speak English? Is it with native speakers?
- Briefly describe your work background in your own country and here.
- What are your plans for the future?
- What do you hope to accomplish in this class?

2. Reading

Choose **one** of the following two paragraphs to record. First read it silently for content. When recording, don't change your pronunciation. Speak naturally. **This is not a test.**

Paying with Plastic

People have always used cash and checks for purchasing things, but in our lifetime things are changing fast. Now, instead of holding cash, people's wallets are stuffed with various kinds of plastic credit cards, debit cards, and ATM cards. It is estimated that Americans charge more than $19 billion a year on credit cards and that there are already more than 900 million cards of various kinds in circulation. Online shopping has expanded card activity even more. Card companies can have problems collecting overdue payments. Although most people intend to record ATM transactions and debits as they spend money, it is easy to use the cards without keeping good records. Cardholders who may be tempted to buy things that they can't afford can end up with high monthly payments beyond their budgets. This explosion in the use of credit cards has brought with it huge amounts of personal debt. Credit card companies are often financially responsible for goods or services illegally charged to businesses. Ultimately, it's not the company that pays. It's the consumer who ends up paying for these losses with increased prices or higher interest charges. Credit card companies are enthusiastic about the switch to a credit card economy because they earn a small percentage of each transaction. But what do *you* think about "paying with plastic"?

[1] To the instructor: See Instructor Worksheet 2, *Identifying Your Targets*, on the website at elt.heinle.com/targetingpron

My Exercise Program

I used to love to sleep late on weekends until I watched my neighbor exercising every day and looking very physically fit. Now I wake up at 5:30 in the morning, put on my exercise clothes and tennis shoes, drink some orange juice, and take off. By 7 o'clock I've walked over sixteen blocks to the gym and worked out for sixty minutes in an aerobics class. Yesterday I also jogged about fifteen minutes on a treadmill and rode my bike five miles to my friend's house. When I finished exercising, I was unusually hungry and enjoyed an early lunch. I ate a cheeseburger, a large green salad, some sliced cucumbers, three bags of potato chips, a milk shake, rice pudding, and five chocolate chip cookies for dessert. That's been my routine for several weeks now, and I have seen signs of improvement. Recently I decided to keep a record of my workouts and record my progress in a notebook. My friend who is a professional trainer doesn't agree with my ABCs for working out. He says I'm better off sleeping late and skipping the huge lunch. What do *you* think? Maybe I *am* better off sleeping late.

3. Describing Pictures

Look at the following four pictures and tell the story they describe. Use the past tense. Add ideas of your own. Tell how you think the story ends.

4. Talking about a Topic

Talk for two or three minutes about **one** of these topics. Think about your topic, but do not write out or rehearse what you are going to say.

- Contrast one aspect of your original culture with American culture, for example, business practices, community/family life, education, or politics/government. What seems the same or different? How has this affected your work experiences or your personal life?

- Talk about an important problem facing the world today. Why did you choose this issue instead of another? How has this affected you or your family? What solutions do you recommend? What do you predict will happen?

- Describe an experience from your past that you will always remember. Talk about the place where it happened and any people involved. Why was this important? How did it influence your life and your decisions? Give details.

1. Listen to your tape. Make sure that the recording is loud enough to hear easily and that you followed the instructions on page 9.

2. Rewind the cassette, and write your name on it. You can either (1) submit the tape for review or (2) schedule a meeting with your instructor to review the tape.[1]

PART 3. MAKING YOUR NEW PRONUNCIATION A HABIT

Where Do I Start?

Learning a new accent requires refining your listening skills and establishing new muscle patterns. This takes time and a plan of action that goes beyond what you do in class. Your instructor will help you develop this plan.

Self-Monitoring

Your plan of action starts with careful, targeted listening. *Monitoring* is targeted listening to the speech of others. Careful listening to your own speech for specific pronunciation features is called *self-monitoring*. Self-monitoring is the only way to discover and correct your own errors and gradually improve your pronunciation. Monitoring the speech of others, whether the instructor, other students in class, or a speaker on TV or in the movies, can help you improve your own self-monitoring.

"Use It or Lose It": Making small talk

You have to use what you learn in class and speak English as often as possible in order to increase your comfort level and improve your pronunciation. One way is to make *small talk*. This is brief, impersonal conversation that can take place anywhere. You can make small talk with someone you don't know at all or with a casual acquaintance. It is a way of greeting people and communicating with them in an informal, safe way.

[1]To the instructor: To provide feedback, see Instructor Worksheet 3, *Instructor Observations*, on the website at elt.heinle.com/targetingpron

Learn By Listening 1: Listen to a teacher talking

Listening plays a big part in learning to pronounce English more clearly. Start by listening to a teacher's taped lecture about a way to improve your pronunciation. As you listen to each part of the teacher's lecture, think about the answers to these questions.

Part 1

- What is small talk?
- What is one of the specific small talk suggestions that the teacher makes?

Part 2

- What does the teacher describe as "tempting"?
- What are two safe topics for making small talk?
- Who should take charge of your pronunciation training?

Partner Practice: Small talk plan

1. Talk to a partner or small group about places where you might make small talk in English. List places and some sentences you might say to start the conversation. Have you already tried any of these?

Places	What to Say to Start a Small, Safe Conversation
_____	_____
_____	_____
_____	_____
_____	_____

2. Check any of the following topics that would be appropriate for small talk with someone you recently met in your native country and in an English-speaking country. Discuss this with your partner.

Appropriate topics for small talk	Your native country	An English-speaking country
weather	____	____
current news event	____	____
politics	____	____
religion	____	____

personal appearance (face, eyes, body)   ____   ____

food/meal you are eating   ____   ____

compliment (clothing, home, accomplishment)   ____   ____

critical comments (appearance, speech, or behavior)   ____   ____

movies/tv/books   ____   ____

family/children/pets   ____   ____

health   ____   ____

how much something costs   ____   ____

sports   ____   ____

work/occupation   ____   ____

your salary   ____   ____

It's a fact   Americans are often uncomfortable with silence, and therefore engage in small talk. They consider it friendly and appropriate to speak about impersonal topics with someone they don't know or have just met. Small talk has become an American pastime.

Making the Most of the *Targeting Pronunciation* Audio Program

Your plan of action includes regular practice with the text tapes or CDs. To make your pronunciation a habit, follow these suggestions for using the audio program for this book.

1. **Practice every day for 10–20 minutes.** This is better than practicing once a week for an hour or more. The more frequently you practice for brief periods, the more quickly you will progress. Keep a record of your practice times until you establish a regular schedule.

2. **Practice in a quiet environment.** Choose a place where you will have few or no interruptions so that you can concentrate on listening to the tape and imitating what you hear.

3. **Do a lot of listening.** Listen to each chapter several times. Replay the tape and go over the exercises that need extra work. Look away from your book and concentrate on listening.

4. **Self-monitor.** Stay alert and focused as you practice. Improving your ability to hear yourself clearly and to discover your own errors is an important part of your progress.

5. **Track the selection.** (Say it with the speaker.)[1]

6. **Practice the same exercises in each chapter many times during the week.** This kind of repetition is needed to train your speech muscles and improve your listening skills.

[1] See page 74, *The Talking Mirror*.

Reflection Journals[1]

As part of your plan of action, you will benefit from keeping a written *reflection journal* about your experiences learning English pronunciation. (To *reflect* is to form or express thoughts about something.) Journal writing not only increases your awareness about your own pronunciation but also provides a record of your progress. Look at a student's sample journal.

Goal: To listen to a TV news program and notice the pausing and thought groups. Try to figure out what is easy and what is hard to understand.

Reflection: I watched Oprah thinking that such a popular TV interviewer would have good speech. I noticed the focus word and that she put in a lot of pauses. She was interviewing a biographer who did a special about Prince William and his father, Charles, and I noticed that British English also puts in a lot of focus words and pauses even though the accent sounds different from American English. I decided that TV is a very good way to learn about pronunciation and what make speech sound clear and it is good to record the program so I can watch it more than once.

For more sample journals and instructions, please visit the Houghton Mifflin ESL website at http://college.hmco.com/esl/students. See Student Worksheet 1.

Overview of Your Plan of Action

The following table provides an overview of the process of improving your pronunciation:

In Class

Gain pronunciation awareness.	Shape your new pronunciation.
• Set realistic goals.	• Learn how to say the target features.
• Learn about English pronunciation.	• Improve your self-monitoring skills.
• Learn what will improve your speech.	• Start discovering and correcting your errors.

On Your Own

Practice what you learn in class.	Make your new pronunciation a habit.
• Work with the text audio program.	• Use your new pronunciation in your daily life.
• Record and listen to your speech.	• Continue self-monitoring and self-correcting.
• Self-monitor and self-correct.	• Gain comfort with your new pronunciation.

---

[1] Thanks to Helen Huntley, "TESOL Matters," *Reflective Journals,* October/November 1999.

FINISHING UP

On Your Own

1. **Audio program.** Listen several times to the teacher discussing small talk. Pay attention to the teacher's voice. Does she use a lot of speech melody by going up and down in pitch, or does she talk near the same pitch? Does she sound friendly, or does she sound bored or uninterested?

2. **Small talk.** Complete three small talk conversations this week. Describe what happened on the *Small Talk Worksheet* or in a *Reflection Journal*. (Please visit the Houghton Mifflin ESL website at http://college.hmco.com/esl/students.) Rate your comfort level from 1 to 10. 1 = least comfortable. 10 = most comfortable. Did your comfort level increase by the third small talk experience?

3. **Phone meeting.** Talk on the phone with another student from this class about some of your experiences and attitudes about English. This is a good way to get acquainted and to practice conversing in English. Discuss the following questions.

   - What is your earliest memory of hearing English? How did it sound to you?
   - How does it sound to you now?
   - Different cultures in the world have had a variety of experiences, both good and bad, with English speakers or English-speaking countries. Think about your culture's experiences. How might these have affected your attitude toward speaking English?
   - Why did you decide to learn to speak English?
   - Do you think English pronunciation will be easy or hard? Why?

   Name and phone number to contact: _____

4. **Recorded practice.** Tape-record your responses to the first three questions that you talked about in your phone meeting above. Speak naturally without reading your answers. Then listen to your tape and start self-monitoring. Take notes on your answers to the following questions:

   - What did you hear or notice about your pronunciation, your voice, or both?
   - What do you like or dislike about listening to your speech on tape?

Web Activities

Go to elt.heinle.com/targetingpron for additional activities related to this chapter.

Pronunciation Basics

Chapter 2 is a brief introduction to the characteristics that make English sound different from other languages. You will have many opportunities to practice the features presented in this chapter as you proceed through the book.

- intonation (speech melody)
- moving your mouth for English
- thought groups
- focus words
- final sounds
- linking
- speech rhythm

Intonation

Every language has its own musical sound—its own melody when the voice goes up and down, called *intonation,* and its own rhythm. Even when you can't understand the words, you can often recognize a language by hearing its intonation. Clear communication in English depends on good intonation.

Listen to the robot. "Do-you-know-who-I-am-I-am-a-pow-er-ful-ro-bot." This robotic speech is very different from English speech, which has exaggerated high and low pitches. Listen to the same phrase with these changes in the melody and the rhythm. "Do you KNOW who **I** am? (pause) I'm a POWerful **RO**bot."

One reason that English speakers use intonation is to contrast information. The arrows show the direction of the speech melody. The melody rises on some words and falls on others.

Example   Anna is driving the **red** car, not the **black** one.

Pay attention to pitch changes and melody as you proceed through this book. You will learn many ways that intonation affects the meaning of English speech.

Moving Your Mouth for English

In every language people move their mouths in ways that make them look and sound like native speakers. For example, relaxing your face and lips and lowering your jaw as you talk can make you look and sound more like a native English speaker

Try three ways that English speakers move their mouths. Use a mirror to watch your mouth move as you listen and repeat some words below.

1. A relaxed jaw

Your jaw can open and close more gently and naturally if you release any muscular tension in your lips.

Lower your relaxed jaw and open your relaxed lips wide as you say *hah*. Use a mirror to see your jaw lower for ɑ , sounding like *ah*. Now say *HOLiday*.

2. A flat, low tongue

Lowering the tongue in the back of the throat moves the sound forward to the center of your mouth, where it belongs for English.

1. Open your mouth as if a doctor is looking at your throat. Relax your lips. Use the muscles in the back of your throat to flatten and lower your tongue and say ɑ , sounding like *ah*. Use a mirror. You may need to gently push the back of your tongue flat with your finger to get the feel of it.

2. Now say *HOLiday*. Lower your jaw and tongue for the stressed vowel ɑ .

3. Relaxed lips

Relaxed lips and face will help you look more like an American speaker.

1. Say uʷ , sounding like *ooo*. Round your lips in a relaxed way without squeezing them tightly.

2. Prepare to say *how*. Start by lowering your jaw for *hah*. Lower the back of your tongue. Then pull your tongue farther back and round your lips into a relaxed *ooo*. Now say *How. How are you? How was your HOLiday?*

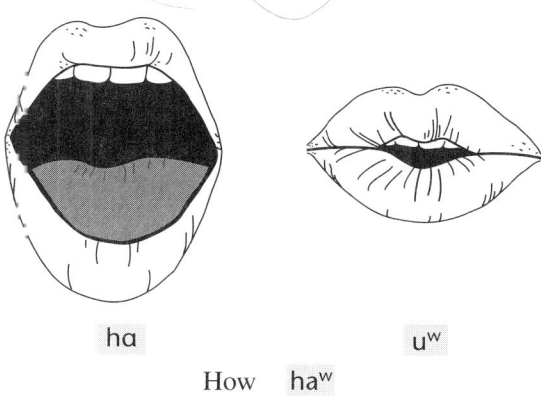

hɑ   uʷ

How   haʷ

pronunciation tips	(1) Try a *yawn-sigh*. Take a deep breath, open your mouth very wide, yawn, and sigh *ahhhh* to relax your mouth for English. Repeat this three times. (2) Try counting to 10, moving your lips as little as possible. Keep the back of your tongue low. Use the back of your tongue to make the sounds. This takes practice, but it is possible. Ventriloquists do it! It will strengthen the back of the tongue for English.

another tip	Turn off the sound on your TV and watch English speakers move their mouths. Watch their jaws, lips, and facial expressions.

Thought Groups

Periods, commas, and paragraph markers make it easier to read and follow written English. Thought groups are *verbal punctuation* that you can hear. They make speech more understandable. You can recognize a thought group when you hear a strongly stressed word (the focus word), a sweep of melody, and a pause.

Learn By Listening 1

Listen to two lines, shown below, from a poem by Edward Lear. The thought groups are separated by slashes. The strongly stressed words are in bold. Trace the lines over the thought groups as you listen to the melody of the words. To learn the rest of this rhythmic poem, go to the *Targeting Pronunciation* webpage.

The owl and the **PUS**sy-cat / went to **SEA** / in a **BEAUT**iful / pea-green **BOAT**. /

They took some **HON**ey / and plenty of **MO**ney / wrapped **UP** / in a five-pound **NOTE**. /

Learn By Listening 2: Public speaker

Public speakers usually have clear speech.

1. Look away from the book as you listen to President Dwight D. Eisenhower deliver the opening lines of his farewell address to the nation on January 17, 1961. What do you notice about his speech? What makes it easy to understand?

Good evening, / my fellow Americans. /

First, / I should like to express my gratitude / to the radio and television networks / for the opportunities / they have given me over the years to bring reports and messages to our nation. My special thanks / go to them for the opportunity / of addressing you this evening. /

Three days from now, after a half-century in the service of our country, I shall lay down the responsibilities of office as, in traditional and solemn ceremony, the authority of the <u>presidency</u> is vested in my successor. This evening I come to you with a message of leave-taking and farewell, and to share a few final thoughts with you, my countrymen.

(2-1)

2. Listen several more times and draw slashes where you hear pauses. Do they always match commas and periods? Underline any strongly stressed words that stand out.

pronunciation tip	Slow speech, many pauses, and short thought groups all make speech easier to understand.

Focus Words

Every language has a way of showing what is important. In English it is the *focus word*. This one strongly stressed word in each thought group is easier to hear than any other stressed words.

Learn By Listening 3: Focus words

1. Listen and repeat what you hear. Lean forward and tap your hand on the desk as you say the focus word. The pitch rises on the focus word and falls at the end of the sentence.

   Here's a glass of **W A T** er.   It's time to **GO**.

   It's a piece of **C A K E**.   I'll see you **L A T** er.

   I like it a **L O T**.   I need some **H E L P**.

   She wants to **S E E** you.   He forgot to **B R I N G** it.

2. Listen and underline the focus word in each phrase.

   Example   some cold <u>water</u>

   walking s<u>low</u>ly   a famous <u>man</u>   the last chance

   an electric <u>light</u>   loves music   a messy paper

a. Partner Practice: New information—old information

The focus word emphasizes important new information. As the conversation proceeds, new information in one sentence may become old information in the next sentence.

1. Listen to the dialogues and underline the focus words.

Example A: I lost my **BOOK**. ("book" is new information)

B: **WHICH** book? ("book" is now old information)

A: My **HIS**tory book. ("history" is new information)

1. A: I found my book.

   B: Which book? Your history book?

   A: No, my math book.

2. A: That must be his house.

   B: The white house?

   A: No. The gray one with the car in front.

3. B: Is that Tom's car?

   A: It looks like his father's car.

2. Compare your answers and practice the dialogues with a partner.

Final Sounds

Some people mispronounce English by leaving off the final consonants from words and syllables. If your native language does not end syllables or words with consonants, you need to pay special attention to this, especially when linking words into phrases or sentences. Dropped or missing sounds can change the meaning. "The pla . . . arrived" sounds as if you are talking about the theater. "The plane arrived" is about an airplane.

b. Partner Practice: Finish the link

1. Sentence (a) in the following example does not make sense because the ending sound in the underlined word is missing. Change the word by adding a final sound and write the correct word on the line.

Example   a. His fee are big.

   b. His *feet* are big.

1. a. It was <u>A</u> hours long.
   b. It was ____eight____ hours long.
2. a. The <u>foe</u> is ringing.
   b. The ____phone____ is ringing.
3. a. The <u>row</u> is closed for repairs.
   b. The ____road____ is closed for repairs.
4. a. Turn <u>rye</u> at the corner.
   b. Turn ____ri____ at the corner.
5. a. I <u>her</u> him laugh.
   b. I _____ him laugh.
6. a. I <u>knee</u> a ride.
   b. I _____ a ride.
7. a. Please <u>moo</u> your car.
   b. Please _____ your car.
8. a. Do you have <u>fie</u> dollars?
   b. Do you have _____ dollars?

2. Compare answers with your partner. Take turns saying sentence (b) correctly. Connect the ending sound to the next word. Monitor your speech and the speech of your partner.

c. Improve Your Monitoring: Missing sounds

1. Listen to each sentence. Check (✓) the word you hear. It may not be the word that you expect to hear or the word that correctly completes the sentence. Replay the tape to check your listening.

Example The <u>pho</u>ne is not installed yet. ____phone ✓ foe

1. I ____ a car wash. ✓ need ____knee
2. The ____ was fun. ✓ hike ____hi
3. I took out a ____ to buy my car. ✓ loan ✓ low
4. The ____ takes off at noon. ____plane ✓ play
5. Take a ____ of the cookie. ✓ bite ____buy
6. I have to ____ in January. ____move ✓ moo
7. Jeffrey got ____ on his way to the highway. ✓ lost ____law
8. There was a long ____ at the post office. ____line ✓ lie

2. Practice saying the sentences correctly. Connect the underlined word to the next word. Self-monitor. Pay attention to the ending sounds and the linking.

d. Improve Your Monitoring: Missing "ed"

1. Listen to each sentence. Decide whether the speaker says the past tense correctly or whether the "ed" is missing. Check (✓) the word you hear. Replay the tape to check your listening.

Example	I <u>looked</u> at my watch.	____ looked	✓ look
1.	He <u>responded</u> to my note.	✓ responded	____ respond
2.	We <u>climbed</u> up the stairs.	✓ climbed	____ climb
3.	Carlos <u>laughed</u> at the joke.	____ laughed	✓ laugh
4.	Anna <u>wanted</u> to read her book.	∅ wanted	✓ want
5.	My mother <u>baked</u> a cake.	✓ baked	∅ bake
6.	I <u>recommended</u> the movie.	____ recommended	✓ recommend
7.	He <u>showed</u> us the way.	____ showed	✓ show
8.	I left after I <u>finished</u> all my work.	____ finished	✓ finish

2. Practice saying the sentences correctly. Self-monitor. Pay attention to the *ed* ending sounds and the linking.

Linking

The words in phrases or thought groups are *linked* together. This means that the consonant that finishes one word connects to the sound at the beginning of the next word. Linking makes speech sound smooth and connected.

Learn By Listening 4

1. Listen to and repeat the following phrases. Hold the last sound of one word until you say the first sound of the next word. Use slow speech to feel the linking. → means "sounds like."

1. turn around → tur-naround
2. turns around → turn-zaround
3. look alike → loo-kalike
4. looks away → look-saway
5. jumps up → jum-psup
6. jumped up → jump-tup
7. calls after → call-zafter
8. called after → call-dafter
9. pulled out → pull-dout

In order to understand spoken English, you have to recognize when words are linked together and sounds are missing. For example, *hot and cold* → *hot'ncold*. The *and* is shortened, or reduced. A phrase can sound like one long word. "There is a bus coming" → *therzaBUScoming*. When listening to conversations, it can be confusing when what you hear does not match what you might see in print.

2. Look at the following words and phrases. They look different but sound the same.

1. missed her → mister
2. spear it → spirit
3. plan it → planet
4. sees an apple → season apple
5. four in jail → foreign jail
6. past or present → pastor present

e. Partner Practice: Linking

Make a list of movies, television programs, or plays with three or more words in the title. Take turns with your partner saying the titles and linking the words.

Examples

Lost in Translation   *The Marriage of Figaro*   *Romeo and Juliet*   *The Wizard of Oz*

Group Practice 1: Finishing numbers and linking

1. Close your eyes and slowly whisper *nine*. Feel your tongue touch the gum ridge for *n* at the beginning and again at the end of the word. Now say *five, seven*. Feel your teeth gently touch the inside of your lower lip at the beginning and at the end of the word. Lower your jaw for the vowel in *five, nine,* and *clock* (as in *o'CLOCK*). Pay attention to the last sound of each number.

2. Whisper these phrases. Link the numbers to the next word. Feel the linking and your jaw lowering.

one o'clock	five eggs	seven avocados	nine hours later
nine o'clock	five oranges	seven animals	nine envelopes
ten o'clock	five elephants	seven o'clock	ninety-five offices

f. Partner Practice: Dictating information

Divide long numbers and Web addresses into thought groups to make your speech easier to understand

1. Listen to the following sentences and draw a slash (/) where you hear a pause. Underline the focus word, number, or letter in each thought group.

Example My **PHONE** number /is **Ar**ea code / 3 1 **0** / 8 5 **9** / 9 7 4 **5**. /

1. My address is 1 5 9 Second Avenue, Freeport, Texas 76951.
2. My credit card number is MasterCard 4 8 8 1 5 7 9 2 6 1 9 7.
3. The website address is http://www.gorilla.org.
4. The number you have dialed, 3 1 0 4 5 8 8 0 9 7, has been changed. The new number is 2 1 3 6 5 9 7 8 6 2. Please make a note of this.

2. With a partner, take turns dictating information. First write down the information you plan to dictate, such as an address, phone number, website, or imaginary credit card number.

3. Dictate your information using complete sentences. Monitor for pauses, focus, and finishing and linking numbers. Exchange suggestions about your pronunciation.

Finishing Consonant Clusters

A cluster is a group of things that are similar, such as a cluster of cherries or a cluster of houses.

Consonants in English are often clustered together at the beginnings and endings of words and across word boundaries. Pronouncing consonant clusters can be challenging if your native language does not group consonants together. You might omit a consonant from the cluster or add a vowel to separate the cluster. People learning English often have difficulty pronouncing final sounds and linking them because of consonant clusters.

1. Clusters at the beginnings and endings of words:

    trip trips stop stops block blocks stripe stripes split slips snaps stopped slipped

2. Clusters across word boundaries

Some consonant clusters result from linking words together in phrases and sentences. For example, in *He likes to talk,* the speaker has to link k s t with no vowel in between. The "e" is silent.

Finished my work ⟶ fini**sht**my work

g. Partner Practice: Consonant clusters

1. Listen and repeat the phrases.

2. Write the underlined clusters that result when words are linked together in the following phrases. The silent vowels are marked with an "x." Compare answers with your partner.

Examples my favoritex̸ movie   t m   Wherex̸'s my wallet?   r z m

1. It's Monday. ____ ____ ____
2. the bus driver ____ ____ ____
3. an electric stove ____ ____ ____
4. five dollars ____ ____
5. That's fine. ____ ____ ____
6. a card store ____ ____ ____ ____
7. stop shouting ____ ____ ____
8. cooked supper ____ ____ ____
9. a word processor ____ ____ ____ ____
10. a television station ____ ____ ____

3. Practice with your partner, monitoring for the clusters.

Speech Rhythm: Stress and Unstress

English speech rhythm has very strong (stressed) and very weak (unstressed) beats. The stressed words are called *content words* because they contain most of the meaning. As you learned, the focus word gets the strongest stress in a thought group. The weak, unstressed words can be hard to hear clearly.

Learn By Listening 5: End-of-the-sentence intonation

Speech rhythm and intonation are closely connected. The voice and the melody line tend to rise on the stressed syllables and words and to fall on the unstressed ones.

```
        PUT           VER            LIKE
 com              un.i                      I
       er              si.ty                     you
```

The melody line of the last word in a sentence is called *end-of-the-sentence intonation*. This often involves the focus word. Most sentences end with a downward pitch line, or melody, called *falling intonation*. Falling intonation lets your listener know that you are finished with the sentence.

1. Listen to the words followed by humming and then to the sentences with falling intonation. (To *hum* is to sing the melody saying *hmmm*.) The melody either steps or glides down. (To *glide* is to move smoothly and effortlessly.) Replay the tape and repeat what you hear.

Glides The pitch on the last stressed syllable jumps up before it glides down.

    aGAIN   I heard it aGAIN.

    MATH   I teach MATH.

Steps If the stressed syllable is not last, the pitch goes up on the stressed syllable and then steps down.

    RAINbow   I can see a RAINbow.

    proFESsor   I'm a proFESsor.

2. Listen and repeat the phrases. Sometimes the focus word is not the last word in the sentence. The melody will step down.

    Glad to MEET you.   The plane hasn't arRIVED yet.

    Let's EAT now.   I've never BEEN there.

---

figure out the guideline Write the word *steps* or *glides* on the line. If the last syllable is stressed, the melody _____ down. If the last syllable is unstressed, the melody _____ down.

---

h. Improve Your Monitoring: Steps and glides

Listen to the speaker hum these sentences. Does the sentence end with a step or a glide? Check (✓) the column that describes the ending. Replay the tape to make sure.

Examples   I bought a comPUter.   ✓ Steps down

                I bought a CAR.   ✓ Glides down

Sentence	Steps Down	Glides Down
1. I bought some equipment.	____	____
2. I need a new pen.	____	____
3. Close your books.	____	____
4. I lost my passport.	____	____
5. It can't compare.	____	____
6. Please pass the sugar.	____	____
7. No smoking allowed.	____	____
8. We need to buy spaghetti.	____	____
9. Let's finish our conversation.	____	____
10. The mail isn't here yet.	____	____

Group Practice 2: Reductions and chunks of speech

Some weak beats in English speech go by so quickly that the words get *reduced*, or shortened. *Chunks of speech* with shortened words or missing sounds are called *reductions*. (A *chunk* is something that is in one thick piece, like a block of wood.)

1. Listen and repeat the following common chunks of speech in *unison*. (To sing or speak in *unison* is to say the same words at the same time.) What you see in print may not be what you hear native speakers say. The arrows show the direction of the end-of-the-sentence intonation.

What You See in Print	What You Hear
1. What do you WANT? ↘	Whad'yaWANT?
2. WHAT do you want? ↗	WHAd'ya want?
3. Give it a TRY. ↘	gividaTRY.
4. Take a CHANCE. ↘	takaCHANCE.
5. Give me a BREAK.[1] ↘	gimme aBREAK.
6. Are you SURE? ↗	are yaSURE?

2. Listen again and repeat the chunk with the reductions. Does the melody rise or fall? The arrows show the direction of the intonation. Tap your hand as you say the focus word.

 ### i. Join the Chorus: Whaddya WANT?

1. Listen and repeat the chant in unison. You will hear linking, reductions, and a strong rhythm pattern. Move your hands and lean forward slightly as you stress the focus words. Then divide into two groups. Say the chant alternating between groups A and B until you sound like a chorus with one voice. Switch groups.

What You See in Print	What You Hear
1. A: What do you want? What do you want? ↘ ↘	whaddyaWANT?
B: I want a piece of candy. ↘	wannapiece[2] aCANdy
B: I want a can of Coke. ↘	wannacannaCOKE
B: I want a cup of coffee. ↘	wannacuppaCOFfee
B: I want to hear a joke. ↗	wannahearaJOKE
A: What do you want? ↘ ↘	WHAddyawant?
B: I want a lot of things! I want it all. ↘	annaLODdathings. wannidALL

[1] **give me a break:** stop trying to fool or bother me

[2] *Wanna* is a common reduction for *want a* or *want to*.

2. B: What do you think? What do you think?   whaddya**THINK**?

    A: I think it's really wonderful.

    A: I think I caught a cold.   caudda**COLD**

    A: I think it's going to rain.   gonna**RAIN**

    A: I think he's getting old.   think'eze getting**OLD**

    B: What do you think?   **WHA**ddyathink?

    A: I think a lot of things. I think about it all.   thinkaboudid**ALL**

3. A: What do you know? What do you know?   whaddya**KNOW**?

    B: I know the world is crazy.   worl diz**CRA**zy

    B: I know the day and date.   day'n**DATE**

    B: I know I'm in _____. (fill in your city, state, or country)

    B: I know it's getting late.

    A: What do you know?   **WHA**ddyaknow?

    B: I know a lot of things,   knowa**LOD**da things

        but I want to know it all.   wannaknowid**ALL**

More Practice

 j. Partner Practice: Two dialogues

1. Listen to the dialogues. Each short sentence is one thought group. Pay attention to the focus words and the final sounds.

Dialogue 1: "Where's the **GATE**?"

A: I'm wondering where to catch my **PLANE**.

B: Let's see your **TICK**et. You need to go to Gate 70-**A**. It's **THAT** way.

A: **THANK** you.

A: Ex**CUSE** me. I can't find Gate 70-**A**. Can you **HELP** me?

B: Gate 70-**A**? There **IS**n't a Gate 70-**A**. Where are you **GO**ing?

A: To Van**COU**ver.

B: You need to go to Gate **78** (seventy-eight). It's in the other di**REC**tion.

Dialogue 2: "Time to **GO**"

A: Hurry **UP**! It's time to **GO**.

B: We don't have to go **YET**. It's too **EAR**ly.

A: **NO**, it's **NOT** too early! It's five o'**CLOCK**. The movie starts at five-**THIR**ty.

B: You're **RIGHT**. We'd better **HUR**ry.

A: That's what I've been trying to **TELL** you!

2. Listen again and repeat one line at a time. Then practice the dialogues with a partner. Monitor for focus words and final sounds. Switch roles.

Sing Along: "Getting to Know You"

In this song from *The King and I* by Richard Rodgers and Oscar Hammerstein, the music echoes the flow of conversational speech. The focus word in each line sounds longer and slower than the other words.

1. Listen to the song and fill in the missing focus words. They are listed here in alphabetical order.

all   breezy   day   easy   know   know   learning   like   me   new   nicely

noticed   precisely   say   tea   way

Getting to _____ you,

Getting to know _____ about you,

Getting to _____ you,

Getting to hope you like _____.

    Getting to know you–

    Putting it my _____, but _____,

    You are _____

    My cup of _____.

Getting to _____ you,

Getting to feel free and _____;

When I am with you,

Getting to know what to _____ –

    Haven't you _____?

    Suddenly I'm bright and _____

    Because of all the beautiful things and _____

    Things I'm _____ about you

    Day by _____.

2. Compare answers with a partner.

3. Discuss the meaning of these expressions.

You are my cup of tea.   free and easy   bright and breezy

k. Partner Practice: Song exercises

Complete the following exercises. Discuss your answers with a partner.

1. Word stress.   Most of the words in the song have one syllable.

Examples   know   you   like

Write the two- and three-syllable words below under the correct pattern on the chart. Trace the pattern as you say the word. The long line shows the stressed syllable. Say it longer and higher in pitch. The long line for *agree* curves down because the melody glides down when the last syllable is stressed.

getting   putting   haven't   noticed   because   suddenly   breezy   beautiful   precisely

 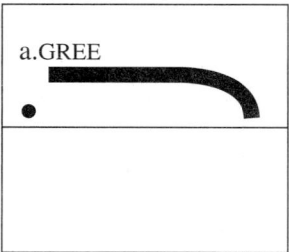  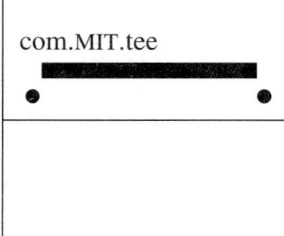

2. Focus words

Say these lyrics from the song and underline the focus words. Lengthen the focus words and change pitch.

Getting to know you . . .[3]	Haven't you noticed? . . .
Getting to like you . . .	Suddenly I'm bright / and breezy . . .
Getting to feel free and easy . . .	Because of all the beautiful and new . . .
Getting to know what to say . . .	Things I'm learning about you . . .
You are precisely / my cup of tea . . .	Day by day . . .

Example   (I'm) getting to know you.

3. Final sounds and linking

Say each phrase in one chunk. Hold the final sound of one word until you are ready to say the next word. Make the focus word easy to hear. These phrases are often reduced in casual speech.

---

[3] The subject of the sentences starting with *getting* is *I*.

cup of **TEA** (cup a'TEA)	bright and **BREE**zy (bright'nBREEzy)
the **BEAU**tiful and **NEW** ('n NEW)	what to **SAY** (what t'SAY)
free and **EA**sy (free'n EAsy)	because of **ALL**

4. Contrastive focus

Listen to these phrases. The words are the same, but the focus is different. Which focus do you hear in the song?

1. I hope you **LIKE** me.
2. I hope **YOU** like **ME**.

Small words such as *you* or *me* are usually not stressed. However, sometimes they are stressed to emphasize new information or to show contrast.

5. Thought groups and end-of-the-sentence intonation

Practice saying the verses of the song using a conversational speech style. Pay attention to the focus words, final sounds, linking, and word stress. Use falling intonation at the end of each sentence.

I. Talk: Getting to know your partner

1. Interview your partner and introduce him or her to the class. Find out your partner's name and native country. Tell at least three important things about your partner. Talk from notes. Emphasize the focus words. Fall in pitch and pause at the end of each sentence.

2. Write three words with more than one syllable that you will say when you introduce your partner. Draw a dot over the stressed syllables. Lengthen them and raise the pitch.

FINISHING UP

Your Targets

Review the pronunciation features listed on page 2. Which two of these features do you think will be most important to improving your English pronunciation? List them below. Explain your choices to your partner and discuss your reasons.

_____

_____

_____

_____

Self-Quiz (Check the answers in the Answer Key, which may be found at http://college.hmco.com/esl/students.)

1. Circle the answer. You can identify a thought group when you hear

    a. a focus word   b. a pause   c. a sweep of melody   d. all of the above

2. True or False? To speak smoothly and clearly, pause only where you would use punctuation such as a period, comma, or paragraph marker.

3. True or False? Missing final sounds can be distracting but do not really affect the meaning.

4. Consonant clusters across word boundaries are a key part of English speech. Write the sounds in the cluster of this phrase. It's Friday. ____ ____ ____ ____

5. In the song "Getting to Know You," several words have more than one syllable. Circle the stressed syllable in these words: getting   noticed   because   suddenly   precisely

Dictation

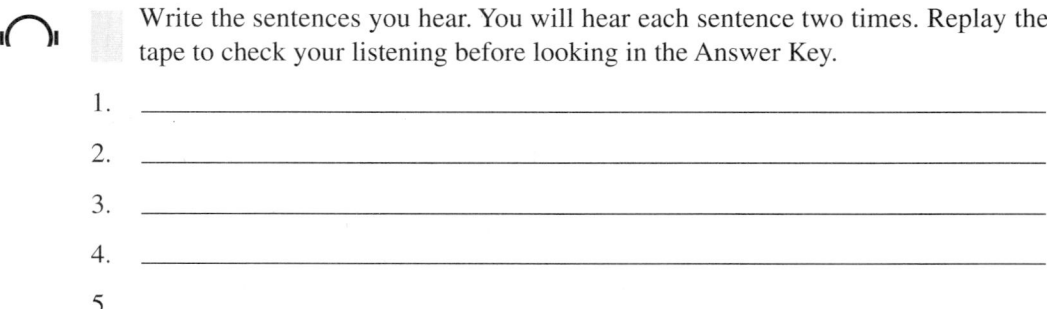

Write the sentences you hear. You will hear each sentence two times. Replay the tape to check your listening before looking in the Answer Key.

1. _____
2. _____
3. _____
4. _____
5. _____

Making Your New Pronunciation a Habit

To make your new pronunciation a habit, you have to use it. Otherwise you may forget what you have learned in class. At the end of every chapter in *Targeting Pronunciation*, you will find an activity called *Talk Times*. This provides an opportunity to practice one or two features of English pronunciation in real-life situations, either over the phone or face-to-face.

Use the *Talk Times* Worksheet (Please visit the Houghton Mifflin ESL website at http://college.hmco.com/esl/students.) for planning and keeping a record of your *Talk Times*. Watch your comfort level increase as you complete more of these activities.

Talk Times in Class

1. Answering machine message

Write a message for your answering machine. Divide your message into thought groups. Emphasize one focus word in each thought group.

Example   You have **REACHED** / 310 / 875 / 2829. / Janet and **I** / are not a**VAIL**able / to answer the **PHONE** right now. / We want to **TALK** to you, / so leave us a **MES**sage / and we'll return your **CALL** / as soon as **POS**sible. / Start **TALK**ing / when you hear the **BEEP** / and speak **SLOW**ly. /

2. Caller message

Write a message to leave on a friend's machine. Decide what information you want to give. Possible topics: a party next weekend; plans for a movie; a mutual friend is in town; a meeting was cancelled; a new class assignment. Include your name, the reason for your call, your phone number, and the best time to reach you.

Example This is your old friend **RO**bert. / I've been trying to reach you for **DAYS**. / What's going **ON**?/ I need to find out about the **MATH** assignment. / Please call me either to**NIGHT** / or to**MOR**row night / at 310 / 829 / 4638. / I'll be home after six o'**CLOCK**. /

3. Partner practice

Take turns saying the answering machine messages and the caller messages you wrote. Emphasize the focus words and pause at the ends of sentences. Ask your partner if your messages were clear. Exchange suggestions. **Suggestion:** Make a tape at home and bring it to class to play. Ask for feedback.

Talk Times in Your Daily Life: The message machine

1. Record a new message that callers will hear on your answering machine. Listen to your message and decide if it is as clear as possible.

2. Call your answering machine. Leave a message 4–6 sentences long, reminding yourself about an event or movie you want to attend, a work task, or a class assignment. Listen several times to your message. Monitor for thought groups, pauses, and focus words. Repeat this assignment and improve your pronunciation.

3. Leave a message on an answering machine for a business or a friend. First use a tape recorder to practice. Listen to your tape and self-monitor. What did you observe? Then record your actual call and message.

Keep track of your experiences on the *Talk Times* Worksheet or in a reflection journal. (See Reflection Journals, page 14.)

On Your Own

1. Audio program

It is better to practice daily for 10–20 minutes than for an hour once a week. Find a time and a place where you will have few or no interruptions so that you can concentrate on self-monitoring. **Suggestion:** Keep a daily record of your practice times. Write them on your daily calendar until you establish a schedule.

2. Recorded practice

Record the following:

(1) the dialogues "Where's the Gate?" or "Time to Go," page 28.
(2) the conversations in Exercise a, page 20, contrasting old information with new information.

Listen to your speech. Is there anything you want to change? Re-record, listen, and notice the improvements.

Note: Your instructor may return feedback about your recorded speech on the Instructor Observations worksheet found on the Houghton Mifflin ESL website at http://college.hmco.com/esl/instructors.

3. Glossary

Collect 3–5 words from your everyday life that you need help pronouncing. Carry a small notebook or packet of sticky notes to write down words as you discover them. Then transfer the words to the Personal Pronunciation Glossary, which may be obtained from the Houghton Mifflin ESL Website at http://college.hmco.com/esl/students. Use your words in sentences.

4. Phone meeting

Call a classmate to talk about this class. It could be the partner you interviewed for the talk "Getting to Know Your Partner."

Write the name and number of someone to call:

Name _____   Phone number _____

5. Small talk

Make short casual conversations in English. Rate your comfort level from 1 to 10 and watch it increase as you make more small talk. 1 = least comfortable 10 = most comfortable. Record your experiences on the *Talk Times* Worksheet or in a reflection journal.

---

a helpful hint

Use a tape recorder to become more comfortable with your own voice speaking English. Listening to your speech on tape gives you a chance to hear things about your pronunciation that you did not hear when you were talking.

Web Activities

Go to elt.heinle.com/targetingpron for additional activities related to this chapter.

Unit II Words

3

Stressing Syllables and Speaking Clearly

Chapter 3 offers practice and some guidelines for pronouncing two-, three-, and four-syllable words, as well as compound nouns. You will learn how pronouncing words correctly becomes the basis for pronouncing short phrases.

Word Stress

English words have one strongly stressed syllable that sounds longer, louder, and higher in pitch than the other syllables. Speech can be hard to understand when the strongly stressed syllable is not clear or when the wrong syllable is stressed.

Learn By Listening 1: Word pairs

Listen and repeat the following sentences. The meaning changes when you change the stress.

Look at the DEsert.

Look at the desSERT.

He gave me a MESsage.

He gave me a masSAGE.

She worked on the **CO**medy.

She worked on the com**MIT**tee.

He lives in a **JEEP** now.

He lives in **E**gypt now.

I'm taking an **AR**abic class.

I'm taking an ae**RO**bics class.

My aunt lives in **MIS**ery.

My aunt lives in Mis**SOU**ri.

Learn By Listening 2: Two-syllable words

Listen, repeat, and tap the rhythm as you say the stressed syllables in the words below.

1. PENcil   DOZen   SOfa

   Most two-syllable words have this pattern.

   Say the phrases: a DOZen PENcils   a NEW SOfa

2. prePARE   apPOINT   reCEIVE

   This pattern is less common.

   Say the phrases: prePARE the DINner   apPOINT the OFficers   reCEIVE a CALL

3. *Trace* the patterns as you say the words in the boxes. (To *trace* is to follow the line and the dots with your finger.) The lines are long and high because the stressed

syllables sound long and the pitch is high. Touch the dot quickly and lower the pitch as you say the unstressed syllable. Then write more two-syllable words under each pattern, and say each word in a phrase.

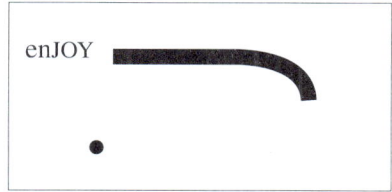

Learn By Listening 3: Nouns

Most two-syllable nouns have stress on the first syllable. Draw a dot over the stressed syllable. Add to the lists.

Examples básket   Álice

Names of Things

table
number
auto
window
office

Names of People

Robert
Betty
Gary
Linda Taylor
David Miller

Note: Some two-syllable names borrowed from French have stress on the second syllable, such as SuZANNE, EuGENE, AnNETTE, ReNEE, and MauRICE.

Group Practice 1: Unstressed syllables and schwa vowels

Unstressed syllables sound weaker than stressed syllables. They are harder to hear clearly because unstressed vowels are low in pitch and short. The vowel sound that native speakers say in most weak syllables is called *schwa*. The symbol for schwa is ə.

Examples DOZən   HUmən   əBOUT

1. To say a schwa, start by relaxing your mouth. Let your tongue rest gently behind your lower teeth. Open your lips a little and say *uh*. The sound is short and low.

2. Listen and repeat these words and sentences in unison until you sound like one voice.

   PRObləm   What's the **PRO**blem?
   MOmənt   **WAIT** a **MO**ment.

SEATed   PLEASE be SEATed.
ROses   I BOUGHT a DOzen ROses.
HUman   It's ONly HUman.

a. Partner Practice: Look-alikes

Some two-syllable nouns and verbs are spelled alike but pronounced differently. Do you see a pattern for which syllable gets the stress?

Examples   PREsent (noun)   It's my birthday PREsent.
               preSENT (verb)   Let's preSENT the idea.

Partner A says either (a), the noun, or (b), the verb. Partner B says the matching sentence. Exaggerate the stressed syllables to make the verbs sound different from the nouns.

1. a. PERmit   You need a PERmit to park here.
    b. perMIT   Please perMIT me to park here.
2. a. INsult   That sounds like an INsult.
    b. inSULT   Don't inSULT the visitors.
3. a. PROduce   They sell PROduce at the market.
    b. proDUCE   Cars proDUCE a lot of smog.
4. a. CONtract   They negotiated a CONtract.
    b. conTRACT   Your muscles conTRACT when you exercise.
5. a. PROgress   He made a lot of PROgress.
    b. proGRESS   Let's proGRESS to the next item.
6. a. OBject   Handle the OBject carefully.
    b. obJECT   Did his boss obJECT to the change?
7. a. INcrease   She got an INcrease in pay.
    b. inCREASE   They tried to inCREASE their profits.
8. a. SURvey   Please answer the questions on the SURvey.
    b. surVEY   Let's surVEY the situation before we decide.
9. a. PROject   We completed the PROject.
    b. proJECT   Please proJECT the slides onto the wall.
10. a. CONduct   The crowd's CONduct was disorderly.
    b. conDUCT   We are planning to conDUCT an experiment.

CHAPTER 3 Stressing Syllables and Speaking Clearly   39

b. Partner Practice: "What am I?"

The suffixes "er" and "or" are not stressed in English.

Examples BETter BIGger MAJor FAVor

1. Listen and repeat the two-syllable names and occupations. Say the stressed syllables longer and higher in pitch.

JAson LIsa RObert KAthy ALlen NANcy MARshall ALice RICHard HANnah
ARTist AUthor BUILDer DOCtor FARMer LAWyer MAYor PLUMBer SAILor TEACHer

2. Choose an occupation from the above list and write it below next to the appropriate job description.

Name	Job Description	Occupation
Jason	writes contracts	Lawyer
Lisa	writes books	Author
Robert	serves in the Navy	Sailor
Kathy	works at a hospital	Doctor
Allen	paints pictures	Artist
Nancy	builds houses	Builder
Marshall	teaches at a kindergarten	Teacher
Alice	fixes plumbing	Plumber
Richard	raises chickens and grows corn	Farmer
Hannah	takes charge of a city	Mayor

3. Say a name and a job description. Then ask your partner, "What am I?" Take turns.

Example   A: My name is JAson. I write CONtracts. What am I?

          B: You're a LAWyer. My name is KAthy. I work at a HOSpital. What am I?

c. Communicative Activity: Interview

1. Interview ten classmates and write down each person's name and current or future occupation. Other students may be interviewing the same ten people.

2. The instructor will say each person's name. If the name is on your list, respond by saying that person's occupation. Speak in unison with others who are responding.

Example Instructor: Pedro   Class: dentist

figure out the guidelines

1. Listen and repeat the phrases with two-syllable words. What parts of speech are the following two-syllable words? (nouns, verbs, pronouns, etc.)

   a FUNny STORy   a PRETty PICture   a FAmous ARTist   PERfect WEAther

   Guideline Stress the first syllable in most two-syllable _____ and _____.
   (fill in the parts of speech)

2. The next two-syllable pattern is much less common. Listen and repeat the phrases.

   I forGOT to apPLY.

   Will they alLOW it or deNY it?

   Let's anNOUNCE it and rePEAT it later.

3. **Figure it out.** What part of speech are the above underlined words?

   Guideline Stress the second syllable in many two-syllable _____.
   (fill in the part of speech)

   Note: Two-syllable adverbs such as *behind, below, ahead,* and *above* also have stress on the second syllable.

---

for your information

More than 90 percent of two-syllable English nouns have stress on the first syllable. More than 60 percent of two-syllable verbs have stress on the second syllable.

---

d. Partner Practice: Predict and pronounce "look-alikes"

Review the look-alike words on page 38. Predict the stress in the underlined words in the following sentences. Take turns saying the sentences. Monitor for word stress.

1. The convict is guilty. The jury voted to convict him.
2. David became a rebel and decided to rebel against the government's unjust policies.
3. The prime suspect in the crime is missing. I suspect he will be found soon.
4. Anna is a convert to the religion, and she is trying to convert all her friends.
5. That's an interesting subject, but please don't subject me to long lectures about it.
6. Let's record the places we visit. I want a record of our vacation.

CHAPTER 3 Stressing Syllables and Speaking Clearly   41

Learn By Listening 4: Three-syllable words

Listen, repeat, and tap the rhythm of the stressed syllables in the words and phrases below.

1. TERrible   WONderful   GOVernment
   a TERrible ACcident   a WONderful iDEa   a GOVernment Agency

2. comMITtee   exAMple   fanTAStic
   a LARGE comMITtee   a GOOD exAMple   a fanTAStic PLAN

3. underNEATH   afterNOON   underSTAND
   underNEATH the umBRELla   this afterNOON   EAsy to underSTAND

4. Trace the pattern with your finger as you say the words in the boxes. Lengthen the stressed syllables and raise the pitch. Touch the dots quickly and lower the pitch on the unstressed syllables. Then write more words below each pattern and say each word in a phrase.

BEAUtiful	exAMple	disaGREE

_____   _____   _____
_____   _____   _____

Learn By Listening 5: Four-syllable words

Listen, repeat, and tap the rhythm of the words and phrases below.

1. occuPAtion   explaNAtion   acaDEMic
   a NEW occuPAtion   a GOOD explaNAtion   an acaDEMic CLASS

2. preOCcupy   aNALysis   asTROLogy
   a psyCHOLogy CLASS   the asTROLogy cHART   a LONG aNALysis

3. SECretary   MEdiator   APpetizer

   an efFIcient SECretary / a COMpetent MEdiator   a deLIcious APpetizer

4. Trace the patterns with your finger as you say the words in the boxes. Write more four-syllable words below each pattern. Say each word in a phrase.

Note: For more examples of words and stress patterns, see the Common Word Stress Patterns worksheet, which may be found at Houghton Mifflin's ESL website at http://college.hmco.com/esl/students. For more practice, complete the Word Stress Chart, also on the website.

---

pronunciation tip To signal the stressed syllable: 1. Lengthen it. (Take your time!) 2. Raise the pitch. (Think high and lift your head!) 3. Emphasize it. (Make it strong!)

Group Practice 2: The Echo Game

Many words in English have the same pattern as short phrases.

repuTAtion	See you LAter.	Glad to MEET you.	How's your FAMily?
compreHEND	in the END	Make a FRIEND.	Pay the BILL.
fanTAStic	It's PLAStic.	Let's FAX it.	The CAB'S here.

1. Divide into two groups. One group is the speaker. The other group is the *echo*. (An *echo* is something that is repeated or imitated.) The echo responds with a phrase that has the same intonation pattern as the word the speaker just said. Work with your group until you sound like a chorus speaking in unison.

   Examples Speaker: acQUAINTed   Echo: He FAINTed.
                 Speaker: underSTAND   Echo: Hold my HAND.

2. Add movement to the echo game. Tap your hands lightly on the unstressed syllables and raise your hands or arms on the stressed syllable. Listen to and watch the speaker. Echo the intonation and copy the hand movements.*

Speaker:	conTENTed	Echo:	He **SENT** it.	Movement:	
Speaker:	interACT	Echo:	It's a **FACT**.	Movement:	
Speaker:	apPROpriate	Echo:	I **NO**ticed it.	Movement:	

3. Alternate between Groups A and B. Group A is the speaker. Group B is the echo.

Examples	Speaker:	satisFACtion	Echo:	It's the **BLACK** one.
	Speaker:	satisFACtion	Echo:	a reACtion
	Speaker:	satisFACtion	Echo:	after **TAX**es

4. Switch speaker and echo roles after each set of three words.

Speaker	Echo	Movement
comMITtee	the CIty	
comMITtee	She's PREtty.	
comMITtee	He's WITty.	
interRUPtion	Let's have LUNCH now.	
interRUPtion	He's my UNcle.	
interRUPtion	in the MIDdle	
accommoDAtion	I'm on vaCAtion.	
accommoDAtion	They're not reLAted.	
accommoDAtion	an obliGAtion	
identifiCAtion	He went on vaCAtion.	
identifiCAtion	Prescribe mediCAtion.	
identifiCAtion	I made the arRANGEments.	
inapPROpriate	I can HOPE for it.	
inapPROpriate	You can Open it.	
inapPROpriate	It's not Over yet.	
comPLEXion	You GUESSED it.	
comPLEXion	He CHECKS it.	
comPLEXion	an EXtra	

*Movement figures were designed by Cathy Davies, Davies Associates.

Speaker	Echo	Movement
aRITHmetic	a BIRTHday gift	
aRITHmetic	I LOOKED at it.	
aRITHmetic	He LIFTed it.	
interACT	It's a FACT.	
interACT	Don't reACT.	
interACT	Here's your HAT.	
macaROni	dozen DOnuts	
macaROni	broken REcord	
macaROni	slice of PIZza	
contraDICtion	Pass the CHICKen.	
contraDICtion	Here's the WINner.	
contraDICtion	science FICtion	

Group Practice 3: Dialogue with movement

Listen and repeat the dialogue. Raise your hands as you say the stressed syllable, as in the Echo Game. For the second pattern, make a gliding movement to the side with your arms.

Listen again and check (✓) the rhythm pattern you hear in each short phrase in the dialogue.

Practice saying the dialogue with a partner. Monitor for word stress.

			Pattern 2	Pattern 3
A:	1.	Excuse me.	✓	
	2.	What's your name?		✓
B:	3.	Betty Ann.		✓
	4.	What's your name?		✓
A:	5.	I'm Tommy.		✓
	6.	Moving in?	✓	
B:	7.	Pretty soon!	✓	
A:	8.	Which unit?		✓
B:	9.	209.	✓	
A:	10.	I'm happy / to meet you!		✓

for your information

The ends of words and sentences are important in English.
- Frequently, the focus word is at or near the end of the sentence.
- Final sounds are important, especially "ed" and final "s."
- End-of-the-sentence intonation tells a lot of information.

e. Improve Your Monitoring: Words and sentences

1. Same or different?
You will hear two words. Listen for the stressed syllables. Is the stress on the same syllable or a different syllable? Circle S (same) or D (different).

Example busy   bigger   (S) D

1. appeal   apple   S (D)
2. appetite   animal   (S) D
3. exercise   excuses   S (D)
4. atlas   at last   S (D)
5. applesauce   apple pie   S (D)
6. possible   possession S (D)
7. ridiculous   radishes   S (D)
8. addendum   added them (S) D
9. subway   subtract   S (D)
10. airport   report   S (D)

2. Which sentence do you hear?
Listen to sentence (a) or (b) from each pair. Check (✓) the sentence you hear

Example a. ___ moved over   b. ✓ move it over

1. a. ✓ Look at the rows of bushes.   b. ___ Look at the rose bushes.
2. a. ✓ It's an integrated school.   b. ___ It's in a great school.
3. a. ___ Was it Colorado?   b. ✓ Was color added?
4. a. ✓ The corporation was helpful.   b. ___ The cooperation was helpful.
5. a. ✓ She speaks her regional language.   b. ___ She speaks her original language.
6. a. ✓ It's numerical.   b. ___ It's a miracle.
7. a. ✓ Simplify your answer.   b. ___ Simply say your answer.
8. a. ___ He marketed the toys.   b. ✓ He marked the toys.

f. Join the Chorus: Limerick

1. Listen and repeat the limerick in unison. Move your hands and lean forward slightly as you stress the focus words.

   A **GLA**morous **IN**ternet User
   Got **MAIL** from an **OB**vious **LO**ser.
   Then **SHE**, in a **DASH**,[1]
   DRAGGED his **NOTE** to the **TRASH**
   In **SPITE** of the **FACT** it a**MUSED** her.

2. Practice linking and reductions in the following phrases.

   from an obvious loser
   dragged his note to the trash
   in spite of the fact it amused her

3. Practice the limerick with a small group until you sound like a chorus speaking in unison. With your group, say the limerick for the class.

Compound Nouns

Compound words are common in English, and new ones are created all the time. They are made up of two parts, often two nouns or an adjective and a noun. For example, air + plane = airplane, or green + house = greenhouse. Compounds have a characteristic intonation pattern that you will learn to recognize.

Learn By Listening 6: Compound noun intonation

1. Listen and underline the strongly stressed words.

   ice cream   cash register   supermarket   fire engine

2. Listen to the melody pattern. Which part sounds higher in pitch? Draw an up-arrow (↑) over the part with the higher pitch.

   grandfather   software   credit card   milk carton

3. Listen and trace the pattern with your finger as you say the words.

   dishwasher   phone call

---

[1] To move in a *dash* means to move quickly.

CHAPTER 3   Stressing Syllables and Speaking Clearly   47

---

guideline   The first word of most compound nouns gets strong stress. Raise the pitch. The second word falls in pitch and gets light stress.[2]

Note: AFterNOON is an exception to the usual compound noun intonation.

4. Computer words are often compounds. Can you add to the list?

DISK DRIVE	KEYBOARD	*mobile phone*
FAX MAchine	comPUter SCREEN	*mouse pad*
CYberSPACE	PRINTer CARTridge	*USB (Universal Serial Bus)*
DESKTOP	WORD PROcessor	*adapter*
SUperDRIVE	DOWNLOAD	*screen capture*

Handwritten additions: Hardware, software, Bluetooth, password, screen saver, laptop, setup

---

for your information

1. Some compounds are spelled as one word. For example:
   roommate • homework • bedroom • doorbell • bookmark • rainfall
2. Some are spelled separately.
   Examples: gas station • swimming pool • trash can • washing machine • bank account • database
3. You cannot tell from listening whether the compound is spelled with one word or two. You must use a dictionary.

---

g. Partner Practice: Compound nouns

1. Match a noun from column 1 with a noun from column 2 to create a compound noun. Write the word in column 3. Take turns saying the compound words in sentences. Raise the pitch noticeably to indicate strong stress.

	1	2	3
Example	cheese	burger	cheeseburger
1.	seat	paper	seatbelt
2.	news	pool	newspaper
3.	super	recorder	supermarket
4.	baby	market	babysitter
5.	tape	belt	tape recorder
6.	swimming	sitter	swimming pool

---

[2] The pronunciation of some compounds can vary occasionally in different regions.

2. Make a list. Add compound nouns that start with the words below. Practice saying them. Raise the pitch on the first part of the compound noun and lower the pitch on the second part.

Car	Book	Coffee	Parking	Sun
car phone	bookshelf	coffee maker	parking lots	Sunday
carseat	bookend	coffee shop	~~lot~~	burn
car wash	bookstore	coffee bean	space	bath
carpool	bookseller	pot / cups	ticket	wash
car insurance	bookkeeper	tab(l)e	meter	sunvisor
Auto		maker machine		

3. Divide into groups of four. Write down as many compound nouns as you and your group can think of in two minutes. Afterward compare lists with the other groups in your class. Monitor the pronunciation of the compounds as you present your list to the class.

Learn By Listening 7: More compound words

1. Listen to find out how the intonation of these compounds differs from the intonation of compound nouns such as CHECKBOOK.

1. Verbs   overSLEEP underSOLD overPRICED overLOADed
2. Adverbs   beHIND beLOW aHEAD aBOVE beSIDE underNEATH
3. Names   New JERsey New BRUNSwick New YORK St. GEORGE San AnTONio
4. Reflexive Pronouns itSELF mySELF himSELF herSELF yourSELF ourSELVES

   It turned itSELF around.   I did it mySELF!   We learned it ourSELVES.

2. Fill in the reflexive pronouns and say the sentences.

She wrote it _herself_. He learned it _himself_. They taught _themselves_.

h. Partner Practice: Short conversations

1. In the following conversations, predict the stress in the compound nouns in brackets. Underline the strongly stressed element. Then listen to the tape to check your predictions.

Example   I lost my <<u>cre</u>dit card>.

1. A: Where is the <<u>sales</u> slip>?

   B: Next to the <<u>cre</u>dit card>.

2. A: I need to make a <phone call>.

   B: There's a <pay phone> at the corner.

3. A: I'd be happy to help with the <home assignment>.

   B: Thank you, but I finished it <myself>.

4. A: Please send the information about your <income tax>.

   B: Do you have a <fax machine>?

5. A: I can't balance my <checkbook>.

   B: You can wait for your next <bank statement>.

6. A: It must be <lunchtime> by now.

   B: I'm dying for a <cheeseburger>.

2. Say all the dialogues with a partner. Be sure to raise the pitch on the first part of the compound.

i. Role play: Visitor with a shopping list

Partner A is a visitor from another country who arrives with a shopping list. Partner B is the host who suggests places to shop.

1. To prepare for the role play, listen to your instructor pronounce the items on the shopping lists and the places to shop. All these are compound nouns.

Shopping List 1	Shopping List 2	Places to Shop
address book	tennis shoes	drugstore
postcards	travel books	snack shop
raincoat	watchband	bookstore
cookbook	razor blades	supermarket
hiking boots	software	department store
sunscreen	blue jeans	shopping mall
hair dryer	candy bar	computer store
printer cartridge	battery pack	
birthday card	cough medicine	

2. Take turns asking and answering questions about where to buy things on the shopping lists. Partner A asks about Shopping List 1. Partner B asks about Shopping List 2. Monitor for compound nouns. Remember to say the unstressed structure words when needed, such as *an, a, the, some, can.*

Examples   an **AD**dress **BOOK**   at a **BOOK**STORE   some **TRA**vel **BOOKS**

Sample Conversation

Visitor: Do you know where I can buy some shoelaces?

Host: They sell shoelaces at the supermarket around the corner.

Visitor: Thank you. Do you know where I can get a toothbrush?

Host: You can buy a toothbrush in the drugstore at a nearby shopping mall.

---

pronunciation tip   Compound nouns often create consonant clusters that cross the boundary between the two words. Be sure to say the final consonant of the first part of a compound noun before saying the second part. Examples: popcorn (pc), sport coat (rtc)

---

j. Join the Chorus: "It's Missing, It's Gone"

Listen and repeat the chant in unison. Move your hands and lean forward slightly as you stress the focus words. Then divide into two groups. Say the chant alternating between groups A and B until you sound like a chorus with one voice. Switch groups. Add more verses.

1. A: I CAN'T FIND my **RAIN**COAT.

    I CAN'T FIND the **PHONE** BOOK.

    WHAT HAPpened to my **BRIEF**CASE?

   B: It's **MISS**ing. It's **GONE**.

2. A: WHERE'd you PUT the **NEWS**PAper?

    I CAN'T FIND the **PEA**nut BUTter.

    Have you SEEN my **BIRTH**day CARD?

   B: You've **LOST** it? It's **GONE**?

Chorus

   A: PLEASE, WON'T you **HELP** me?

   B: I'm **SOR**ry, but I'm **BUS**y now.

   A: WON'T you HELP me **FIND** it?

   B: MAYbe LAter **ON**.

3. B: I CAN'T FIND my **CRE**dit CARD.

    I CAN'T FIND my **HIK**ing BOOTS.

    What HAPpened to my **CHECK**BOOK?

    A: It's **MISS**ing! IT's **GONE**!

4. B: I CAN'T FIND my **SHOP**ping LIST.

    Have you SEEN my **CAR** KEYS?

    What HAPpened to my **TEN**nis SHOE?

    A: It's **MISS**ing. It's **GONE**.

Chorus

B: PLEASE, WON'T you **HELP** me?

A: I'm **SOR**ry, but I'm **BUS**y now.

B: WON'T you HELP me **FIND** it?

A: **MAY**be LAter **ON**.

FINISHING UP

Self-Quiz   (Check the answers in the Answer Key.)

Complete the following word stress charts. They show common stress patterns for two-, three-, and four-syllable words. Each word has one strongly stressed syllable. Listen to the words in each group and write them under the correct pattern. Replay the tape and listen again to make sure.

Two-syllable words

connect letter receive modem houses compare movie surprise

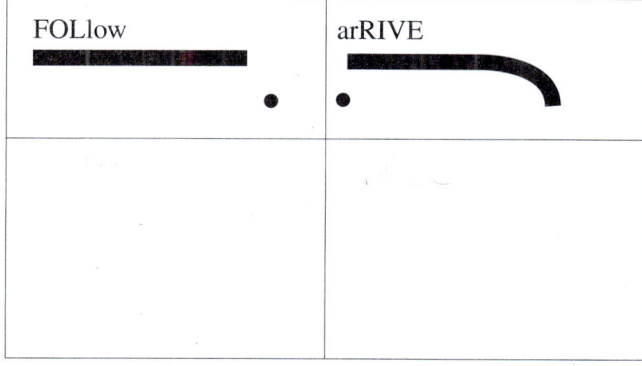

Three-syllable words

important   appointment   introduce   company   engineer   visitor
September   popular   comprehend

OCcupy	comMITtee	underSTAND

Four-syllable words

secondary   population   millennium   television   enjoyable   politician
cemetery   entertainment   exceptional

imMEDiate	introDUCtion	HONorary

Compounds

sky miles   myself   tablespoon   checkbook   themselves   New York
behind   beehive

PHONE CALL	HIMSELF

Making Your New Pronunciation a Habit

Talk Times in Class: Role play

Partner A is shopping at a market. Partner B works at the market. The shopper asks for help finding items on his or her shopping list.

1. Before you begin the role play, look at the shopping list below. Write the number of syllables for each word. Draw a dot over the stressed syllables.

Examples toothpicks 2   tomatoes 3   cucumbers 3   avocados 4

Shopping List   **Compound Nouns**

detergent ___   cranberry juice ___

pepper ___   tuna fish ___

spaghetti ___   peanut butter ___

hamburger ___   coffee cake ___

salami ___   blueberries ___

shampoo ___   ice cream ___

2. Make your own shopping list. Include items with two, three, or more syllables and compound nouns. Write the number of syllables next to each item on your list, and draw a dot over the stressed syllables. When you finish your list, see if you and your partner agree about the stressed syllables on both your lists.

My Shopping List   **Compound Nouns**

_____ ___   _____ ___

_____ ___   _____ ___

_____ ___   _____ ___

_____ ___   _____ ___

_____ ___   _____ ___

_____ ___   _____ ___

3. Role play with your partner. Switch roles. Listen to the sample conversation. The focus words are in bold type.

Shopper: I'm looking for the **CE**real. Do you know where I can **FIND** it?
Clerk: The cereal is on aisle **NINE**.
Shopper: I **LOOKED** on aisle nine, but couldn't **FIND** the cereal I **WANT**ed.
Clerk: I'll check to see if we're **OUT** of it. Is there anything **ELSE**?
Shopper: **YES**, I need some **PEP**per. Do you have fresh ground **PEP**per?

Talk Times in Your Daily Life: Shopping at a store

Use what you have learned about word stress and compound nouns in a real-life situation at a market or other store.

1. Go to a store. Take your shopping list with you. Ask for help finding 4–5 items on your list per visit. Self-monitor. Pay close attention to word stress, pauses, and focus words to make your speech easy to understand.

2. When you finish, describe your experience on the *Talk Times* Worksheet or in a reflection journal.

Making the Most of Your Recorded Practice

Recording and listening to your speech on tape is the quickest way to improve your self-monitoring and your pronunciation. Speech goes by too quickly to hear everything in real time. Throughout *Targeting Pronunciation* you will have regular opportunities to tape and listen to your speech.

Follow these instructions when you are recording from a written script that has a recorded model. For example, you might be taping a dialogue or paragraph from your text that is recorded on the audio program.

1. **Listen to the selection at least four times before you record it.** Pay attention to the pronunciation, one line at a time. Look away from the script whenever possible.

2. **Mark the key pronunciation features on the script.** For example, underline focus words, separate thought groups with slashes, and draw dots over the stressed syllables on longer words. Mark any features you plan to monitor, such as final sounds.

3. **Make a recording.** Self-monitor for one or two features at a time.

4. **Listen to your recording.** Compare it to the original taped selection, line by line.

5. **Decide what you want to improve.** What are your targets? Mark these on the script or take notes.

6. **Re-record and listen again until you are satisfied.** Notice your improvement.

On Your Own

1. **Audio program.** Practice this chapter for 10–20 minutes each day. This is better than practicing once a week for an hour or more. Keep a record of your practice times.

2. **Recorded practice.** Follow the instructions on page 54 for making the most of your recorded practice. Submit your tape to your instructor or send your recording by voiced e-mail. Record the following:

   - Sentences. Use a dictionary to figure out the stressed syllable on the underlined words.

     a. The <u>company</u> has a good <u>reputation</u>.

     b. The <u>restaurant</u> was <u>advertised</u> in the <u>newspaper</u>.

     c. The <u>station</u> has <u>problems</u> with <u>reception</u>.

     d. They <u>speculated</u> in the <u>stock market</u>.

     e. The <u>activity</u> is good for the <u>economy</u>.

     f. She forgot her <u>umbrella</u> <u>underneath</u> the sofa in the <u>waiting room</u>. (Divide this sentence into thought groups.)

   - Either Exercise a, "Look-alikes," page 38, or Exercise h, "Short Conversations," page 48.

3. **Glossary.** Write down hard-to-pronounce words from your everyday life as you discover them. Then transfer them to your Personal Pronunciation Glossary (see page 34).

4. **Small talk.** Look for opportunities to make brief conversations in English every day. Get to know people in class so that you can talk about pronunciation. Call a classmate!

---

a helpful hint

1. Improve your listening by recording your favorite TV program on video so that you can listen again. The more familiar you are with the content, the easier it is to hear the pronunciation. Don't skip the commercials! They can be good for hearing natural pronunciation.
2. Make a list of five longer words you hear on the video, and mark the stressed syllables.

Web Activities

Go to elt.heinle.com/targetingpron for additional activities related to this chapter.

4

More Intonation Patterns: More Words

In the previous chapter you learned that two-, three-, and four-syllable English words and short phrases all have one strongly stressed element. This strongly stressed element stands out because it sounds longer and louder. It also changes pitch noticeably. In this chapter, you will learn how your dictionary can help you pronounce words and predict word stress in groups of related words. You will also learn common intonation patterns for two-word combinations that contrast with the compound noun intonation presented in chapter 3.

Predicting Stress: Which Syllable Should I Stress?

Dictionaries and Pronunciation

The only sure way to know which syllable to stress when you see a new word is to use a dictionary. Dictionaries vary in the ways they show pronunciation so it is important to learn about your dictionary.

Stress. Figure out how your dictionary shows word stress and the number of syllables.

1. Look up the word *banana* in your dictionary and copy the pronunciation below. Here are ways that four different dictionaries show the stressed syllable.

   bə nan´ə   bə **nan**´ə   bə'nan ə   bə.NAN.ə   Your dictionary: _____

2. Look up the word *Canada*. Copy the pronunciation below.

   _____

   Compare the stress patterns for *Canada* and *banana*.

These words are both spelled with a consonant–vowel pattern. Are the stressed syllables the same? ____ yes   ____ no

CHAPTER 4   More Intonation Patterns: More Words   57

Unstress.   Most dictionaries do not mark unstressed syllables, but many do show a schwa vowel ə in unstressed syllables. Does your dictionary show a schwa?
____ yes   ____ no

Look for the ə in the unstressed syllable in *about* ə bout´ and *absent* ab´ sənt. Copy the way your dictionary shows these two words.

_____   _____

Sounds.   Dictionaries vary considerably in the ways they show vowel and consonant sounds. Your dictionary may use a combination of letters or phonetic symbols. These symbols are different from letters. They indicate the pronunciation, but not the spelling, of the word.

Locate the pronunciation key that explains your dictionary's symbol system. For now, the only symbol to learn is the *schwa*, or ə.

Note: The symbols used in *Targeting Pronunciation*, shown in gray boxes, are similar to the International Phonetic Alphabet (IPA). See page xiii.

Secondary stress.   Some dictionaries show two stress marks for longer words. The smaller mark indicates lighter stress, called *secondary stress*. This lightly stressed vowel does not sound like a schwa even though it is always low in pitch compared to the strongly stressed syllable. Look for the lightly stressed syllables below.

appreciate   ə prē´ shē āt´   patriotic   pat´ ri ot´ ik

Look up the following words in your dictionary and copy the pronunciation below. Do you see a secondary stress mark? Locate the schwa vowels.

confidential _____   hippopotamus _____

for your information   You may hear native speakers dropping a middle syllable in some common words.
Examples   family → fam´ly   camera → cam´ra   vegetable → veg´table
salary → sal´ry   chocolate → choc´late   interesting → int´resting
different → diff´rent   favorite → fav´rite   scenery → scen´ry
Most dictionaries show two pronunciations for these words.

a. Partner Practice: Comparing dictionaries

Write the following words on the chart below. Then copy the way your dictionary shows the pronunciation for these words. Draw a dot over the stressed syllables.

allow   application   department   consonant   exceptional   guarantee

58 UNIT II Words

Compare your list with your partner's. Say the words in phrases.

Example pajamas   pə jä′məz

1. _____

2. _____

3. _____

4. _____

5. _____

6. _____

---

pronunciation tip The most important thing you can learn from a dictionary about pronouncing words is which syllable to stress strongly.

Learn By Listening 1: Prefixes and suffixes

Some longer English words fall into patterns. Learning the intonation of these patterns can help you predict stress when you find a similar word and can make the pronunciation of longer words more natural. The following chart shows words with prefixes (syllables at the beginnings of words) and suffixes (syllables at the ends of words).

1. Listen to the words and discover the patterns. Draw a dot over the stressed syllables.

2. Replay the tape many times. Say the words along with the speaker until the pattern becomes automatic. Move your hands and lean forward slightly as you say the stressed syllable. Can you think of more words for each pattern?

Suffixes

Pattern I Where is the stress? On the suffix? Before the suffix? On which syllable? How are the -ary words different from the others?

1. -sion -tion   2. -ic -ical   3. -ian   4. -ary
   decision (3-2)   magic (2-1)   Cambodian (4-2)   secretary (4-1)
   occasion (3-2)   Atlantic (3-2)   Indian (2-1)   voluntary (4-1)
   inflation (3-2)   identical (3-2)   Colombian (4-2)   vocabulary (5-2)
   preposition (4-3)   symmetrical (4-3)   technician (3-2)   contemporary (5-2)

CHAPTER 4 More Intonation Patterns: More Words 59

(handwritten top:) orbital, horizontal, ornamental, instrumental (4-3)

5. -logy   6. -ity   7. -tal   8. -ium -imum
   psychology (4-2)   reality (4-2)   dental (2-1)   aquarium (3-1)
   biology (3-2)   minority (4-2)   accidental (4-3)   auditorium (4-2)
   ecology (3-2)   possibility (5-3) developmental (5-4) maximum (3-1)

9. -graphy   10. -cian (shən) 11. -cial (shəl)   12. -able -ible
   photography (4-2) physician (3-2) commercial (3-2)   memorable (3-1)
   oceanography (5-2) optician (3-2)   official (3-2)   dependable (4-2)
   geography (4-2)   mortician (3-2) financial (3-2)   sensible (3-1)

---

guideline The suffix is not stressed in Pattern I words.
Examples: aTOMic popuLARity anthroPOLogy satisFACtion   *critique*

Pattern II Where is the stress? On the suffix? Before the suffix? On which syllable?

(handwritten:) Japanese engineer. Boutique, technique.
(handwritten left:) employer

1. -ee   2. -ese   3. -eer *volunteer* 4. -ique   5. -ette *kitchenette*
   employee (3-3)   Vietnamese (3-3) pioneer (3-3)   unique (2-2)   cassette (2-2)
   trustee (2-2)   Japanese (3-3)   auctioneer (3-3)   antique (2-2)   marionette (4-4)
   refugee (3-3)   Chinese (2-2)   career (2-2)   physique (2-2)   cigarette (2-1) or (3-3)

(handwritten:) Mantee, Roteree, guarantee, appointee,

---

guideline Stress the suffixes in the Pattern II words.
Examples: traiNEE volunTEER techNIQUE

Prefixes   *NO*

Is the stress on the prefix?

1. un-   2. in-   3. pre-   4. ex-   5. mis-
   unhealthy (3-2)   intolerant (4-2)   prevent (2-2)   explain (2-2)   misplace (2-2)
   unwise (2-2)   insufficient (4-3) prefer (2-2)   expose (2-2)   mistake (2-2)
   unnecessary (5-2) indifferent (3-2) predict (2-2)   experience (4-2) misrepresent (4-4)

---

guideline Prefixes are not usually stressed in English.
Examples: atTRACT preTEND misLEAD

60 UNIT II Words

pronunciation tip	All pronunciation guidelines in English have exceptions!
	Examples of common words that do not follow the above patterns:
	COFFee TELevision aRITHmetic NAturalize PERmeate
	Some words have two pronunciations: *Employee* can be emPLOYee or employEE

Learn By Listening 2: Related Words

1. Listen and repeat the related words listed across the following chart until they become natural.

Base Word	Related Noun	Adjective + (al)ly = Adverb	Verb
1. NAtion	nationALity	NAtional + ly	NAtionalize
2. PSYche	psyCHOLogy, psyCHOLogist	psychoLOGical + ly	psyCHOLogize
3. eCONomy	ecoNOMics, eCONomist	ecoNOMical + ly	eCONomize
4. SYMpathy	SYMpathies	sympaTHEtic + ally	SYMpathize

2. Then say the following related words. Monitor for the stressed syllable.

5. Edit	ediTORial	ediTORial + ly	ediTORialize
6. aSTRONomy	aSTRONomer	astroNOMical + ly	
7. PHOtograph	phoTOgrapher	photoGRAphic + ally	PHOtograph
8. MAGnet	MAGnetism	magNEtic + ally	MAGnetize

Suggestion: Look in a dictionary to discover more groups of related words. Notice the parts of speech for each set.

b. Partner Practice: Predict the stress

Look at the word lists with prefixes and suffixes on pages 58 and 59. Predict the pronunciation of the words in the following phrases. Draw a dot over the stressed syllables. Compare answers with your partner.

Example   identification

a usable cassette   Lebanese engineer   enormous popularity
Peruvian refugee   Japanese antiques   magnetic personality
maximum security   indifferent majority   financial possibilities

c. Role Play: Tuesday night at the planetarium

Partner A wants to go to the planetarium and calls for information. Partner B answers the phone at the planetarium.

1. To prepare for the role play, use what you learned about prefixes, suffixes, and compound nouns to predict the stress in the underlined words on the planetarium webpage below. Draw a dot over the stressed syllables. Then practice saying the words. Raise the pitch and lengthen the stressed syllables.

2. In the role play, Partner A calls to find out more about the Tuesday evening program. Partner B answers the questions and directs Partner A to the planetarium website.

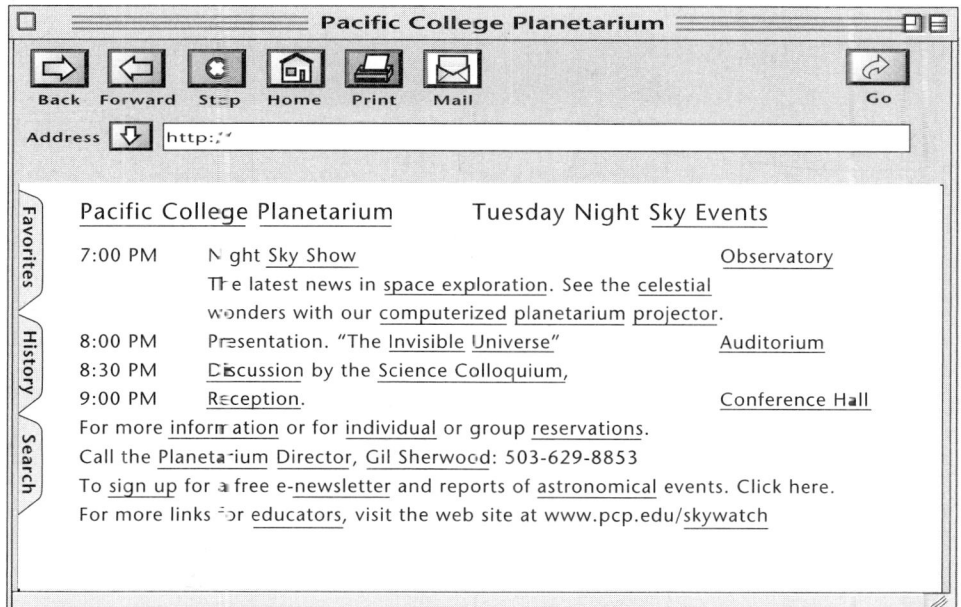

Sample Dialogue

B: Pacific College Planetarium. May I help you?

A: Yes, I would like information about your Tuesday night program.

B: OK. At 7 P.M. we have our night sky show in the observatory. This show features our computerized planetarium projector, which provides the latest information about space exploration. You can find more information on our website.

Descriptive Phrases

Learn By Listening 3

In chapter 3 you learned the pattern for pronouncing compound nouns. Now you will learn the pattern for *descriptive phrases*. Descriptive phrases are two-word combinations with the stress on the last word.

1. Listen and repeat the phrases. Where is the focus?

   WALKing SLOWly   a RAINy DAY   APple PIE   COlor COPies   SOFT PILlow

2. Contrast the above descriptive phrases with compound nouns. Notice the difference in focus and intonation. Replay the tape until you can say the phrases with the speaker.

   WALKing SLOWly   WALKing SHOES   COlor COPies   COlor BLIND
   a RAINy DAY   a RAINCOAT   SOFT PILlow   SOFTWARE
   APple PIE   APple JUICE

d. Improve Your Monitoring: Two-word combinations

Listen to the two-word combinations. For each combination, decide if you hear the pattern for a descriptive phrase or a compound noun. Which word gets more stress?

				Compound Noun	Descriptive Phrase
Examples		applesauce	I ate some applesauce.	✓	
		apple pie	I ate some apple pie.		✓
1.	a.	fresh bread	Here is the fresh bread.		✓
	b.	French bread	Here is the French bread.	✓	
2.	a.	sleeping bear	I saw a sleeping bear.		✓
	b.	sleeping bag	I saw a sleeping bag.	✓	
3.	a.	orange juice	I'd like some orange juice.	✓	
	b.	orange sherbet	I'd like some orange sherbet.		✓
4.	a.	fresh cream	I want some fresh cream.		✓
	b.	ice cream	I want some ice cream.	✓	
5.	a.	space shuttle	Let's wait for the space shuttle.	✓	
	b.	last shuttle	Let's wait for the last shuttle.		✓
6.	a.	golf course	We met at the golf course.	✓	
	b.	new course	It was a new course.		✓

e. Partner Practice: Finish the descriptive phrases

The first sentence in each pair ends with a compound noun. The other ends with a descriptive phrase. The focus and the intonation should sound different.

1. Add an adjective of your choice to complete the descriptive phrase.

Example   I bought a **SWEAT**SHIRT.

   I bought a *green* **SHIRT**. (other choices: *blue, new, striped, silk*)

Compound Nouns

1. I bought some **SUN**GLASses.
2. They went on a **BUS** RIDE.
3. Here's some to**MA**to JUICE.
4. I made a **PHONE** CALL.
5. I like your **TEN**nis SHOES.
6. John gave me a **COOK**BOOK.

Descriptive Phrases

1. I bought some ___new___ **GLAS**ses.
2. They went on a ___free___ **RIDE**
3. Here's some ___fresh___ **JUICE**
4. I made a ___private___ **CALL**
5. I like your ___new___ **SHOES**.
6. John gave me a ___interesting___ **BOOK**.

2. Partner A says the sentence with the compound noun. Partner B says the sentence with the descriptive phrase. Take turns. Remember to glide or step down in pitch at the end of each sentence.

f. Partner Practice: Compound nouns and descriptive phrases

Partner A asks either (a) or (b). Partner B answers. The focus words are shown in bold type.

Examples   A: Where do you like to sleep?   in a DARK **ROOM**.

   B: Where is he developing the pictures?   in the **DARK**ROOM?

1. a. What are you doing with the **CHALK**?   writing on the **BLACK**BOARD
   b. What are you using to build the **BOOK**CASE?   a BLACK **BOARD**
2. a. What's the fastest **ROUTE**?   the **FREE**WAY.
   b. What is the **CHEAP**est way to **GET** there?   a free WAY with no **CHARGE**.

3. a. What are you doing with the **WA**ter?   Giving a drink to the hot **DOG**.
    b. What do you want for **LUNCH**?   a **HOT** DOG and a cold DRINK.
4. a. Where does the U.S. **PRES**ident live?   In the **WHITE** HOUSE.
    b. Where do you **LIVE**?   In the WHITE HOUSE.
5. a. Where does your rich **UN**cle live?   He lives on a REAL e**STATE**.
    b. What kind of **WORK** does he do?   He sells REAL eSTATE.
6. a. Why are you **LATE**?   I made a SHORT STOP on the WAY.
    b. Does **JA**son play **BASE**BALL?   Yes, he plays **SHORT**STOP.
7. a. Where did you grow the **PLANTS**?   In a **GREEN**HOUSE.
    b. Where does your **COU**sin live?   In the GREEN HOUSE.

for your information

You can't tell from looking whether two words that go together should sound like a compound noun or a descriptive phrase. You have to listen. You might think that the following phrases are compound nouns. In reality, the intonation and the stress sound like descriptive phrases or names, not like compound nouns.

fast food   science fiction   iced tea   instant coffee   clock radio   frozen yogurt

Historically words can change. Some of these phrases may sound like compound nouns in the future.

Phrasal Verbs

Phrasal verbs have two words that are pronounced as a unit. *Turn on. Pull over.* The first word is a verb. The second word is called the *particle*. (A *particle* is a very small piece, a fragment.) In a phrasal verb the particle is usually an adverb or a preposition that comes after the verb.

Examples   Put **ON** your hat.   Clean **UP** the mess.   Take **OFF** your shoes.

CHAPTER 4 More Intonation Patterns: More Words 65

Learn By Listening 4: Contrast phrasal verbs and compound nouns

1. Listen and compare the stress and intonation of the phrasal verbs and the compound nouns below. Underline the stressed words.

Phrasal Verbs	Compound Nouns
work out	workout
drop out	dropout
print out	printout
cover up	cover-up
run off	runoff
tear off	tear-off

2. Sometimes the particle can be separated from the verb.

   Examples Take it a**WAY**.   Put them **DOWN**.   Print it **OUT**.   Clean it **UP**.
   Turn it **ON**.

figure out the guideline   Circle the answer:
In phrasal verbs, the (verb–particle) gets the strong stress.

g. Partner Practice: Phrasal verbs and compound nouns

Partner A says either (a), the compound noun, or (b), the phrasal verb from each pair. Partner B says the matching sentence.

Example   A: WORK OUT   B: How did the plan work out?

1. a. **WORK**OUT   That was quite a workout.
   b. WORK **OUT**   How did the plan work out?
2. a. **DROP**OUT   He's a college dropout.
   b. DROP **OUT**   Did he drop out of the race?
3. a. **PRINT**OUT   The ink on the printout is faded.
   b. PRINT **OUT**   I need to print out some extra copies.
4. a. **CO**ver-UP   The criminals were involved in a cover-up.
   b. COver **UP**   Please cover up the baby.
5. a. **RUN**OFF   The runoff is from the melting snow.
   b. RUN **OFF**   The thief tried to run off with my wallet.
6. a. **TEAR**-OFF   There is a tear-off at the bottom of the page.
   b. TEAR **OFF**   Don't tear off the label.

h. Cartoon: Drabble

Read the cartoon and emphasize the focus words.

Find and write the compound noun: _____

the descriptive phrase: _____

the phrasal verbs: _____ _____

DRABBLE by Kevin Fagan

DRABBLE reprinted by permission of United Feature Syndicate, Inc.

i. Join the Chorus: "Wishes"

Listen and repeat the chant in unison. Move your hands and lean forward slightly as you stress the focus words. Then divide into two groups. Say the chant alternating between groups A and B until you sound like a chorus with one voice. Switch groups.

A: What do you do with a hungry tiger?

B: Keep it away from the sleeping baby.

A: What do you do with a shiny car?

B: Cover it up on a rainy day.

A: What should I do with an apple pie?

B: Put it down on the kitchen table.

A: What do you think of the gorgeous sunset?

B: I like it better than the cloudy sky.

A: What did you order with the mushroom omelet?

B: Buttered toast and some fried potatoes.

A: Did you make a wish on a falling star?

B: I made a wish on a falling star.

A–B: I wished for—a gorgeous sunset, a mushroom omelet, a sleeping baby, a shiny car, and an apple pie.

CHAPTER 4   More Intonation Patterns: More Words   67

j. Communicative Activity: Your ideal weekend

1. Below is a list of phrasal verbs that you can use to talk about your ideal weekend. Read them with correct stress. Add your own verbs. Plan which verbs you will use.

2. Describe your weekend to your partner, and listen to your partner's description.

call up	get away	try out	_____
camp out	get up	ride over	_____
close up	go out	set up	_____
climb out	lock up	sit down	_____
drive over	pick up	stay out	_____
eat out	plan out	walk over	_____
flake out[1]	take it easy[2]	work out	_____

3. Change partners and take turns telling your new partner about your ideal weekend.

Names

Learn By Listening 5

Listen and repeat the names and descriptive phrases. These have the same pattern. The last name and the last word in the phrase get stronger stress than the first name or word. The pitch steps or glides down.

SHIRley TEMple	The ROCky MOUNTains	FROzen PIZza
MICHael JORdan	AMERican AIRLINES	DIet COla
MOther TeREsa	NiAGra FALLS	BOILing WAter
THOmas JEFferson	MEXico CIty	WINter JACKet

k. Partner Practice: Conversation with names

Make a list of the names of your favorite performers, writers, or artists. Draw a large dot over the stressed syllables. Underline the focus words. Talk about your choices with your partner.

Examples   John S̱teinbeck   Elton J̱ohn

---

[1] **flake out:** to lie down; to rest
[2] **take it easy:** to proceed at a comfortable pace without rushing

l. Communicative Activity: Talk about where you live

1. Listen and say these names of places and streets. Underline the word with strong stress.

    Se**A**Ttle, **WASH**ington   **CAL**gary, Al**BER**ta   **TREN**ton, New **JER**sey

    FIFTH **AVE**nue   LINcoln **BOUL**evard

    Note: Names ending with the word *street* sound like compound nouns.
    FOURTH STREET   **NINTH** STREET   **GIN**ger STREET

2. Write down the names of six streets and places in your community, including the nearest cross streets to your home. Check with your instructor to find out the correct pronunciation. Draw large dots over the stressed syllables and underline the words with strong stress.

    Examples: Princeton <u>Avenue</u>   MacDougall's <u>Drugstore</u>   Creative <u>Computers</u>
    Arizona <u>Avenue</u> and <u>Third</u> Street

3. Tell your partner about where you live. Talk about the city, state, nearby cross streets, and places in your community. Monitor your own and your partner's pronunciation. Exchange suggestions about what you notice.

m. Communicative Activity: Interview

You are going to interview your classmates about their job or their school.

1. Prepare by filling in your workplace and school information below. Ask your instructor how to pronounce key names.

Place name _____

- **Location**   (include address, city, state, cross streets, part of city/town)

    1162 El Abra Way, San Jose, California
    Willow glen, near willow st crosses Lincoln Ave

- **Workplace description**   *I work at home*

_____

- **Your job title (what do you do?)** _____

CHAPTER 4 More Intonation Patterns: More Words 69

School name _____

- **Location** (include cross streets, city, state, part of city/town)
  3000 Mission College Blvd, Santa Clara, California
- **Your major, minor, special interests** Graphic Design, Digital Illustration, Art & Food
- **Plans after graduation** an licensing artist, specia[lize] in illustration & surface pattern design

2. Make a list of questions for the interview based on the items above. Write four questions for the school interview and four for the workplace interview.

3. Divide into groups of three or four for the interview. Each person takes one of these roles: (1) interviewer, (2) person interviewed, (3) observers. (The observers take notes on the pronunciation and offer suggestions to each speaker.) When it is your turn to be interviewed, tell the interviewer whether you want to talk about your school or your workplace.

4. Change roles after each interview.

🎧 Sing Along: "This Land Is Your Land"

During the Great Depression of the 1930s Woody Guthrie roamed across many states on his way to California to look for work. He wrote this and other songs as he traveled on foot with his guitar. The lyrics of this song translate easily into conversational speech.

1. Listen to the song. Fill in the missing focus words. They are listed here in alphabetical order:

   above   around   below   forest   deserts   island   lifting   me   rolling
   shining   valley   walking   waters   your   my

2. Compare answers with a partner. Replay the song.

1. As I was _____ that ribbon of **HIGH**WAY,

   I saw _____ me that endless **SKY**WAY,

   I saw _____ me that golden _____.

   This land was **MADE** for you and _____.

Chorus

This land is _____ land, This land is _____ land,

From Cali**FOR**nia to the New York _____

From the redwood _____

To the Gulf Stream _____

This land was **MADE** for you and **ME**.

2. I've roamed and **RAM**bled and I followed my **FOOT**STEPS,

    To the sparkling **SANDS** of her diamond _____

    And all _____ me a voice was **SOUND**ing,

    "This land was **MADE** for you and _____."

    Chorus

3. When the sun came _____, and I was **STROLL**ing

    And the wheat fields **WAV**ing and the dust clouds _____,

    As the fog was _____ a voice was **CHANT**ing,

    "This land was **MADE** for you and _____."

    Chorus

3. Discuss the vocabulary.   roam   ramble   fog   chant   stroll   dust   clouds

Note: In the song you hear this intonation: This land is **MY** land. This land is **YOUR** land. The pronouns are stressed to show contrast and to emphasize that the country belongs to everyone.

n. Partner Practice: Song exercises

1. Word stress. There are many two-syllable words in this song. Some are compound nouns. Write the two-syllable words from the song on the chart. Say the words as you trace the pattern with your finger.

PAper ●	beLIEVE ●	Compound Nouns

2. **Descriptive phrases.** Add the focus word to these phrases from the song and practice saying them. Focus on the last word. In the last two phrases below you will see a compound noun in brackets. This compound noun becomes part of the descriptive phrase.

   a golden _____   her diamond _____

   an endless _____   the [dust clouds]_____

   the sparkling _____   the [wheat fields]_____

3. **Important endings: "ed" and final "s."** Fill in the missing endings. Practice saying these phrases from the song. Slow down and lengthen the focus words, but link them to the next word in the sentence.

   1. I've roam____ and ramble____ / and I follow my footstep____ /
   2. to the sparkling sand____ / of her diamond desert____ /
   3. and the wheat field____ waving / and the dust cloud____ rolling /

4. **Song lyrics.** Practice saying each verse as if you are telling a story. Lengthen the focus words and signal the end of the sentence by falling in pitch. Join in with a small group to say one of the verses for the class.

   1. As I was **WALK**ing / that ribbon of **HIGH**WAY, / I saw a**BOVE** me / that en**d**less **SKY**WAY. / I saw be**LOW** me / that golden **VAL**ley. / This land was **MADE** / for you and **ME**. /

   2. I've roamed and **RAM**bled / and I followed my **FOOT**STEPS / to the sparkling **SANDS** / of her diamond **DE**serts / and all a**ROUND** me / a voice was **SOUND**ing / "This land was **MADE** / for you and **ME**."/

   3. When the sun came **SHIN**ing / and I was **STROLL**ing / and the wheat fields **WAV**ing / and the dust clouds **ROLL**ing / as the fog was **LIFT**ing / a voice was **CHANT**ing / "This land was **MADE** / for you and **ME**."/

o. Dialogue: "A Great Weekend"

1. Listen and practice the following dialogue with a partner. Pay attention to the phrasal verbs, the compound nouns, the descriptive phrases, and the names.

   1. A: I'm going away for the weekend. Would you and your roommate like to come along?

   2. B: My roommate usually can't get away. She's an X-ray technician at Memorial Hospital and only gets off one weekend a month.

   3. A: Sounds like a hard work schedule!

   4. B: It is, but she likes her job. Where are you planning to go?

   5. A: Sightseeing in the countryside near Angel's Ranch. I need some sunshine. I'm tired of the traffic jams and the car exhaust.

6. B: Sounds good to me. There's a phone booth across the street from Charlie's Market. I'll try to get ahold of my roommate.

7. A: (*B returns.*) So what did she say? Can she take off for the weekend?

8. B: Yes! She can! The good news is that her backache is almost gone. And her headaches aren't a problem anymore. She still gets carsick, but not if we pull off the highway every ten or fifteen minutes and let her walk around.

9. A: Terrific! It sounds like a great weekend.

2. Replay the tape and listen to A's comment in line 9 again. The intonation gives you extra information. Do the words mean what they say or do they mean the opposite?[3]

3. There are six phrasal verbs, three names, and fifteen compound nouns in this dialogue. How many can you find? Make a list of these two-word combinations, and compare lists with your partner.

4. Prepare to present the dialogue to the class with a partner. Use the correct focus and intonation. Practice both roles A and B.

FINISHING UP

Self-Quiz (Check the answers in the Answer Key.)

1. a. Underline the compound nouns.

     greenhouse   green house   White House   white house

   b. The strong stress is on the (__first __second) element.

2. a. Underline the descriptive phrases.

     white house   new glasses   broken glasses   sunglasses

   b. The strong stress is on the (__first __second) element.

3. a. Underline the strongly stressed element in the following names:

     John Adams   Brooke Shields

   b. The strong stress in a name is on the (__first __ last) name.

4. True or False? The main verb in a phrasal verb gets strong stress.

5. Underline the strongly stressed element in the following phrasal verbs:

   slow down   speed up   print out   check it out   set it down

---

[3] You will learn more about this kind of intonation in chapter 7.

Making Your New Pronunciation a Habit

Talk Times in Class: Role play

Partner A works for the "Y" (YMCA, a community organization with a health club). You are enthusiastic and try to interest people in the program as well as answer questions. Partner B is considering joining the "Y" and wants to find out about the program and what classes fit into his or her schedule.

1. Listen, repeat, and practice the following list of classes with compound noun and descriptive phrase intonation.

    Compound Nouns
    EXercise CLASS   VOLley BALL   CPR
    aeRObics CLASS   BOdy SCULPTing
    STRETCH CLASS   POwer WALKing
    SWIMming CLASS   WAter WORKout
    YOga CLASS   RACquetBALL

    Descriptive Phrases

    CARdioVAScular **JAZZ**

    FITness after FIFty-**FIVE**

2. Role play with your partner. Then switch roles.

Partner A: Look at the "Y" schedule below. Your partner will be asking for information about it. Describe some of the classes, and try to convince your partner to join.

TIME	MON.	TUES.	WED.	THURS.	FRI.	SAT.	SUN.
7 AM	aerobics	swimming	yoga	water workout	CPR	water workout	stretch class
10 AM	power walking	water workout	body sculpting	fitness after 55	swimming	volley ball	exercise class
NOON	cardio/jazz	swimming	stretch class	aerobics	volley ball	CPR	racquetbal
5 PM	aerobics	power walking	cardio/jazz	water workout	body sculpting	fitness after 55	water workout
7 PM	swimming	cardio/jazz	racquetball	yoga	aerobics	cardio/jazz	yoga

Partner B: Look at the list of available classes, and decide which ones you would like to take. Inquire about the classes available during your free time, marked by asterisks. Fill in your personal calendar below.

TIME	MON.	TUES.	WED.	THURS.	FRI.	SAT.	SUN.
7 AM	*	*	*	*	*	*	*
10 AM						*	*
NOON	*	*				*	*
5 PM			*		*	*	*
7 PM	*	*		*		*	*

Sample Conversation

A: I am interested in taking a yoga class in the morning. Do you have one available at 7 or 8 A.M.?

B: We have a yoga class on Wednesday mornings at 7 A.M. The instructor is excellent, so I hope that time will work for you.

Talk Times in Your Daily Life: Choosing a health club

1. Call or visit two or three health clubs in your community, including a YMCA, if possible. Make a list of questions to ask.

   Sample topics

   - the activity schedule
   - the cost (dues, the payment plan)
   - how to see the facilities
   - hours
   - child care
   - parking

2. Self-monitor and assess what happened in order to improve the next call. Decide what targets you are going to monitor. Describe your experience on the *Talk Times* Worksheet (see page 32).

The Talking Mirror

A technique called *mirroring* (sometimes known as *tracking* or *shadowing*) can improve your speech and help you sound and look more like a native speaker. To mirror, watch a speaker on video and copy the speaker's words and movements as you see and hear them.

1. **Choose a model.** This should be a person whom you admire and want to imitate. Your instructor may provide help selecting your model.

   a. Select a speaker from a TV program (lecture, interview, drama, or situation comedy)

   b. Select a video of a native English speaker or lecturer from your school or workplace.

2. **Mirror five minutes of the speaker you choose.** Replay the five-minute selection many times as you try to copy everything the speaker says a few seconds after you hear it. Imitate the speaker's hand, face, and body movements. Notice how the movements go with the speech.

3. **Gain experience.** Don't worry if at first you cannot mirror everything. The more you watch the same tape, the easier it will get. Hum along with the speaker when you cannot repeat the words.

Mirroring has proven to be a highly effective practice strategy. **The more times you repeat each mirroring or tracking activity, the more it will help you.** Once you learn the technique, you can mirror silently in your head as you watch and listen to speakers in real-life situations.

Adapted from "Mirroring Project," presented at TESOL 2003 by Colleen Meyers, Jeff Lindgren, and Monica Monk.

On Your Own

1. **Audio program.** Practice this chapter frequently for short periods of time. For variety, say short segments of speech from memory.

2. **Recorded practice.** See how to make the most of your recorded practice on page 54. Listen first and then record the dialogue "A Great Weekend" on page 71. Compare your recording, line by line, to the taped speakers. Submit your tape to your instructor or send your recording by voiced e-mail.

3. **Glossary.** Keep collecting words from your everyday life. This week concentrate on names of streets and places in your community. Ask a native speaker how to say them.

4. **Mirroring.** Read the directions for mirroring above. Mirror five minutes of the movements and speech of a videotaped speaker from TV or another source. Write a reflection journal about this experience.

---

a good idea   Become your own best teacher. Decide what parts of your accent you need to target. Look at the targets on page 2. Then make a list of the three that will make the biggest difference in your speech.

1. _____
2. _____
3. _____

Unit II Progress Check

Make a tape to turn in or to review in a scheduled conference with your instructor. Before you start, look at the tips for recorded practice on page 54.

1. Record the following sentences. Monitor for word stress, focus words, pauses, and end-of-the-sentence intonation. Pay attention to the look-alike nouns and verbs.

   1. If you record your progress in a notebook, you will have a record of it.
   2. The secretary indicated a problem with the equipment. She called the technician to check out the fax machine, the computer screen, and the word processor.
   3. His cell phone did not work out so he decided to return it. When he needed to make a phone call, he looked for a pay phone.
   4. I ordered some new glasses. Meanwhile, I'll have to use my sunglasses.
   5. She is deciding between a career in psychology, biology, or economics. The opportunities for employment will affect her decision.
   6. We discussed a plan to increase our profit without an increase in our cost.

2. Record the information about your school or workplace that you provided in the group interview, Exercise m, page 68. Talk for 1–2 minutes. Monitor for word stress, pauses, final sounds, and names. Re-record until you are satisfied.

Unit III   Phrases and Sentences

5

Speech Rhythm: [rɪðəm]
Stress and Unstress

In chapter 5 you will learn how speech rhythm in English sentences is similar to speech rhythm in words. Both words and sentences have one strongly stressed element. The stressed words are higher in pitch and are held longer. Weak words go by more quickly in English than you might expect from your original language. The pitch differences are also more extreme. You will also learn guidelines for speech rhythm in sentences and how to use speech rhythm, focus words, and contrastive stress to emphasize meaning.

Sentence Rhythm: Strong Stress, Normal Stress, and Unstress

There are three levels of stress in English sentences: (1) strong stress (focus words), (2) normal stress (content words), and (3) unstress (structure words). The stressed words, levels 1 and 2, are important. They tell most of the meaning and stand out like headlines in a newspaper.

CHAPTER 5 Speech Rhythm: Stress and Unstress 77

Learn By Listening 1: Focus words (level 1) and content words (level 2)

1. Look at the drawing. Tap the elephants as you say each stressed syllable. You will hear each sentence twice.

   I FOUND a DOLlar in my POCKet.

   I FOUND a DOLlar in my POCKet.

   - FOUND DOLlar POCKet are all content words. They tell the main meaning.
   - POCKet gets the strongest stress. It is the focus word.

2. Look at the drawing. Tap the elephants as you say each stressed syllable. You will hear each sentence twice.

   I forGOT to SET the aLARM.

   I forGOT to SET the aLARM.

   - forGOT SET aLARM are all content words. ___alarm___ is the focus word.

---

figure out the guideline

Which parts of speech are the following content words?
FOUND DOLlar **POCK**et   forGOT SET a**LARM**
Are they nouns, pronouns, verbs, articles or adjectives?

Content words are often ___Nouns___, ___verbs___, or adjectives.
(fill in the parts of speech)

Learn By Listening 2: Unstress: Structure words (level 3)

The unstressed words in between the content words are called *structure words*. They are important to the grammatical structure of speech and to the rhythm. Structure words can be hard to hear clearly because the vowels are weak and short.

Listen for the structure words in these sentences and write them below.

I am PLANning to TAKE a TRIP.   She LIKES SALT and PEPper on her EGGS.

Structure words: _____
_____

UNIT III Phrases and Sentences

figure out the guideline

Which parts of speech are the following structure words?
I she her his you am are have to the and from
Are they nouns, pronouns, verbs, articles, adjectives, or another part of speech?

Structure words are often ___articles___ ___pronouns___, helping verbs, and other small grammatical words. (fill in the parts of speech)

Group Practice 1: Tap the rhythm

Tap the desk for each stressed word as you say the sentences with the class in unison.

Keep tapping the beats evenly. Notice how the number of words per beat increases.

BEAT 1 (tap)		BEAT 2 (tap)		BEAT 3 (tap)
DOGS		CHASE		CATS
The DOGS		CHASE	the	CATS.
The DOGS are		CHASing	the	CATS.
PEOple		PLANT		TREES
The PEOple	are	PLANTing		TREES.
The PEOple	have	PLANTed	some	TREES.
The PEOple		should have PLANTed	some more	TREES.

Group Practice 2: "Where's Bob?"

Sentences with the same number of words can have different rhythms. The stressed syllables shown in capital letters on the following dialogue get the beat.

1. Listen first and tap the desk for the focus words. Count and compare the number of words, syllables, and beats.

		Words	Syllables	Beats
1.	A: GO FIND BOB.	3	3	3
2.	B: I FOUND him.	3	3	2
3.	A: WHAT'S he DOing?	3	3	3

4. B: **LOOK** at him! 3

5. He's **REA**ding the **ADS**. 4

6. A: **WHAT'S** he **LOOK**ing for? 4

7. B: A **BEAU**tiful **NEW** a**PART**ment. 4

8. A: That's **NOT** so **EA**sy to **FIND**. 5

9. B: **ESPE**cially because he **WANTS**
   CHEAP RENT that in**CLUDES**
   u**TIL**ities and a **GOOD** lo**CA**tion
   that's **NEAR** transpor**TA**tion. 16

10. A: I **HOPE** he **FINDS WHAT** he **WANTS**. 7

2. Divide into groups A and B. Say the dialogue in unison with your group. Switch groups.

Learn By Listening 3: Rhymes

Most English-speaking children learn Mother Goose rhymes at an early age. Although these children don't always understand or say the words correctly, they learn the rhythm.

Linking The words in the rhyme are linked together. Phrases sound like one long word. *Jack and Jill* → *JACK'nJILL*. *Could eat no fat* → *c'dEATnoFAT*.

Listen and repeat the rhymes in unison until you can say them along with the speaker. Tap the desk to keep up with the rhythm. Find the phrasal verbs in the first rhyme.[1]

Two Mother Goose rhymes

JACK and **JILL**	JACK **SPRAT**
went UP a **HILL**,	could EAT no **FAT**.
to FETCH a PAIL of **WA**ter.	His WIFE could EAT no **LEAN**.
JACK fell **DOWN**	and SO be**TWIXT**
and BROKE his **CROWN**,	the **TWO** of them
and JILL came TUMBling **AF**ter.[1]	they LICKED the PLATter **CLEAN**.

[1] Phrasal verbs: go **UP**   fall **DOWN**   TUMble **AF**ter

a. Partner Practice: Match the rhythm

Notice how the sentences match the rhythm of the nursery rhyme. Finish line 3 and add a new line for each rhyme. Practice the sentences with your partner. Tap your hand for the rhythm.

JACK and JILL / went UP a HILL   JACK SPRAT / could EAT no FAT (2-2)

1. Maya Jones is out of town.   1. Bob left before the show.
2. Print it out before you leave.   2. Jane's phone is off the hook.
3. Call a cab and _before I left_.   3. Tom's car is _red_.
4. _Ride a bike for exercise_.   4. _My coat is white_.

to FETCH a PAIL of WAter. (3-3)   His WIFE could EAT no LEAN (3-3)

1. I lost my watch on Sunday.   1. The market closed at nine.
2. We'd rather leave tomorrow.   2. I ran around the block.
3. My sister _is on fire yesterday_.   3. The cat _ran away after frighting a dog_.
4. _She likes to eat pie_.   4. _The dog barks in the fall moon night_.

Predicting Stress: Chart

You can predict stress and unstress in sentences by looking at the parts of speech on the following chart. Study the examples and add more examples to the categories.

Stress: Focus Words (Level 1) and Content Words (Level 2)

Nouns	Main Verbs	Adjectives	Adverbs	Question Words	Numbers and Negatives
phone, paper	call, walk	happy, large	slowly, fast	what, when	don't, won't, ten
_____	_____	_____	_____	_____	_____
_____	_____	_____	_____	_____	_____
_____	_____	_____	_____	_____	_____

Unstress: Structure Words (Level 3)

Pronouns	Helping Verbs	Articles	"To Be" Verbs	Prepositions	Conjunctions
he, her, it	will, have	the, a, an	is, were	on, of, to	and
_____	_____	(There are only three articles.)	_____	_____	but
_____	_____		_____	_____	if — subordinators
_____	_____		_____	_____	because

Group Practice 3: Identifying stressed words

1. Listen and repeat each sentence several times in unison. Underline the content words and circle the focus words.

   Example I put my foot on the brakes.
   1. What would you like for dessert?
   2. I haven't received the bill yet.
   3. Our professional staff will be happy to assist you.
   4. He planted a variety of vegetables in his garden.
   5. Ethnic foods such as bagels and pizza are popular.

2. Now work with a partner. Using the chart on page 80, discuss the parts of speech of the words you underlined. Then say the sentences. Monitor for content and focus words.

b. Partner Practice: Structure words

1. Add structure words to the following sentences. There may be several good choices.

   Example I CALLED you on the TELephone.

   1. WHAT ___did___ ___you___ THINK ___of___ ___the___ MOvie?
   2. ___My___ CAR ___had___ ___a___ FLAT **TIRE**.
   3. ___I___ BOUGHT ___a___ BOX ___of___ CANdy ___for___ ___my___ MOther.
   4. ___I___ SAILED ___my___ BOAT ___in___ ___the___ LAKE ___at___ ___the___ **MOON**LIGHT.
   5. ___Did___ ___you___ FIND ___a___ SHORTCUT ___to___ ___the___ **AIR**PORT?
   6. ___There___ ___is___ ___a___ BIG DENT ___on___ ___the___ DOOR ___of___ ___my___ NEW **CAR**.
   7. ___He___ STOPPED HOME ___on___ ___the___ WAY ___to___ ___the___ **LI**brary.
   8. ___He___ LISTENS ___to___ ___the___ PHONE MESSAGES ___in___ ___the___ **MORN**ing.

2. Compare answers with your partner and practice the sentences. Emphasize the content words. Say the structure words softly. Glide or step down in pitch at the end of the sentence.

practice tip Whisper the structure words to yourself and say the content words out loud. This will highlight the contrast between the stressed and unstressed words.

Group Practice 4: Walking the rhythm

Pausing in the right place and marking stress with some kind of movement will make your speech more effective, especially when you are speaking to an audience. When giving a talk, you need to think in thought groups, or chunks of speech, rather than in single words. You also need to move your arms, head, or body.

1. Listen and repeat the following selection several times in unison. Move your hands and lean forward slightly to get the feel of where to focus and pause. Movements can be tiny or large.

   People who **LAUGH** a lot / are much **HEALTH**ier /

   than those who **DON'T**. /

   That makes **SENSE**, / But did you **KNOW** /

   that people hardly **EVER** laugh / when they are a**LONE** /

   or that we laugh **MORE** /

   when we are **TALK**ing / than when we are **LIS**tening? /

   Can you **GUESS** / why **LAUGH**ter /

   might have seemed **DAN**gerous / to our **AN**cestors? /

   That's because when people **LAUGH** / they often show their **TEETH**. /

   And millions of **YEARS** ago, / showing your **TEETH** /

   was a sign of being **FIERCE**, / not **FUN**ny. /

   Perhaps that makes **SMIL**ing /

   somehow "safer" than **LAUGH**ing. /

2. Now, stand up and walk the rhythm of the thought groups as you and the class say the selection together.[2] Step to the rhythm of the words. Slow down on the focus words and pause on one foot at a slash.

3. Write a paragraph about a funny experience. Divide it into thought groups and start a new line for each chunk. Walk the rhythm of the thought groups as you say your paragraph for the class.

[2] Thanks to William Acton for the idea of walking thought groups.

Focus Words: The Basic Stress Pattern

English speakers use speech rhythm and intonation to emphasize meaning. It would be confusing if all the content words were stressed equally or were said at the same pitch. The focus words change pitch and get the strongest stress to call attention to what is most important.

Learn By Listening 4: Guidelines for focus words

Listen and repeat some examples for each guideline. Tap the desk as you say the focus words.

guideline 1 — The focus word is usually the last content word in each thought group or short sentence.

Basic way.

Add focus words to the incomplete sentences:

We DROVE in the DARK.   I SAT in the LAST ROW.   I WALKED to the __City__.
I WENT to the MOvies.   She WORKS at the BANK.   He inVITed his __girlfriend__.

guideline 2 — The focus word is an important part of speech.

Add focus words to the incomplete sentences. Say the sentences.

The focus word is a (Noun)
JIM is a GOOD TEACHer.
My FAvorite CIty is __Chicago__.
I forGOT to CALL my __wife__.

Verb
It's TIME to EAT.
It's TIME to __work, sleep__.
She JUST LEARNED how to __speak__.

Adjective
The FLOWer is DELicate and BEAUtiful.
The MOvie was VEry __funny__.
His MONTHly rePORT was __bad, awesome__.

Adverb
She FINished QUICKly.
She SPEAKS __slowly, clearly__.
TELL me the ANSwer __completely__ly.

productivity
productive
instant
instantaneous
instantaneously

UNIT III Phrases and Sentences

guideline 3 If there are several content words in a row, the last one gets the focus.

Is basic

| a BUsy SCHEDule | It STOPPED SNOWing. | RED, WHITE, and BLUE |
| reCOvered QUICKly | the LAST YELlow BUS | BLUE, WHITE, and RED |

guideline 4 Adverbs at the end of the sentence that answer the questions *where* and *when* are often unstressed and fall in pitch.

Add focus words to the incomplete sentences. Say the sentences.

I'm planning to **LEAVE** now.   Should we _leave_ now?
I've never **BEEN** there.   There are a lot of _____ here.
We're expecting **RAIN** today.   I'm planning to _____ today.
It's not **FIN**ished yet.   I _____ yesterday.
There are a lot of **TREES** here.   They keep _____ here.
It should have ar**RIVED** already.   He didn't _____ it yet.

guideline 5 Structure words at the ends of sentences in the basic pattern are unstressed and fall in pitch.

Add focus words to the incomplete sentences. Say the sentences.

I'll **WAIT** for you.   I took a _____ of it.
What **BANK** is it in?   I'd like _____ of them.
There's a lot of **CREAM** in it. Whose _____ is this?
We bought **FOUR** of them.   He _____ it to you.

guideline 6 Speakers usually divide longer sentences with more than five or six words into more than one thought group with a focus word in each.

around grammar

Some credit card **COM**panies / offer low **IN**terest / but they charge an annual **FEE**. /
She wants to become an in**TER**preter / and work for an international **COM**pany. /

c. Dialogue: "Fix the Roof"

1. Listen and underline the focus word in each sentence in the dialogue.

A: What's the **matter**?

B: My roof is **leaking**.

A: Why don't you **fix** it?

B: It's **raining**. I don't want to get **wet**.

A: You could **wait** until it stops **raining**.

B: Then I **won't** have to fix the **roof**.

2. Compare answers and practice saying the dialogue with a partner.

d. Join the Chorus: Two poems

1. Listen and repeat two poems in unison. Move your hands and lean forward slightly as you stress the focus words. Then divide into two groups. Say the poems alternating between groups A and B until you sound like a chorus with one voice. Switch groups.

Happy Thought

Group A: The world is so full / of a number of things, /
Group B: I'm sure we should all / be as happy as kings. /

Rain

Group A: The rain is raining all around, /
It falls on field and tree, /
Group B: It rains on the umbrellas here, /
And on the ships at sea. /
—Robert Louis Stevenson

2. Work with a small group to learn one of the poems. Practice until you sound like a chorus speaking in unison. Present your poem to the class.

e. Partner Practice: Focus words

1. Listen and repeat these short conversations in unison as you underline the focus words. Notice where the focus word falls. Is it at the end of the sentence?

1. A: I got a call from Jennifer.

   B: Really? I wonder how her father is.

2. A: I'd like to find out about the college.

   B: Here's some information for you.

UNIT III Phrases and Sentences

3. A: John isn't feeling well.
   B: What's the matter with him?
4. A: How long have you been here?
   B: About an hour.
5. A: Peter finally arrived.
   B: Good. We've been waiting for him.
6. A: Did you remember to cash the check?
   B: No. I forgot about it.

2. After you listen and repeat numerous times, say the dialogues with a partner. Switch roles.

3. Review the guidelines on pages 83–84. Then underline the focus words in the following short conversations and compare answers with your partner. Listen to check your predictions. Practice saying the short conversations.

1. A: We're expecting visitors today.
   B: I would like to meet them.
2. A: Why did your friend decide to go to Guatemala?
   B: Because he's never been there.
3. A: Do you have any information about skiing in Utah?
   B: Yes. Here are some brochures for you.
4. A: I hope you've considered all the possibilities.
   B: I've considered all of them.
5. A: We are not quite prepared for the meeting today.
   B: Perhaps we should cancel it.
6. A: We have to install a new phone line here.
   B: I hope we won't have to wait a long time for it.
7. A: Did the check come?
   B: No. The mail hasn't arrived yet.

f. Join the Chorus: "What's Happening?"

Listen and repeat the chant in unison. Move your hands and lean forward slightly as you stress the focus words. Then divide into two groups. Say the chant, alternating between groups A and B until you sound like a chorus with one voice. Switch groups.

A: How are you **DO**ing today, **ANNE**?

B: I'm doing **FINE**, and **YOU**?

A: Nothing much is **HAP**pening.

B: Nothing much is **NEW**.

1. A: Things have been going **SMOOTH**ly,

   Time has been flying **BY**.[3]

   B: I'm feeling on top of the **WORLD**.[4]

   And I don't know exactly **WHY**.

2. A: What's going **ON** these days? What's **NEW**?

   How are things working **OUT**?[5]

   B: This has been a fantastic **YEAR**.

   It's **GREAT**, without a **DOUBT**.

3. A: Oh, I'm **BU**sy, I'm **DIZ**zy,

   Everything's in a **SPIN**.

   B: I **THINK** I'm ready for a **CHANGE**.

   My patience is wearing **THIN**.

4. A: Well, I've been very **HAP**py.

   Things have been going **WELL**.

   B: I'm delighted to **HEAR** that.

   I can **LOOK** at you and **TELL**.

A: How are you **FEEL**ing today, **PAUL**?

B: How about **YOU**—what's **UP**?

A: There's a **LOT** that's going **ON**,

B: There's a **LOT** that's shaping **UP**.[6]

[3] **flying by:** to pass quickly
[4] **on top of the world:** feeling very happy, delighted
[5] **working out:** progressing, turning out
[6] **shaping up:** developing, taking shape

Learn By Listening 5: The weather report

1. Read the weather report and underline the focus words. The longer sentences will have more than one focus word. Use the parts of speech to help predict the stress. Then listen to the report to see if you predicted correctly.

   [1]Good afternoon. [2]Here is the latest weather news on this wet Tuesday. [3]Heavy rain is falling throughout the Southland. Cloudy skies and showers will continue until Friday. [4]The low yesterday was fifty-six. [5]The high was sixty-eight. [6]Temperatures in the same range are expected today and for the next few days. [7]Keep your umbrellas handy. [8]You'll need them.

2. Circle the final **s** sounds and the letter "x" in the numbers *six* and *sixty* as a reminder to say these sounds. ("X" is pronounced **ks**.) Listen again and track the speaker. Then practice saying the report. Monitor for pauses, focus words, and final sounds.

g. Role Play: TV weather reporter

You are a TV weather reporter. Prepare a short weather report for the class. Write out the report and underline the content words. Start by announcing your name, the day, the time, the TV station, etc. Lengthen the focus words. Change pitch and pause at the end of each sentence.

Example And now for the 11 o'CLOCK WEAther rePORT. This is Jody CHAN with CHANnel **4** NEWS and WEAther. I'm BRINGing you the LAtest WEAther rePORT for TUESday, April SEcond. You can expect SUNSHINE toDAY and the REST of the WEEK. The TEMperature will conTINue to RISE.

h. Communicative Activity: Planning a party

Partners A and B are giving a party for a friend who just got a great new job. They are both busy and wish to take care of as much as possible in advance. They divide the responsibilities and make a list.

1. Discuss the list with your partner. It is not in order. Talk about which things can be done in advance (that is, one or two weeks before), a day or two ahead, or on the day of the party. Lengthen the focus word at the end of each phrase. The pitch lines either glide or step down at the end of the phrase.

Example A: When should we borrow some dishes?

B: Let's do it a day or two ahead.

"to do" list	in advance	a day or two ahead	the day of the party
make a list of the GUESTS	____	____	____
address the inviTAtions	____	____	____
borrow some CHAIRS	____	____	____
arrange the FLOWers	____	____	____
set the TAble	____	____	____
clean the aPARTment	____	____	____
buy the FOOD	____	____	____
plan the MEnu	____	____	____

2. Add two or three additional things that need to be done before the party.

Changes in Focus

 Learn By Listening 6: Guidelines for shifting the focus

As conversations proceed, speakers use focus to respond appropriately to the previous statement or question. They shift away from the basic pattern to highlight new information. The speakers may stress words that would not normally receive strong stress at the beginning of the conversation.

Listen and repeat some examples for each guideline. Nod your head or move your hands as you say the focus words. Jump up in pitch.

---

guideline 1   Use focus to highlight new information.

Stress the word that provides new information.

1. A: I need to borrow some **MO**ney. (Basic pattern: *money* is new information and the last content word.)

   B: How **MUCH** money? (*money* is old information; *much* is new)

   A: Well, not **TOO** much money. (*much* and *money* are both old information)

   B: I have about TEN **DOL**lars. (*dollars* is new information, basic pattern)

   A: I was hoping to borrow **TWEN**ty dollars. (*ten dollars* is old; *twenty* is new information and shows contrast)

---

guideline 2   Use focus to respond to a question.

Stress the word that answers the question.

2. A. Jerry lost his **BOOK**. (basic pattern)

   B. **WHO** lost his book? (*book* is old information)

   A. **JER**ry lost his book. (answers the question *who*)

3. A. Jerry lost a **BOOK**. (basic pattern)

   B. **WHOSE** book? (*book* is old information)

   A. He lost **HIS** book. (answers the question *whose book*)

guideline 3 — Use focus to disagree.

Stress the word that highlights the disagreement.

1. A: I think that the movie ends at NINE-THIRty. (basic pattern)
   B: I read that the movie should end at TEN-THIRty.
2. A: Monica is going to win the gold medal for gymNAStics.
   B: I think JANE is going to win the gold medal for gymNAStics.
   A: I don't aGREE. I think Jane is going to win the SILver medal.

guideline 4 — Use focus to emphasize agreement.

Stress the helping verb.

1. A: That was a marvelous FILM.
   B: That WAS a marvelous film.
2. A: That sounds like a great iDEa.
   B: That DOES sound like a great idea.

guideline 5 — Use focus to return a question.

Stress the pronoun.

1. A: How is your FAMily? (basic pattern)
   B: Fine, thank you. How's YOUR family?
2. A: What would you LIKE? (basic pattern)
   B: An apple. What would YOU like?

guideline 6 — Use focus to show contrast.

1. A: That shirt would look good with a green TIE. (basic pattern)
   B: I don't HAVE a green tie. What do you think of this BLUE one? (shows contrast)

2. A: I like to swim in hot **WEA**ther. (basic pattern)

   B: I'd rather swim in **HOT** weather than in **COLD** weather. That's for **SURE**!

3. A: Let's buy **DIN**ner tonight. I'm tired of **COOK**ing.

   B: I **LIKE** to cook. I'd rather **COOK** dinner than **BUY** it.

| **guideline 7** | Use focus to show compound noun contrast. |

---

1. A: Here is the **CAR** phone charger / that you **LOST**. (basic pattern)

   B: I lost the car **PHONE**, not the car phone **CHAR**ger. (contrasting stress)

2. A: Let's park in a **PARK**ing lot. (basic pattern)

   B: I don't see a parking **LOT**, but there is a parking ga**RAGE**. (contrastive stress)

i. Partner Practice: Short conversations

Complete the following short conversations. Speaker A starts with the basic focus pattern. Speaker B responds by using a shift in focus. Complete the sentences and circle the focus words. Then practice the conversations with a partner.

Example A: The book costs e**LE**ven **DOL**lars. (basic pattern)

  B: With the tax, it will probably cost _closer to twelve dollars_.
  (contrastive stress)

Old information/new information

1. A: Guess **WHAT**? I bought a **CAM**era.

   B: What **KIND** of camera?

   A: _____ camera.

2. A: I just heard from your **SIS**ter.

   B: **WHICH** sister? I have **THREE** sisters.

   A: _____ sister.

Responding to a question

3. A: How many **LANG**uages does your friend's father **SPEAK**?

   B: _____.

4. A: Would you like a **COU**pon to save $1.00 on a **CAR**WASH?

   B: No, thank you. I already _____.

5. A: Which **SWEAT**er are you planning to **BUY**?

   B: _____ sweater.

Showing disagreement

6. A: There were four people **WAIT**ing.

   B: Are you sure? I thought _____.

7. A: It's EIGHT o'**CLOCK**.

   B: **REAL**ly? I thought it was about _____.

8. A: Baseball tickets cost about TWENty-FIVE **DOL**lars.

   B: That sounds ex**PEN**sive. I thought they cost about _____.

Emphasizing agreement

9. A: That was a long **WALK.**

   B: You're right! That _____.

10. A: The new schedule is a real im**PROVE**ment.

    B: I agree. _____.

11. A: That was an exciting **SOC**CER GAME.

    B: I know! That _____.

Returning a question

12. A: Who's your favorite **ACT**or?

    B: I'm not sure. Who's _____?

13. A: What's your **MA**jor?

    B: I'm majoring in computer science. What _____?

Showing contrastive stress

14. A: Did you hear that Amy started a new **BUS**iness?

    B: Yes, and she likes her **NEW** business better than _____.

15. A: I usually get up at six o'**CLOCK**. What time do **YOU** get up?

    B: _____.

16. A: Here is your small cheese **PIZ**za.

    B: I didn't order a _____. I ordered a _____.

j. Partner Practice: Contrast the basic pattern with changes in focus

In these short conversations, responses (a) and (b) have the same words, but the focus changes to match the initial statement or question. Response (a) is the basic focus pattern. Response (b) shows a shift in focus.

Before you listen, predict the focus words in the following responses. Listen to check your predictions. Practice saying the sentences.

Initial Statement or Question   **Response**

Example
- a. What's the matter?
- b. Give me your keys, and I'll move your car.

- a. I can't find my keys. (basic pattern)
- b. I can't find my keys.

1.
   - a. You seem busier than usual.
   - b. Are you still looking for a new job?

   - a. I have a new job. (basic pattern)
   - b. I have a new job.

2.
   - a. Where are you from?
   - b. I thought you were from Brazil.

   - a. I am from Brazil. (basic pattern)
   - b. I am from Brazil.

3.
   - a. What are you doing tonight?
   - b. Would you like baseball tickets for tonight?

   - a. We have baseball tickets. (basic pattern)
   - b. We have baseball tickets.

4.
   - a. Why weren't you at work last week?
   - b. Are you planning to go to Japan?

   - a. I went to Japan. (basic pattern)
   - b. I went to Japan.

5.
   - a. We have been waiting a long time.
   - b. John suggested that we leave.

   - a. Maybe we should leave. (basic pattern)
   - b. Maybe we should leave.

6.
   - a. Have you tried any new restaurants?
   - b. Jane said you had a great dinner at Tami's.

   - a. We had a great lunch at Tami's (basic pattern)
   - b. We had a great lunch at Tami's

7.
   - a. When did Maria graduate?
   - b. Is Maria graduating this year?

   - a. She graduated last year. (basic pattern)
   - b. She graduated last year.

8.
   - a. Where is the mail?
   - b. Please put the mail on my desk.

   - a. It's on your desk. (basic pattern)
   - b. It's on your desk.

k. Partner Practice: Two dialogues

Listen and underline the focus words in the following dialogues. The focus words emphasize the new information. Then replay the tape to check your answers. Practice the dialogues with a partner.

Where Are You Going?

A: Where are you going?

B: To buy a car.

A: What kind of car?

B: A used car. A cheap used car. Where are you going?

A: I'm going to a meeting.

B: The staff meeting?

A: No, the director's meeting.

A Fearful Shopper

A: I'd like to look at a printer, a laser printer.

B: Do you want a color printer or a black and white printer?

A: I don't care about the color. I'd like to see that one, the laser printer with the carrying case. It looks like a portable laser printer.

B: I'm sorry, but that's not a portable printer. It's a laptop computer. Would you like to look at a laptop computer? They're great for airplanes.

A: I'm sure they are great for airplanes. Thank you, but not today. I'm still afraid to fly.

l. Partner Practice: Giving a choice

The appropriate answer to a *choice question* is not *yes* or *no*. When someone gives you a choice, you might answer by picking one thing, by picking them both, or by rejecting them both. The focus changes for each answer. Listen to four possible answers to A's question, *Do you want cake or ice cream?*

Example   A: Do you want **CAKE** or **ICE** CREAM?

B¹: I want cake **AND** ice cream. I want them **BOTH**.

B²: I'd like **CAKE**, please.

B³: I'd like **ICE** CREAM, please.

B⁴: I don't want cake **OR** ice cream. I've stopped eating des**SERT**.

1. Listen to A's choice questions below and several of B's possible responses. Underline the focus word you hear in B's answers. Write another answer for B on the line.

1. A: Do you prefer the <u>black</u> coat or the <u>striped</u> coat?
   B¹: I don't like the black coat or the striped coat.
   B²: I like the black coat and the striped coat. I'll buy them both!
   B³: _I prefer the black coat / I prefer the striped coat._

2. A: Would you like <u>meat</u> or <u>fish</u>?
   B¹: I don't want meat or fish. I'm a vegetarian (OR)
   B²: I'd like fish, please. (OR)
   B³: _I like meat and fish. I like them both._

3. A: Should we go by <u>plane</u> or drive the <u>car</u>?
   B¹: Let's go by plane and car. We can drive there and fly home. (OR)
   B²: I don't want to go by plane or drive the car. I want to stay home. (OR)
   B³: _I would go by plane._

4. A: Do you want to eat <u>before</u> the movie or <u>after</u>?
   B¹: I want to eat before the movie and after. I'm really hungry.
   B²: _I want to eat before._

5. A: What do you prefer to be called, <u>Andy</u> or <u>Andrew</u>?
   Write your response. Discuss all the possible responses with your partner.
   B: _____

2. Write a new choice question to ask your partner. Respond to your partner's question. Discuss the possible responses to both of your questions.

m. Talk: You're the expert

Tell the class how to do something that you know very well. Pick something with about ten or twelve steps. Start with an introduction and end with a conclusion. Use transition words, such as *first, next, then, after that,* and *finally*. Speak conversationally to make your talk interesting. Interact with your listeners and encourage questions. Monitor for pauses, thought groups, and focus words.

Sample Topics

How to eat a healthy diet, wash your car, cook your favorite recipe, plan a trip, be a good shopper, quit smoking.

> Plan your talk and write out the steps.

- Make a list of the longer words and draw a dot over the stressed syllables.
- Underline the focus word in each phrase or sentence. (See sample below.)
- Practice walking to the rhythm of the thought groups. (See Group Practice 4, page 82.) Slow down your walk as you say the focus words.
- Use a tape recorder to practice your talk. Listen to your recording and self-monitor.

Sample Introduction and Steps: How to make a pot of tea

Drinking tea with a <u>friend</u> is one of my favorite ways to <u>relax</u>. Here's how I like to <u>make</u> it.

First step: First, decide how many cups of <u>tea</u> you want to <u>make</u>.

Next step: Then, measure the water.

Last step: Finally, serve with <u>milk</u> or <u>lemon</u> or <u>sugar</u>, along with your favorite <u>cookie</u> or <u>cake</u>.

Word stress: relax decide lemon sugar favorite cookie

> When giving your talk, speak from memory or from notes. If you need to look at your paper, look at your audience before you speak. Monitor for focus words and end-of-the-sentence intonation. For things to consider when planning your talk, see the Checklist for Talks, which may be found on Houghton Mifflin's ESL website at http://college.hmco.com/esl.

---

pronunciation reminder   There are three levels of stress in English sentences.

- strong stress (focus words)
- stress (content words)
- unstress (structure words)

FINISHING UP

Self-Quiz   (Check your answers in the Answer Key.)

1. Fill in the blanks. There are three levels of stress in English sentences.

   Level 1—strong stress—_____ words. (Choose one: content, structure, focus)

   Level 2—normal stress—_____ words. (Choose one: content, structure, focus)

   Level 3—unstress—_____ words.   (Choose one: content, structure, focus)

2. How would you say the following sentence? Write the stress level 1, 2, or 3 over each word. Draw a slash to show the thought groups.

   Our professional staff will be happy to assist you.

3. Circle the true statements about structure words such as *the, an, at, to, from, his,* and *her*.

   a. Structure words are necessary to the meaning of a sentence.

   b. Structure words are important to grammatical structure and speech rhythm.

   c. Structure words are never stressed.

4. Predict the focus. Underline the focus word in each line of the dialogues. Some of the longer sentences have two focus words.

Which Bus?

A: When is the next bus?

B: Which bus?

A: The bus to the shopping mall.

B: There are two shopping malls. Do you want the best mall or the closest mall?

A: I want to go to the best mall, of course!

B: That bus should be here soon. You can walk to the closest one.

The Loud Dog

A: I think your dog needs a walk.

B: Which dog? I have three dogs.

A: The loud dog. The barking dog. That's the dog that needs a walk!

B: Unfortunately, they are all barking.

Making Your New Pronunciation a Habit
Talk Times in Class: Role play

A friend has recommended a restaurant. Partner A wants to find out more about it before taking a guest there for dinner and calls the restaurant for information. Partner B answers the phone.

1. Plan the conversation between the customer and the restaurant. Write the questions you will ask. Possible topics:

- the price range of the entrees
- what is included (salad, dessert, etc.)
- the dress, formal or informal
- the appropriateness for children
- the location (include cross streets)
- the parking (street parking or parking lot)
- reservations needed

2. Role-play the conversation. Monitor for word stress, focus words, and end-of-the-sentence intonation.

Talk Times in Your Daily Life: Choosing a restaurant

Call or visit at least three different restaurants to ask for information.

1. Choose two or three things to ask about during each call. Write down the questions you plan to ask, and practice them before you make the call. Decide what targets you are going to monitor.

2. Make notes about what happened and how well you monitored for your targets. Rate your comfort level. Plan your next call. Use the *Talk Times* Worksheet (see page 32).

On Your Own

1. **Audio program**

   Repeat the same exercises on several different days during the week. Replay small sections of the tape several times, especially the parts that need work.

2. **Recorded practice**

   Learn to discover and correct your own errors. See the tips for recorded practice on page 54.

   - Record the sentences in Group Practice 3, page 81, and one of the dialogues in Exercise k, page 94. Listen and compare your recording to the speaker on the audiotapes. Improve your pronunciation and re-record.

   - Write a rhyme to the rhythm of one of the nursery rhymes on page 79 and record your rhyme. Listen and re-record until you are satisfied.

3. **Glossary**

   Add words to your glossary. **Reminder:** The words should come from your daily experience, not a dictionary.

4. **Mirroring**

   Review the directions on page 74. Mirror a speaker's movements and speech for five minutes of a videotaped selection. Write a reflection journal about your mirroring experience.

5. **Converse in English as often as possible**

   This will build your confidence and make you more comfortable with the language and the pronunciation.

---

something to remember Keep congratulating yourself. It takes courage and effort to change the way you speak. Many people feel self-conscious when they try talking differently. This probably means that their pronunciation is improving. Your efforts and successes, large and small, are all important.

Conversation Strategies

Use what you learn about pronunciation targets to avoid problems and clear up misunderstandings when you are having a conversation. Discuss these conversation strategies:

1. **Use eye contact.** Conversations are easier to understand when you are looking at the other person. Furthermore, to native speakers of English, eye contact establishes trust and confidence. It makes your listener feel that you are interested and attentive.

2. **Look for clues that your listener does not understand what you are saying.** Does your listener seem annoyed or unfriendly? This may be a cue that he or she does not understand what you are saying. Is your listener responding inappropriately to your questions or comments? This may not be cue to your accent. It could be happening because you are not using the right words.

3. **Don't be afraid to ask to make sure you are being understood.** You might say, *Can you understand me?* or *Please tell me if I say anything that you don't understand.* This puts everyone at ease. Some people are hesitant to let you know directly when they are having trouble understanding.

4. **When your listener asks *what?* you probably need to do something more than repeat what you said.** Think about ways you can say it more clearly. Try changing the word stress or focus. Frequently, just by lengthening the stressed syllable and raising its pitch, a word will be easier to understand. Emphasizing the focus words more strongly can often make a whole sentence easier to understand.

5. **Provide extra information.** Rephrase what you said using different words. Explain the meaning. For example, "I work at a senior center, *a place where older people go.*" Use gestures. Spell or write down unfamiliar names.

6. **Pay attention to the stressed words.** They provide most of the meaning whether you are the listener or the speaker.

7. **Talk more slowly in English than you do in your native language.** Pause more often. Slow down at the ends of sentences and on focus words.

8. **Find out how to pronounce frequently misunderstood words and phrases.** This might be your address or workplace name.

9. **Don't worry about your mistakes.** Hearing your own mistakes is a sign of progress. If you make a mistake, correct it casually without apologizing. If this is not comfortable, make a mental note of your mistake. Later when you are practicing, say that word or phrase correctly.

Vowels and Speech Music

In chapter 6 you will learn how closely English speech rhythm is tied to vowel sounds. It is the contrast between the stressed and unstressed vowels that gives English speech its characteristic rhythm. English has at least fifteen stressed vowel sounds but only five vowel letters. Each of these letters has a number of possible pronunciations, and this can be confusing to learners of English. Fortunately, clear speech depends more upon the rhythm and intonation of vowels than on how nativelike they sound.

Unstress: Shortening the Vowels in Weak Syllables

As you learned in chapter 3, the vowels in *weak,* or unstressed, syllables are short and low in pitch, and often known as *schwa*. Believe it or not, schwa is the most common sound in English! Any unstressed vowel can be reduced to ə, and most of them are, especially in informal, rapid speech. But all schwas do not sound exactly alike. They are hard to hear clearly and are often called *unclear vowels*.

Review how to say ə

- Let your whole face, lips, and tongue relax.
- Open your mouth just a little and let your tongue rest gently behind your lower teeth.
- Say a quick "uh." Make it lower in pitch and quieter than the stressed syllable.

 Learning By Listening 1: Two-syllable words

1. Listen to the words and sentences. Trace the word pattern. Touch the dot lightly and quickly for the unstressed syllable with the schwa vowel.

1. sucCESS (ə)   It's a sucCESS.   5. SALad (ə)   I like SALad.
2. dePART (ə)   It's TIME to dePART. 6. FAmous (ə)   She is FAmous.
3. tøDAY (ə)   ToDAY is MONday.   7. ADDed (ə)   I ADDed the TIP.
4. tøNIGHT (ə)   Let's GO toNIGHT.   8. WALlet (ə)   Where's my WALlet?

2. Replay the tape. Look away from the book as you say the words and sentences with the speaker.

a. Partner Practice: Compare clear vowels and reduced vowels

1. Say *pen*. It has a clear vowel. Say *HAPpen*. The vowel in the syllable *pen* is reduced to schwa.

2. Listen and repeat the words on the following chart. Exaggerate the difference between the stressed and the unstressed syllables.

Clear Vowels	Reduced Vowels	Clear Vowels	Reduced Vowels
1. man	WOman (ə)	6. fin	MUFfin (ə)
2. fast	BREAKfast (ə)	7. stage	HOStage (ə)
3. band	HUSband (ə)	8. sip	GOSsip (ə)
4. ad	adVICE (ə)	9. pro	proDUCtive (ə)
5. ban	URban (ə)	10. no cent	INnocent (ə ə)

3. Practice the word pairs and use the words with schwa in your own sentences. Take turns with your partner.

Example   Partner A: man   WOman (ə)   The woman stood in line.
             Partner B: fast   BREAKfast (ə)   Do you want some breakfast?

b. Communicative Activity: Countries and names

Most two- and three-syllable names in English have at least one unstressed schwa vowel.

1. To prepare for the activity, listen and repeat these names. Monitor for the schwa vowels in the unstressed syllables.

JaPAN (ə)   KøREa (ə)   GERmany (ə)   CHIna (ə)   FINland (ə)   MøROCco (ə)   POLand (ə)   ITaly (ə)

ALice (ə)   NORman (ə)   MARsha (ə)   KARen (ə)   ALlan (ə)   MARvin (ə)   ReBECca (ə)   KENneth (ə)

2. You and your partner are in charge of hosting a reception. You each have a chart telling who in your group is going to greet students from different countries. Ask each other questions until you both have all the information. Use the unstressed schwa in the names. Lengthen the stressed syllables.

Example

A: Who is going to greet the student from Finland?

B: I believe it's Alice. Who is going to host the student from Morocco?

A: Karina doesn't have anyone to greet. Let's ask her to host the student from Morocco.

Partner A's List

Greeter	Country
	Finland
Karina	
Hye Soo	
Allen	Poland
	Italy
Ryoko	China
Norman	
Emilio	Korea

Partner B's List

Greeter	Country
Alice	Finland
	Morocco
Hye Soo	Germany
Allen	
Marco	
Ryoko	
Norman	Japan
Emilio	

Reductions and Schwa Vowels

When native speakers converse, they shorten many unstressed structure words used in everyday speech. They may omit certain consonants. As you learned in chapter 2, these shortened words are called *reductions*. The vowels in these shortened, or reduced, words often sound like a schwa. The same word said alone has a full clear vowel.

Example Word alone: *and* Reduction: *One ənd two equals three.*

Learn By Listening 2: Reducing structure words

1. Listen and compare some structure words said alone and in phrases or sentences.

Structure Words	Sentences with Reductions
1. your	WHAT'S yər FAVorite STORy?
2. you	Are yə REAdy?
3. and	FUN ənd GAMES

4. are, than   ComPUters are FASter than EVer.
5. an   I WANT an ORange.
6. a, of   HAVE a glass of JUICE.
7. at   Let's LEAVE at NOON.
8. to, the   They WENT to the MOVies.
9. from, to   It's from FOUR to FIVE.
10. or   ONE or TWO TIMES a DAY

2. Replay the tape, and look away from your book to hear the sound of the reductions. After you have listened several times, say each phrase with the reduced structure words.

c. Improve Your Monitoring: Listening for reductions

It's important to understand these reductions even if you don't always say them. Listen to the sentences. Decide whether the speaker uses nativelike speech with reduced structure words or all clear vowels. Check (✓) the appropriate answer.

		Reduced Structure Words	All Clear Vowels
Example	Does the bus go to the beach?	✓	
	Does the bus go to the beach?		✓
1.	You have to sit down.		✓
2.	He said that he was sorry.	✓	
3.	I can tell that you want to go.		✓
4.	Please pass the sugar and cream.		✓
5.	Put them on top of the copy machine.	✓	
6.	Would you like to read the paper?		✓
7.	He was interested in her story.	✓	
8.	What do you think of that?		✓
9.	Did you read the end of the book?	✓	
10.	We have to try to save money.	✓	

questions and answers

1. Do native speakers always reduce the same words?
   Not necessarily. When native speakers talk more slowly or more formally, they may use fewer reductions and fewer schwa vowels.
2. Do I have to say a schwa in unstressed syllables and use reductions to speak English clearly?
   No. You need to shorten the unstressed syllables and lower the pitch.
3. Do I have to say schwas and use reductions to sound like a native speaker?
   Yes.

Learn By Listening 3: What's the difference between *can* and *can't*?

Even native speakers get confused at times and need to ask for clarification. One key is lengthening the vowel and raising the pitch for *can't* because negatives get stress in English. The other key is lowering the pitch and reducing the vowel for *can*.

1. Listen and compare these sentences. You will hear the basic focus pattern in both examples.

   can ⟷ / kən /
   Reduced, Unstressed, Lower Pitch

   Melinda can SING.
   She can SPEAK SPANish.
   Adam can TELL the DIFference.

   CAN'T ⟷ / kænt /
   Not Reduced, Stressed, Higher Pitch

   Melinda CAN'T SING.
   She CAN'T SPEAK SPANish.
   Adam CAN'T TELL the DIFference.

2. Listen to the sentences. Check (✓) the word you hear. Is it *can* or *can't*? Pay attention to the vowel and the pitch.

   Example   We <u>can</u> buy milk at that store.   ✓ can   ___ can't

   1. Carlos ___ cook anything.   ✓ can   ___ can't
   2. I ___ be there tomorrow.   ___ can   ✓ can't
   3. The mechanic ___ fix my car today.   ___ can   ✓ can't
   4. I ___ finish my paper on time.   ✓ can   ___ can't
   5. The babysitter ___ sit tonight.   ___ can   ✓ can't
   6. His uncle ___ come as planned.   ___ can   ✓ can't
   7. You ___ borrow my laptop computer.   ✓ can   ___ can't
   8. Everyone that we invited ___ come.   ✓ can   ___ can't
   9. The chairman ___ conduct the meeting today.   ___ can   ✓ can't
   10. The salesman ___ deliver the order tomorrow. ✓ can   ___ can't

d. Partner Practice: Can and can't

Partner A says either *can* or *can't* in a sentence. Use the basic focus pattern by giving focus to the main verb. Underline the word you say, but keep it hidden.

Partner B responds with either (a) *That's great!* or (b) *That's too bad*, depending on what the partner said. B adds another comment to the response. Switch roles.

Examples

A: I can **GO** with you tomorrow.   B: That's great! I'll pick you up.

A: I can't **GO** with you tomorrow.   B: That's too bad. Maybe next time.

1. A: I (can-can't) **CALL** you later.   B: Say (a) or (b). Add a comment.
2. A: You (can-can't) **BOR**row my car.   B: Say (a) or (b). Add a comment.
3. A: She (can-can't) speak **RUS**sian.   B: Say (a) or (b). Add a comment.
4. A: I (can-can't) find your **BOOK**.   B: Say (a) or (b). Add a comment.
5. A: I (can-can't) finish the **PAP**er today.   B: Say (a) or (b). Add a comment.
6. A: We (can-can't) **BRING** the salad.   B: Say (a) or (b). Add a comment.
7. A: She (can-can't) **TAKE** the job.   B: Say (a) or (b). Add a comment.
8. A: I (can-can't) **FIX** your car by noon.   B: Say (a) or (b). Add a comment.
9. A: You (can-can't) **BUY** it at a supermarket.   B: Say (a) or (b). Add a comment.
10. A: I (can-can't) **LOAN** you the money.   B: Say (a) or (b). Add a comment.

e. Communicative Activity: Making appointments

Take turns finishing the following conversations. When your partner says *I can* or *I can't*, what will you say? Then role-play more conversations.

1. Friend A: Jerry is coming in for the weekend. Can you join us for lunch on Saturday?

   Friend B: I'd love to see you and Jerry. I (can-can't) join you for lunch on Saturday.

   Friend A: _____

2. Caller: Can I have a reservation for dinner for four at 7 o'clock tonight?

   Restaurant: I (can-can't) give you a table at 7. _____

   Caller: _____

3. Patient: Can I please have an appointment this week with Dr. Adams?

   Receptionist: Can you come tomorrow at 4:30? I can work you in at the end of the day.

   Patient: I (can-can't) make it at 4:30 _____ .

> **pronunciation tip**
>
> To say *can't*, push your tongue against the gum ridge for the final t. Hold it there and stop the air. Native speakers often hold this final t without releasing a puff of air. If you don't push your tongue to stop the air completely, *can't* might sound like *can*.

f. Dialogue: "Phone Confusion"

Listen and underline the focus words. Replay the tape and listen for the reduced *can*. Practice the dialogue with a partner.

A: Can you hear me?

B: Yes, I can hear you. Can you hear me?

A: We must have a bad connection. I can't hear you at all.

B: Well, I can hear you! You're the one who can't hear.

A: What did you say? I guess you can't hear me, either.

B: I can hear you. Listen, I'm hanging up. I'll call you back on another line.

Learn By Listening 4: Knock-knock jokes

American children love *knock-knock jokes*. These jokes depend on understanding linking, reductions, and schwa vowels. Listen and decide what the name in the last line stands for. See the first joke as an example.

1	2	3
A: Knock-knock!	A: Knock-knock!	A: Knock-knock!
B: Who's there?	B: Who's there?	B: Who's there?
A: Susan.	A: Willy.	A: Parker.
B: Susan who?	B: Willy who?	B: Parker who?
A: Susan Love and she's telling everyone.	A: Willy stay or Willy go?	A: Parker car in the driveway!
Susan Love = <u>Sue's in love</u>	Willy = _____	Parker = _____

g. Partner Practice: How many syllables?

Adding or omitting a schwa can change the number of syllables and the meaning of a word. Compare *blow* (one syllable)—*Blow the HORN*—and *beLOW* (two syllables)—*It's beLOW the WINdow.*

1. Listen and repeat the items on the left. Pay attention to the syllables in the underlined words. Do you hear a schwa vowel?

   1. a. Do you have an <u>I.D.</u>?   Yes, I have my driver's license.
      b. Do you have an <u>idea</u>?   Yes, I think we should cash the check.
   2. a. The thief was <u>rested</u> this morning.   He got a good night's sleep.
      b. The thief was <u>arrested</u> this morning.   The police took him to jail.
   3. a. It's <u>cute</u>.   You mean her puppy?
      b. It's <u>acute</u>.   You mean her illness?
   4. a. His <u>state</u> is large.   He is from Texas.
      b. His <u>estate</u> is large.   He has a lot of money.
   5. a. It's not <u>fair</u>.   The man got paid more than the woman for the same job.
      b. It's not <u>a fair</u>.   It's not a trade exhibit or a carnival.
   6. a. I've been learning about <u>signs</u>.   Are you talking about billboards?
      b. I've been learning about <u>science</u>.   Physics and chemistry?
   7. a. Use <u>surfs</u> in a sentence.   He surfs the Internet daily.
      b. Use <u>surface</u> in a sentence.   The surface of the desk needs cleaning.
   8. a. We sat near the <u>center</u>.   Which row were you in?
      b. We sat near the <u>senator</u>.   Did you ask her any questions?

2. Partner A says either sentence (a) or (b). Partner B says the response.

   Example   A: Do you have an I.D.?   B: I have my driver's license.

h. Partner Practice: Finish the sentences

Partner A says one pair of words. Partner B fills in the blanks and says the sentence. Monitor for syllables and the schwa vowels. Take turns.

Example A: I.D. idea B: I haven't any <u>idea</u> what happened to my <u>I.D.</u>

1. state   estate   1. The _____ is in the _____ of Washington.
2. sport   support 2. The _____ fans enthusiastically _____ the team.
3. steam   esteem   3. His self-_____ ran out of _____ when he lost the race.
4. rested   arrested 4. John _____ quietly after the thief was _____.
5. signs   science 5. The _____ in front of the _____ building are green.
6. surfs   surface 6. He _____ on the _____ of the waves.
7. organ   Oregon   7. A man from _____ donated the _____.

Clear Vowels

Clear vowels are vowels that are not reduced. Native English speakers from different countries and with different dialects can vary in the way they pronounce individual vowel sounds. However, all native speakers emphasize stressed syllables with clear vowels and use schwas in unstressed syllables.

Learn By Listening 5: Overview of American English vowels

1. Cover the box below with a piece of paper before you listen. Listen and repeat fifteen American vowels in key phrases without seeing the words.[1]

1 2	3 4	5 6	7 8	9 10	11	12	13 14 15
SEE IT.	SAY YES.	a FAT BIRD	at a BUS STOP	TWO BOOKS	SHOW the BOSS		HI COWBOY

2. Notice the number over each word. The number represents the vowel sound in that word. You can use these numbers to label the vowels in words you want to pronounce.

---

[1] These key phrases were adapted by permission of Joan Morley. Joan Morley, *Improving Spoken English* (Ann Arbor, University of Michigan Press, 1979).

The next few exercises give you a chance to hear the fifteen clear vowels in words with American English pronunciation. The clear vowels are divided into (1) long vowels that glide and (2) short vowels that don't glide. (See the Vowel Chart showing fifteen clear vowels in appendix B.)

Learn By Listening 6: Long vowels

Long vowels sound longer because the tongue glides from one place to another and then tightens as you say them. This takes longer than it does to say the short vowels that do not glide or change positions. Long vowels have two parts and are more complex than short vowels. Therefore, these can also be called *complex vowels*.

Listen to sentences with words that have long vowel sounds. Pay attention to the vowels that sound like the names of the letters "a" "e" "i" "o" and "u." Listen for the word *cowboy* to hear the other two long vowels. Find the matching numbers for each vowel sound in the column to the right of the sentences.

Vowel Symbols	Sentences with Long Vowel Words	Vowel Numbers
e^y	CHANGE the DATE to the **EIGHTH**.	3
i^y	LEAVE the KEYS on the **SEAT**.	1
a^y	MIKE would LIKE some **RICE**.	13
o^w	He TOLD me an OLD **JOKE**.	11
u^w	The NEW SHOES are **HUGE**.	9
a^w	I FOUND the TOWN in an **HOUR**.	14
$ɔ^y$	The BOY enJOYs his **TOY**.	15

Moving Your Mouth for English: Contrast three long vowels

Saying long vowels is different from saying short vowels because you have to move your lips and jaw and tighten your tongue. The part of the tongue that moves is the fat blade behind the tip.

Look at pictures below showing how the mouth glides from the position on the left to the position on the right for these vowels. Use a mirror to check your mouth as you follow the directions in the boxes.

Vowel 3 e^y as in SAY

1. Smile slightly. Push the tongue forward. Start to say the letter "a."
2. Widen the lips a bit further while gliding the tongue farther up and forward. Tighten the tongue to say y.

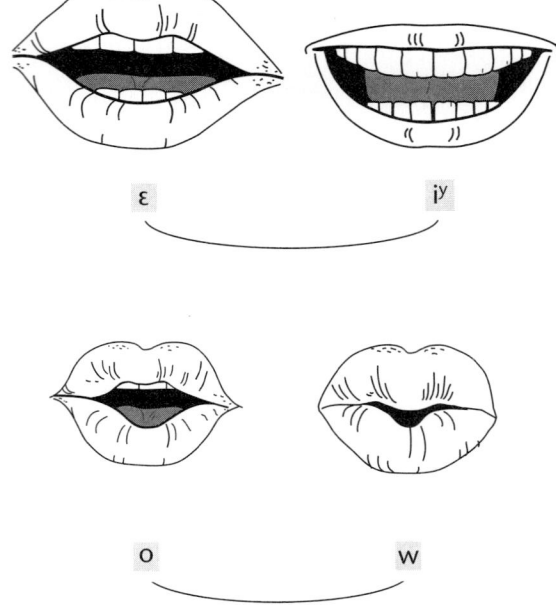

ε   i^y

Vowel 11 o^w as in SHOW

1. Open the mouth and round the lips slightly. Start to say the letter "o."
2. Glide the tongue backward and tighten it. Round the lips more to say w.

o   w

Vowel 13 a^y as in HI

1. Lower the jaw and say a.
2. Glide forward with the tongue and tighten it to say y.

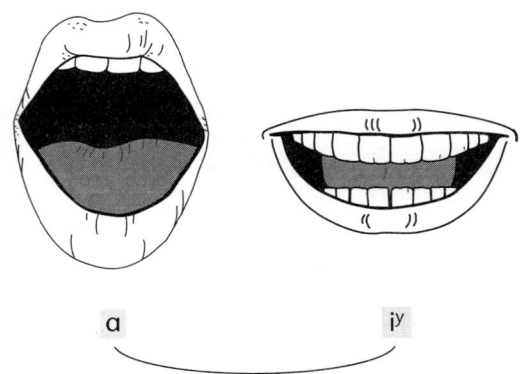

a   i^y

Learn By Listening 7: Short vowels

Short vowels do not have two parts, so they are shorter and take less time to say than long vowels. The tongue stays in one place and does not glide. They can be thought of as *simple vowels*. They sound slightly different from the names of any letters.

 Listen to the sentences with words with short vowel sounds. Find the matching numbers for each vowel sound to the right of the sentences.

Vowel Symbols	Sentences with Short Vowel Words	Vowel Numbers
ɪ	GIVE him a SIP of MILK.	2
ɛ	The GUESTS LEFT at SEven.	4
æ	I was MAD at the MAN in the CAB.	5
ɚ	SIR, can you LEARN the WORK?	6
ʌ	Can you COME for LUNCH on SUNday?	7
ɑ	My FAther GOT the JOB.	8
ʊ	LOOK! I TOOK a COOKie!	10
ɔ	I BOUGHT some COFfee at the MALL.	12

important information All vowels, short and long, sound even longer when they are stressed.

Note: For more practice with clear vowels, see appendix B.

think about this
- Most languages have between five and nine vowels. How many vowel sounds and vowel letters does your language have? _____
- Do any of these vowels glide? Most languages do not have complex vowels that glide.
- Compare the American vowels to similar vowels in your language. How are they different?

Moving Your Mouth for English: Contrast three short vowels (4, 5, 10)

#4 ɛ Men (neutral jaw)   #5 æ Man (open jaw)   #10 ʊ Look (neutral jaw)

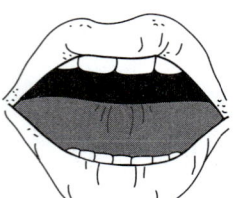

Mouth barely open.　　　　Mouth open. Jaw lowered.　　Mouth barely open.
Lips slightly spread.　　　Lips slightly smiling.　　　　Lips slightly rounded.
Tongue pushed forward.　　Tongue flat and central.　　　Tongue pulled back.

Look at the <u>men</u>. (more　Look at the <u>man</u>.　　　　<u>Look</u>! The man waved
than one person)　　　　　(one person)　　　　　　　at the men.

　　Listen and repeat the phrases. Emphasize the focus words.

- Vowel 4 ɛ

  TEN RED **PENS**　　　　My FRIEND is **REA**dy.　　I SENT the LETter **YES**terday.

- Vowel 5 æ

  an atTRACTive **PLAN**　a fanTAStic **ACT**or　a roMANtic **MAN**　a MATter of **FACT**

Many learners of English have difficulty with the #5 vowel. Opening your mouth and smiling slightly helps. æ is often spelled with the letter "a."

- Vowel 10 ʊ

  a GOOD **COOK**　　　　I TOOK a **LOOK**.　　　She STOOD near the **BOOK**

Moving Your Mouth for English: Contrast two more short vowels

Vowel 7 ʌ Shut (neutral jaw)　　　　　**Vowel 8 ɑ Shot (jaw open)**

ʌ and ə are made in the same way.　　　Lower the jaw and back of the tongue
The tongue and the jaw are completely　more for ɑ than for any other
relaxed and barely open.　　　　　　　vowel. Say *ah*.

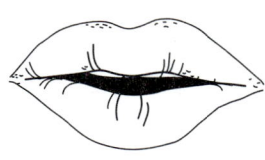　　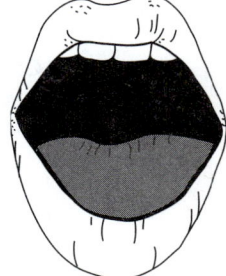

He <u>shut</u> the door (with his hand).　　　He <u>shot</u> the door (with a gun).

Listen and repeat the phrases. Emphasize the focus words.

ʌ	COME for **LUNCH**	my MOther COUNtry	ONCE a **MONTH**
ɑ	LOCK the **BOX**	STOP the **CLOCK**	a POPular **TO**pic

---

pronunciation tip — Practicing the neutral sound ʌ can help you to learn the sound of schwa. ə goes by more quickly, but has the same sound as ʌ.

---

 i. Partner Practice: ʌ and ɑ (vowels 7 and 8)

1. Listen to the sentences contrasting vowels 7 and 8. Write the vowel number over the stressed syllables in the underlined words.

   Example
                  7
   a. This <u>cut</u> is uncomfortable.   a. Would you like a bandage?
                  8
   b. **This <u>cot</u> is uncomfortable.**   b. **Would you rather sleep on a futon?**

   1. a. You look good in that <u>COLor</u>.   Thanks! I like red.
      b. You look good in that <u>COLlar</u>.   It feels a bit tight.

   2. a. I was <u>WONdering</u> about the city.   Would you like some information?
      b. I was <u>WANdering</u> about the city.   Were you lost?

   3. a. Is your <u>luck</u> good?   Yes, I have a good job and a big apartment.
      b. Is your <u>lock</u> good?   Yes, but I lost the key.

   4. a. I hear a loud <u>pop</u>.   Is it a balloon bursting?
      b. I hear a loud <u>pup</u>.   Has he been barking long?

   5. a. He's in the <u>bucks</u>.   When did he get all the money?
      b. He's in the <u>box</u>.   What's he doing in a carton?

   6. a. There's a <u>duck</u> over there.   It is swimming away.
      b. There's a <u>dock</u> over there.   Let's tie up our boat.

2. Partner A says either sentence (a) or (b). Partner B says the appropriate answer. Relax your mouth for ʌ. Lower your jaw for ɑ.

spelling and pronunciation tip	**Vowel 8.** Many common words spelled with an "o" in the stressed syllable are pronounced with an α. For example: POSsible OPposite FOLlow microSCOpic TOpic POverty aTOMic psyCHOlogy Add more examples: _____

more spelling tips	1. Long vowels are often spelled with two letters. The vowel sounds like the first letter in these words.
	   main seat bean pie toe boat
	2. The vowels in words with a final "e" sound like the name of the vowel.
	   lake Pete fine lone mute
	3. Short vowels are often spelled with one letter.
	   hat pin ten pot but

Learn By Listening 8: Unstressed syllables with clear vowels

Not all the unstressed vowels are reduced to schwa. An unstressed clear vowel will be quieter and <u>lower in pitch</u>. Listen and compare. The first word in each pair has an unstressed schwa vowel in the underlined syllable. The second word has an unstressed clear vowel.

Unstressed Schwa	**Clear**
1. COMm<u>ø</u>n (ə)	COM<u>ment</u>
2. MAN<u>age</u> (ə)	MAN<u>date</u>
3. BA<u>cø</u>n (ə)	BA<u>King</u>
4. PRO<u>mise</u> (ə)	PRO<u>gress</u>
5. WEAK<u>ø</u>ned (ə)	WEEK<u>end</u>
6. c<u>ø</u>nCLUDE (ə)	<u>con</u>CRETE

j. Improve Your Monitoring: Schwa or clear vowel?

Most unstressed syllables have schwa vowels, especially in rapid conversation. Listen for the unstressed syllable in these two-syllable words. Decide whether you hear a schwa or a clear vowel in the unstressed syllable. Check (✓) the correct column.

Example

COOKie ____ schwa ✓ clear   FASHion ✓ schwa ____ clear

		Schwa	Clear			Schwa	Clear
1.	hoTEL	___	___	6.	transMIT	___	___
2.	camPAIGN	___	___	7.	ELbow	___	___
3.	RANdom	___	___	8.	colLECT	___	___
4.	URban	___	___	9.	PROfit	___	___
5.	WAITed	___	___	10.	BARgain	___	___

k. Partner Practice: Look-alikes

1. Some English words are spelled the same but pronounced differently. What is the difference between the following look-alike nouns, verbs, and adjectives, which all end with "ate"? (*Hint:* Listen closely to the vowel in the "ate" syllable.) Check (✓) whether you hear a clear vowel or a schwa.

		e^y	$ə$
DUplicate (noun)	I need a duplicate of my birth certificate.	___	___
DUpliCATE (verb)	Can you duplicate this report?	___	___
DUplicate (adjective)	This is a duplicate bill.	___	___

2. Listen to the following words and sentences. Partner A says either word (a) or (b). Partner B says the matching sentence. Take turns.

   1. a. GRAdu$ə$te (noun)   Tony is a college graduate.
      b. GRAduATE (verb)   When did he graduate?
   2. a. EStim$ə$te (noun)   Here is an estimate of the costs.
      b. EStiMATE (verb)   Can you estimate the cost per square foot?
   3. a. ADvoc$ə$te (noun)   Michael is a women's rights advocate.
      b. ADvoCATE (verb)   He advocates a change in the law.
   4. a. asSOci$ə$te (adjective) Eleanor is an associate professor.
      b. asSOciATE (verb)   She associates with people from her department.
   5. a. apPROXim$ə$te (adjective) That's an approximate amount.
      b. apPROXiMATE (verb)   Let's approximate the costs.
   6. a. SEPar$ə$te (adjective)   That's a separate subject.
      b. SEParATE (verb)   Let's separate the clothes before we wash them.

Learn By Listening 9: "Ate" verbs and related words

1. Although verbs ending in "ate" are very common, they do not always have noun or adjective look-alikes. In chapter 4, page 60, you learned patterns for related forms of words. Listen to the stress in the following:

   DEMonstrATE—DEMonstrates—DEMonstrated—demonSTRAtion

   INtegrATE—INtegrates—INtegrated—inteGRAtion

   eVALuATE—eVALuates—eVALuated—evaluAtion

2. Use the above patterns to predict the stress for related forms of these "ate" verbs.

   exaggerate   indicate   facilitate   communicate   evaporate

Summary: Rules for Stressed and Unstressed Vowels

Rules	Word Stress	Syllable Length and Pitch
Strongly stressed syllables all have clear vowels. • These syllables have one of the fifteen clear vowels.	1. HAMburger reVIEW	←———→ high pitch and long
Most unstressed syllables have unclear schwa vowels. • These vowels are hard to hear clearly.	2. əBANdøn BANdɨt	←—→ low pitch and short
Some unstressed syllables have clear vowels. • These syllables have clear vowels, but they are shorter and lower in pitch than stressed vowels.	3. camPAIGN PROgram	←—→ low pitch and short
Lightly stressed syllables in longer words have clear vowels. • These syllables are low in pitch, but longer than unstressed syllables.	4. SATisFACtion inVEStiGATE	←——→ low pitch and moderate length

More Practice

l. Story: "Breakfast Conversation"

1. Listen to the story and draw a slash where you hear a pause. Then listen and repeat each line in unison until you sound like a chorus with one voice.

¹The man and the **WO**man were having **BREAK**fast. ²"I hope we can finish breakfast **FAST** because I don't want to be late for **WORK**." ³The man started to eat his bacon **OM**elet. ⁴The woman took a bite of her **MUF**fin, but got dis**TRAC**ted. ⁵They began to **GOS**sip about the woman's **BOSS**. ⁶"Can you i**MA**gine? He has a lot of ad**VICE** about being pro**DUCT**ive and making a **PRO**fit. ⁷Then he leaves **EAR**ly on **FRI**day before things are **FIN**ished." ⁸"Well, I can be**LIEVE** it! He never seems to **WORK** very **HARD**." ⁹"And did you notice his **SHOES** at the open **HOUSE**? Ex**PEN**sive, but not **PO**lished." ¹⁰"**NO**. I didn't **NO**tice. But I **DID** notice that he wasn't very **FRIEND**ly." ¹¹**MEAN**while, the omelet was getting **COLD** and the minutes were ticking a**WAY**.

2. Practice these words from the story. In casual conversation unstressed syllables are likely to be reduced to schwa. Lower the pitch on the unstressed syllable.

WOmən   BREAKfəst   FINish   STARTəd   MUFfin   BAcən
OMələt   disTRACTəd   iMAGinə   ədVICE   prəDUCTive
PROfit   NOtice   POlished   MINutəs   əWAY

3. Alternate reading the lines from the story. Monitor your own speech and the speech of the other readers. Pay attention to lengthening the stressed vowels. Monitor for focus.

m. Proverbs

Listen and fill in the missing structure words. Notice the schwa vowels. Replay the tape and repeat each proverb. Discuss the meaning of each proverb.

1. ____ bird ____ ____ hand / ____ worth two ____ ____ bush./
2. ____ stitch ____ time / saves nine./
3. Don't put all ____ eggs / ____ one basket./
4. Necessity / ____ ____ mother ____ invention./
5. Money ____ ____ root / ____ all evil./
6. Grab ____ bull / ____ ____ horns./
7. Rome ____ built / ____ ____ day./
8. ____ err ____ human, / ____ forgive ____ divine./
9. ____ apple doesn't fall far / ____ ____ tree./
10. ____ grass ____ always greener / ____ ____ other side ____ ____ fence./

n. Partner Practice: Scrambled proverbs

The proverbs below are divided into two thought groups. Partner A says the first part from column 1. Partner B completes the proverb from column 2. Emphasize the focus words, and shorten the vowels in the structure words.

Group 1

	1	2
1.	A bird in the **HAND**	saves **NINE**.
2.	A stitch in **TIME**	is the mother of in**VEN**tion.
3.	Don't put all your **EGGS**	of all **E**vil.
4.	Ne**CES**sity	in one **BAS**ket.
5.	Money is the **ROOT**	is worth two in the **BUSH**.

Group 2

1.	Grab the **BULL**	to forgive is di**VINE**.
2.	Rome wasn't **BUILT**	on the other side of the **FENCE**.
3.	To err is **HU**man,	by the **HORNS**.
4.	An apple doesn't fall **FAR**	from the **TREE**.
5.	The grass is always **GREEN**er	in a **DAY**.

o. Dialogue: "The Optical Shop"

Listen and repeat each line of the dialogue in unison. Underline the focus words. The first line is done as an example. Compare answers with your partner.

CHAPTER 6 Vowels and Speech Music   **119**

1. A: I need new contact <u>lenses</u> and <u>glasses</u>.
2. B: I know a couple of good optical shops that are not far from here.
3. A: What are their names?
4. B: I think one is I-Care Optical and the other one is Eye-Care Optical.
5. A: What are you talking about? Both those names sound alike to me.
6. B: They may sound alike, but not exactly alike. They're not spelled alike, either. That makes them different,[2] don't you think?
7. A: That's possible, but what about their prices? I want to know if they're expensive.

2. Look at the names of the two shops. How are they different? (Hint: Which one is a compound noun?)

3. List two-syllable words from the dialogue. Figure out which ones have schwa in one syllable and which ones have two clear vowels. Check (✓) the chart.

Two-Syllable Words	Schwa Syllable	Two Clear Vowels
Example contact		✓
different	✓	
1. _____	_____	_____
2. _____	_____	_____
3. _____	_____	_____
4. _____	_____	_____
5. _____	_____	_____
6. _____	_____	_____

4. In the dialogue, find two words with three syllables. Mark the unstressed syllables where native speakers say a schwa as shown below.

Example optical   _____   _____

5. Practice the dialogue with a partner. Switch roles.

---

[2] *Different* is usually said as a two-syllable word in informal conversation.

p. Talk: A proverb and a personal experience

1. Give a 1–2 minute talk about one of the proverbs on page 117. Start by saying the proverb and explaining it in your own words. You might compare the proverb to a similar proverb in your language. Describe a personal experience that relates to the proverb.

2. Write out your talk and mark the targets. Draw slashes to show the thought groups and underline the focus words. Then practice with a tape recorder.

3. Speak from notes. Do not read your talk. Choose your own monitoring targets from the target list on page 2 and review the Checklist for Talks, which may be obtained from the Houghton Mifflin ESL website at http://college.hmco.com/esl/students.

FINISHING UP

Self-Quiz (Check the answers in the Answer Key.)

1. Circle all true statements about schwa vowels.
    a. They are important for understandable speech.
    b. You can recognize a schwa vowel by the way it is spelled.
    c. They are important for speech rhythm.
    d. They are critical for nativelike speech.

2. Circle all the true statements about *can* and *can't*.
    a. *Can* when used as a helping verb ("I can go") has a schwa vowel.
    b. *Can't* is said with a full, clear, no. 5 vowel.
    c. Native speakers also have trouble with *can* and *can't*.
    d. *Can't* is reduced when it is used as a helping verb.

3. True or False? Until you can pronounce all fifteen clear vowels accurately, your English speech will be difficult to understand.

4. True or False? The fifteen vowels are divided into long (complex) vowels and short (simple) vowels. Short vowels glide from one position to another as you say them.

5. True or False? Opening the mouth and lowering the jaw when saying a schwa vowel will make the speaker look and sound more nativelike.

Dictation

Write the sentences you hear. You will hear each sentence two times. Replay the tape to check your listening before looking in the Answer Key.

1. _____
2. _____
3. _____
4. _____
5. _____

Making Your New Pronunciation a Habit

Talk Times in Class: Role play

1. Partner A is a customer who needs information about moving. Partner B works for either a moving company or a truck rental company. You both need information. What do you need to find out? Write a list of questions that the customer and the company might ask.

Moving Company Questions	**Customer Questions**
• the number of rooms to move	• cost
• what is being moved (furniture, belongings)	• availability on a certain date
• the distance of the move	• experience of the company
• who will pack (need help or do it yourself)	• insurance to protect against loss/damage

2. Listen to the sample dialogue with your partner.

1. A: Good afternoon, Peacock Van and Storage. How can I help you?
2. B: I'm planning to move soon. How much do you charge?
3. A: That depends. How far are you moving, and how many rooms?
4. B: I have a one-bedroom apartment and I'm moving to Portland.
5. A: Do you need help packing?
6. B: I can pack everything myself. So what do you think it will cost?
7. A: We can come over tomorrow and give you an estimate.

3. Role-play a conversation with your partner. Call either a moving company or a truck rental agency. Monitor your own and your partner's speech. Switch roles.

Talk Times in Your Daily Life: Calling about moving

You live in a one-bedroom apartment and plan to move to another city. Make three calls to decide between using a mover or renting a truck. Get information and compare prices. Choose one or two things to ask about during each call. Write your questions and practice saying them before calling. Mark the stressed syllables and the focus words.

On Your Own

1. **Audio program.** Regular practice is important to your progress. For variety, try slow speech on one exercise. Close your eyes and speak very slowly. Concentrate on what your mouth and tongue feel like as they form the words.

2. **Recorded practice.** To become independent and able to correct your own errors, follow the tips for recorded practice on page 54. Record the dialogue "The Optical Shop," page 118, or the paragraph "The Photographer" below.

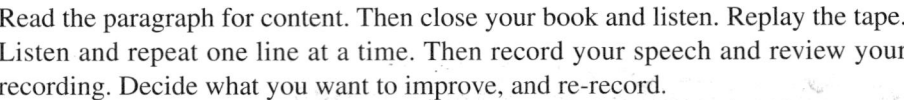

Read the paragraph for content. Then close your book and listen. Replay the tape. Listen and repeat one line at a time. Then record your speech and review your recording. Decide what you want to improve, and re-record.

The Photographer³

¹Anything is possible. ²My brother Adam just won a North American photography competition. ³He specializes in taking pictures of desert animals. ⁴He exhibited his photographs in communities across the United States and Canada. ⁵After some local television appearances, he immediately sold some of his photographs for exceptionally good prices. ⁶Until a few years ago, Adam didn't even own a camera.

3. **Glossary.** Keep collecting words, names, and places in your community that you need help pronouncing. Get help from a native speaker. Mark the stressed syllables.

4. **Mirroring.** Review "The Talking Mirror" on page 74. Mirror five minutes of a televised or videotaped speaker whom you admire and want to imitate. Describe your experience in a journal.

---

a helpful hint Close your eyes. Visualize a TV screen and a channel changer. Switch the channel to English. You are now an English-speaking actor in an English program. Breathe English. Move English. Use the English channel when you are doing Talk Times. Later, switch back to your native language channel for speaking your original language.

---

³ Notice how frequently this speaker says ə and ʌ.

Sing Along: The Melody of Speech

In earlier chapters you learned that stressed words and syllables rise in pitch. Chapter 7 discusses additional functions of intonation. English speech melody serves many purposes. Various linguistic forms, such as questions and abbreviations, have their own melody. Melody can provide information beyond the meaning of the words themselves. For example, it can indicate when someone is finished talking, or it can give emotional information such as how confident or friendly the speaker sounds.

How Much Melody Do People Use?

Cultures have different rules about how much speech melody is appropriate. In some cultures, using a lot of speech melody can indicate anger, rudeness, or lack of refinement. In contrast, both male and female English speakers who use a lot of speech melody tend to sound friendly, concerned, and interesting. Too little melody can make an English speaker seem distant, bored, or insincere.

 Listen to two speakers talking about winning the lottery. Which speaker sounds friendlier and more interesting?

Speaker 1. Expressive speech melody

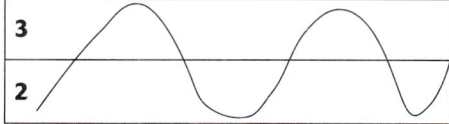

Speaker 2. Very little melody

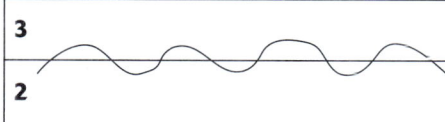

The Four Pitch Levels of English Speech

You hear more highs and lows in English than in most other languages. Most learners of English, both male and female, need to use more pitch variation. The following chart shows some ways that pitch levels are used in English speech. Most of the time English speech flows between levels 2 and 3.

Level 4 **Extra high pitch**	• emphasis and contrastive stress • strong emotions such as surprise, anger, elation, or disbelief	
Level 3 **High pitch**	• stressed words and syllables • the ends of questions or thought groups with rising pitch	
Level 2 **Middle-low pitch**	• unstressed words and syllables • reductions with schwa vowels	
Level 1 **Extra low pitch**	• the ends of most sentences • the completion of a speaker's turn talking	

Group Practice: Conversation with melody

Melody can carry meaning, even without words. In this short conversation between neighbors, Neighbor B uses intonation to communicate.

Listen several times and track the speakers. Then divide into two groups: Neighbor A and Neighbor B. Practice the conversation with the class until each group sounds like a chorus speaking in unison. Switch groups.

	Neighbor A	**Neighbor B**		**Meaning**
1.	Have you seen Snowball?	Huh?		lack of understanding
2.	My cat! Have you seen my cat?	Uh-uh!		no
3.	I can't find her anywhere in the house.	Oh!		mild surprise
4.	She's been missing since yesterday.	Oh!		mild pain or discomfort, empathy
5.	The cars drive very fast up and down my street.	Uh-oh!		indication of trouble or danger
6.	Maybe Snowball was run over by a car.	Oh!		great concern
7.	(later in the day) My cat came home this afternoon, safe and sound.	Aahhh!		sigh of pleasure or relief
8.	I should probably be more careful about keeping Snowball inside at night.	Mmmm.		agreement with unexpressed judgment or feeling

Some Guidelines for Intonation

The rules for speech melody are not clearly defined. The many variations take time to figure out. Although changing the pitch does not change the definition of a word, it can change the meaning in other ways. You will learn the melody of English speech in the same way that you learn the melody of a new song. With time and practice the song becomes automatic. Start by learning the following guidelines.

---

guideline 1   The focus word always changes pitch.

Often the focus word jumps up in pitch before it glides or steps down in pitch at the end of the sentence.

     Throw the ball to the CATCHer. (step)   He's in the CAR. (glide)

---

guideline 2   One word in each thought group jumps up to the highest pitch.

Other stressed words will rise in pitch, but not as high. The highest pitch is often on an early content word, but sometimes it is on the focus word. Individual speakers make this choice.

     The proFESsor was LATE.   I SAT on the BLACK CHAIR.

---

guideline 3   Falling intonation sounds finished.

The speaker may be finished with a thought, or possibly finished talking altogether. This can signal another speaker to take a turn talking.

     We waited for the MAIL.   I forgot my NOTEBOOK.

     My notebook was in the SCIence LAB.

a. Improve Your Monitoring: Finished or unfinished?

1. Listen to the sentences. Speaker A sounds finished and Speaker B sounds unfinished.

1. A: I plan to go on a diet . . . (for the New Year). ___ finished _✓_ unfinished
2. B: I plan to go on a diet. _✓_ finished ___ unfinished
3. A: She is a professor . . . (at a large university). ___ finished _✓_ unfinished
4. B: She is a professor. _✓_ finished ___ unfinished

2. Now listen to the short conversations. How does Speaker B sound? Check (✓) the answer.   1 = finished   2 = unfinished

Example   We close at five.   _✓_ 1   ___ 2

1. A: Are you going away?   B: Yes, we're leaving for London.   ___ 1   _✓_ 2
2. A: You look excited.   B: I'm going to buy a new car.   ___ 1   _✓_ 2
3. A: Who won the contest?   B: The winner will be announced   _✓_ 1   ___ 2
4. A: Why did Pedro call?   B: He had an important message.   _✓_ 1   ___ 2

Learn By Listening 1: Different messages for intonation

Intonation can give messages beyond the meaning of the words themselves. As you learned, falling intonation sounds finished. It can also make a speaker sound confident, convincing, and believable. In contrast, somewhat level pitch lines, that is, melody that does not clearly rise or fall, express little emotion or opinion. Level pitch can also make a speaker sound hesitant or uncertain.

Listen to the following sentences contrasting level and falling intonation. Speaker A sounds confident and believable. Speaker B sounds hesitant and uncertain.

1. A: I'm sure we can handle your problem.   _✓_ confident   ___ hesitant

   B: I'm sure we can handle your problem.   ___ confident   _✓_ hesitant

2. A: Let's try to get together again.   _✓_ believable   ___ uncertain

   B: Let's try to get together again.   ___ believable   _✓_ uncertain

b. Improve Your Monitoring: Confident or hesitant?

1. Listen to the short conversations. How does Speaker B sound? Check (✓) the answer.   1 = confident, believable   2 = hesitant, uncertain

		1	2
1.	Our shop has been in business for more than twenty years.	✓	
2.	Hello, everyone. I am going to be your guide today.		✓
3.	Our company is committed to protecting the environment.	✓	
4.	I hope you'll visit us again soon.		✓
5.	I'm so sorry, but I have other plans on Sunday.		✓
6.	We're going to make a profit.	✓	
7.	It was very nice meeting you.	✓	

2. Take turns practicing each sentence two ways. First, sound confident or sincere, and then sound hesitant or unconvincing. Discuss the intonation with your partner.

---

guideline 4 Yes–no questions usually have rising intonation.

The speaker shows little emotion but wants a response.

Are you **FIN**ished?   Would you like to leave a **MES**sage?

Sometimes yes–no questions are made as statements with rising intonation.

It's **COLD** outside?   You're planning to **WORK** today?

---

guideline 5 Wh-questions asking for information usually have falling intonation.

Where are you **GO**ing?   When is the **PAR**ty?   Who's **COM**ing?   What **TIME** is it?

c. Partner Practice: End-of-the-sentence intonation

1. Listen and repeat the following conversations. Check (✓) the direction of the end-of-the-sentence intonation.

	Rising Pitch	Falling Pitch
Example		
A: Would you like some coffee?	✓	—
B: Maybe later.	—	✓
1. A: What are you doing?		✓
B: I am giving my dog a bath.	—	✓
A: Do you need any help?	✓	—
2. A: Did you lose your umbrella?	✓	—
B: Yeah—have you seen it?	✓	—
A: No—when was the last time you had it?	—	✓
3. A: When are your parents going back to India?	✓	
B: Probably this week.	—	✓
A: Can't they stay any longer?	✓	—
4. A: Where did your friends go?	—	✓
B: They went for a walk.	—	✓
A: Do you think they'll be back soon?	✓	—

2. Listen again and repeat the conversations. Raise your arms for rising pitch. Lower your arms for falling pitch.

3. Practice the conversations with a partner. Monitor for end-of-the-sentence intonation.

| guideline 6 | Wh-questions rise in pitch when speakers seek clarification or show surprise. |

The wh-word gets the focus.

WHAT did you say?   **WHY** did he leave?   **WHICH** book do you prefer?

d. Partner Practice: Dialogues with wh-questions

1. Listen first. Then practice the dialogues with a partner.

Dialogue 1

A: Where are you **GO**ing? (needs information)

B: I'm going to **EUR**ope.

A: **WHERE** are you going? (needs clarification)

B: To **EUR**ope.

Dialogue 2

A: What did the airline **TELL** you? (needs information)

B: The planes are all **CAN**celed due to bad **WEA**ther.

A: **WHAT** did they tell you? (shows surprise, disbelief)

B: The **PLANES** are all **CAN**celed.

2. Create a four-line dialogue with your partner. First ask for information and then ask for clarification or show surprise at your partner's response. Switch roles.

e. Partner Practice: Rising and falling wh-questions

Partner A makes a statement. Partner B responds with a wh-question. Rising intonation will show surprise or seek clarification. Falling intonation will ask for more information. Partner A responds accordingly. Switch roles.

Example A: Julia's baby was born last week.

B: When? (clarification) | B: When? (asking for more information)
A: Last week. | A: On Tuesday.

---

1. A: Yoshi moved back to Japan.

    B: Where? 问清楚 | B: Where?
    A: To Japan. | A: To Kyoto.

---

2. A: Paco is graduating next year.

    B: When? | B: When?
    A: Next year. | A: In June.

---

3. A: We are saving to buy a condo.

    B: Why? | B: Why?
    A: To buy a condo. | A: We want our own home.

---

4. A: Tami is leaving tomorrow evening.

    B: When? | B: When?
    A: Tomorrow evening. | A: At 7 o'clock.

---

5. A: Elena is from Mexico.

    B: Where? | B: Where?
    A: Mexico. | A: Oaxaca.

CHAPTER 7　Sing Along: The Melody of Speech　**131**

Learn By Listening 2: Answering questions with a slightly rising pitch line

People who answer questions with a rising intonation sound uncertain and less confident. Self-monitor your intonation at the ends of sentences to make sure you give the message you intend. Listen to each conversation read two ways. Which response sounds more confident?

Conversation 1

1. A: Where do you work?
   B: At a bakery.

2. A: Where do you work?
   B: At a bakery.

Conversation 2

1. A: Where are you from?
   B: From Canada.

2. A: Where are you from?
   B: From Canada.

Intonation Variations

Learn By Listening 3: Abbreviations

Abbreviations have a specific intonation pattern. Each letter has a clear vowel and receives stress. The last letter gets the focus, and the pitch glides down.

Example　TV (television)

　　　　　　PDQ (pretty darn quick)

　　　　　　ASAP (as soon as possible)

1. Write the abbreviations on the line. Then listen and repeat what you hear. Add more abbreviations. Speak slowly. Be sure to say each letter clearly.

   1. _____ chief executive officer　CEO
   2. _____ Certified Public Accountant　CPA
   3. _____ Automatic Teller Machine　ATM
   4. _____ Digital Versatile Disc (original name)　DVD
   5. _____ grade point average　GPA
   6. _____ University of California, Los Angeles　UCLA

   Add More Abbreviations

2. Write the abbreviation on the line. Then listen and repeat. Say either a **y** or a **w** between two-letter abbreviations linking two vowel sounds.

   1. _____ you^wes United States　US
   2. _____ ee^yar emergency room　ER
   3. _____ a^yem midnight to noon　AM
   4. _____ see dee compact disc　CD
   5. _____ pee^yar public relations　PR
   6. _____ i^ydee identification　ID

f. Partner Practice: Using abbreviations

1. Partner A says the abbreviation. Partner B says a sentence. Take turns.

   Example   A: CNN (Cable News Network)

   B: My friend is a reporter for CNN.

2. Take turns asking and answering five questions using abbreviations from Learn By Listening 3 or your own list. Say the abbreviation in both the question and the answer.

   Example   A: How much TV do you watch?

   B: I watch about 5 hours of TV a week.

---

pronunciation tip   Say each letter in an abbreviation with a full clear vowel. Abbreviations said too quickly or with reduced vowels are hard to understand, especially four-letter ones such as UCLA.

---

g. Join the Chorus: "Get to the Airport Early"

Listen and repeat the chant in unison. Move your hands and lean forward slightly as you stress the focus words. Then divide into two groups. Say the chant alternating between groups A and B until you sound like a chorus with one voice. Switch groups.

A: I'm going on vaCAtion.

B: Gotta make a reserVAtion.

A: I wish you could come aLONG.

B: I wish I could come aLONG.

   A: A.M., P.M.,[1] day or NIGHT.

   Gotta get to the airport EARly.

   Don't want to miss my FLIGHT.

   B: DeTROIT, NEWark

   WASHington, BOSton

   ChiCAgo, ToRONto

   J-F-K.

---

[1] In this context **A.M.** and **P.M.** show contrast. Usually the focus is on the last letter: 4 **A.M.**, 2 **P.M.**

A: Find the **TICK**et. Stand in **LINE**.

B: Check the **LUG**gage. Get a **SEAT**.

A: Buckle **UP.** Settle **DOWN**.

B: Taking **OFF.** Up and a**WAY**.

    A: **A.M., P.M.,** day or **NIGHT**.

        Gotta get to the airport **EAR**ly.

        Don't want to miss my **FLIGHT**.

    B: SeATTle, MiAMi

        PORTland, **DAL**as

        VanCOUver, **PHOE**nix

        L-A-**X.**

A: C-E-**O**, V-I-**P**, CPA, or Ph.**D**.

B: LA**X** or JF**K**, PD**Q** ASA**P**

A: I wish you could come a**LONG**.

B: I wish I could come a**LONG**.

    A: **A**.M., **P.**M., day or **NIGHT**.

    B: Gotta get to the airport **EARL**y.

    A: Oh, **NO**! I missed my **FLIGHT**!

    B: That's 'cause you didn't take **ME** along!

New Abbreviations

LA**X** = Los Angeles International Airport

JF**K** = John F. Kennedy Airport

V**IP** = very important person

Ph.**D**. = Doctor of Philosophy

Phrasal Verbs

COME a**LONG** = accompany someone

BUCkle **UP** = buckle your seat belt

SETtle **DOWN** = get calm and comfortable

TAKing **OFF** = plane leaving the ground

Learn By Listening 4: More emotion

Native speakers use a bigger-than-usual change in pitch to show emphasis or increased emotion, such as great concern, surprise, disapproval, or enthusiastic approval. Listen and compare different versions of the same statement or question. Notice the changes in meaning.

The Basic Pattern

1. A: Is he **SICK** again?
2. A: I need to start **STU**dying.
3. A: That was an exciting **GAME**.
4. A: They'll return our money in a **MONTH**. (surprise)

Emphasis (More Emotion)

1. B: Is he sick a**GAIN**? (surprise, concern)
2. B: I **NEED** to **START STU**dying! (emphasis)
3. B: That **WAS** an exciting game. (enthusiastic agreement)
4. B: They'll return our money in a **MONTH**? (disapproval)

h. Partner Practice: Conversations at the office

1. Listen to two conversations between people who work together in an office. Conversation 1 shows the emotions expressed in parentheses. For conversation 2, write whether the speaker is expressing strong emotion, mild surprise, or a simple statement.

Conversation 1

First worker:	I came to pick up the report.	
Second worker:	Can you come back later? It's not finished.	1. (simple statement)
First worker:	It's not finished? OK, I'll come back later.	2. (question/mild surprise)
Third worker:	It's not finished! I needed it an hour ago!	3. (exclamation)

Conversation 2

First worker:	I'm ready to go to the meeting.	
Second worker:	The meeting was canceled.	1. _____
First worker:	The meeting was canceled? I wonder what happened.	2. _____
Third worker:	The meeting was canceled! I changed my whole day around because of that meeting.	3. _____

2. Work in groups of three. Practice the conversations. Switch roles.

| **pronunciation tip** | Fall low enough in pitch at the ends of sentences to sound finished. Otherwise your speech may seem uncertain or hesitant. |

---

i. Dialogues: More practice with questions

Listen to the dialogues. Underline the focus words. Notice the end-of-the-sentence intonation and the changes in focus.

Dialogue 1: "Not My Bag"

Is speaker B asking questions to seek clarification, show surprise, or express emotion?

1. A: That's not my bag. Those aren't my groceries.
2. B: That's not your bag? Those aren't your groceries?
3. A: No. I bought cheese, chips, salsa, and Coke.
4. B: You bought cheese, chips, salsa, and Coke? I didn't know you liked salsa.
5. A: I don't. I'm having a party, and I'm serving salsa.
6. B: You're having a party? And you didn't invite me?

Dialogue 2: "Trip to Paris?"

The wh-questions in lines 4, 5, and 6 have the same words. How does the intonation differ?

1. A: Would you like to take a trip?
2. B: What kind of trip?
3. A: A short trip, an inexpensive trip. One without a lot of hassle.[2]
4. B: That sounds good. Where would you like to go?
5. A: I'd like to go to Paris. Where would you like to go?
6. B: Where would you like to go? Did you say Paris? That's not a short trip, or an inexpensive trip. That's a long trip.
7. A: Haven't you heard of Paris, Texas? We can fly there in an hour.

---

[2] bother or trouble

Learn By Listening 5: Beyond the words

Intonation changes the meaning of these sentences. Listen to each sentence read different ways. Replay the tape and repeat each sentence one line at a time.

Sentence	Meaning
1. That new restaurant was pretty **GOOD**.	good (statement, little emotion)
That new restaurant was pretty **GOOD**!	excellent (exclamation, surprise)
That new restaurant was **PRET**ty good.	mediocre (statement, little emotion)
That new restaurant was pretty **GOOD**?	not good (ironic question showing doubt)
2. I'll bet she wants to work all **WEEK**end.	words mean what they say
I'll **BET** she wants to work all weekend.	words mean the opposite (ironic)
I'll bet **SHE** wants to work all weekend.	She wants to work, but no one else does.
3. That was a great way to spend an after**NOON**.	words mean what they say
That was a **GREAT** way to spend an afternoon.	words mean the opposite (ironic)
THAT was a **GREAT** way to spend an afternoon.	exclamation, emphatic speech

Longer Sentences

As you learned, English speakers organize sentences with more than four or five words into thought groups. Within certain guidelines, they make individual choices about the intonation patterns for these longer sentences.

 Sing Along: "Home on the Range"

The songs of a culture can tell you a lot about the intonation of the speech. Speech is another kind of song. Both the speaker's voice and the singer's voice move up and down in pitch to make melody.

1. Listen several times to this traditional cowboy song from the mid-1880s. Each verse is one long sentence with several thought groups. Fill in the focus words shown here in alphabetical order.

   amazed   bright   day   deer   gazed   heard   home   night   ours   play   range   roam   stars   word

1. Oh, give me a ___Home___,
   where the buffalo ___roam___,
   And the deer and the antelope ___play___,
   Where seldom is ___heard___,
   a discouraging ___word___,
   And the skies are not cloudy all ___day___.

Chorus:

   Home, home on the ___range___,
   Where the ___deer___ and the antelope ___roam___,
   Where seldom is ___heard___ a discouraging ___word___,
   And the skies are not cloudy all ___day___.

2. How often at ___night___ when the heavens are ___stars___
   With the light of the glittering ___play___,
   Have I stood there _____ and I asked as I _____
   "Does their glory exceed that of _____?"

2. Listen to verse 1 again and say the words with the speaker. Tap your desk for the focus words. Say the final sounds for *home*, and *roam*. Link the final d on *heard* and *word* to the next vowel.

Oh, give me a **HOME** / where the buffalo **ROAM** /

Where the **DEER** / and the antelope **PLAY** /

Where seldom is **HEARD** / a discouraging **WORD** /

And the **SKIES** / are not cloudy all **DAY**. /

3. Divide into two groups. Practice until you can say or sing one verse with your group for the class. Everyone says or sings the chorus.

j. Partner Practice: More to say

When you are saying a series of two or more things, use a slight pitch rise after the focus words to signal that you have *more to say*. Fall in pitch at the end of the sentence to signal that you are finished. Pause at the end of each thought group in the series.

1. Listen to the sentences with a series.

1. I'm taking history, math, and beginning English.
2. We're going to plant daisies, rose bushes, and tulips.

2. Listen and draw pitch arrows over the focus words in the series below. Then take turns saying the sentences. Monitor for intonation, indicating when you have more to say and when you are finished.

1. I'd like the soup of the day, a Caesar salad, and the tomato pasta.
2. Please fill in your name, birth date, and passport number.
3. When I move into the new apartment, I'll need a rug, dining table, and sofa.
4. My boss requested a starting date, cost estimate, and production schedule.

3. Give your partner three reasons why you need a vacation and then three places you want to go or things you want to do. Monitor for intonation for a series.

Example

I need a vacation because I'm tired of my job, I have to get away, and I want to see the world. I want to go to Spain, to Alaska, and to Thailand.

Learn By Listening 6: Two-part sentences

The intonation for a two-part sentence indicates when you have more to say and when you are finished. Listen and repeat what you hear. Draw arrows.

1. I believe you, but I'd like more proof.
2. He can fix the printer, but not today.
3. I can see you're planning to leave, so please turn off the lights.

k. Partner Practice: Two-part sentences

Say the first part of the sentence below. Use intonation and pausing to show that you have more to say. Then finish your sentence. Take turns.

Example   She spent all her money <u>before she knew what happened.</u>

1. It may rain this afternoon _____.
2. I've been living in California _____.
3. The bus came around the corner _____.
4. We're going to make a profit _____.
5. My car needs washing _____.

l. Partner Practice: An ad

1. Listen to the ad. Draw a slash (/) every time you hear a pause. Listen to the pitch lines.

   1. We don't make the mattress, / we make it softer.
   2. We don't make the boots, / we make them drier.
   3. We don't make the house, / we make it livelier.
   4. We don't make the snowboard, / we make it stronger.
   5. At BASF / we don't make a lot of the products you buy, / we make a lot of the products you buy / better.[3]

2. Practice saying the ad. Pay attention to the pitch lines and the abbreviation.

m. Communicative Activity: Talk about yourself

1. Partner A says a phrase from column 1. Use intonation that shows that you have more to say. Finish the sentence with any phrase from column 2. Use falling intonation.

2. Then ask Partner B, "What about you?" Partner B responds.

Example

A: Ordinarily, I am very early. What about you?

B: As a matter of fact, I'm never early. But when I get a chance, I'm extremely neat. What about you?

Column 1

1. As a RULE,
2. You may not beLIEVE it, but
3. In GENeral,
4. OrdiNARily,
5. As a matter of FACT,
6. As you can iMAgine
7. When I get a CHANCE
8. Under most CIRcumstances

Column 2

I eat / don't eat meat.
I am usually / very / never early.
I would / wouldn't like to fly a helicopter.
It's hard / easy for me to be on time.
I read / don't read newspapers.
I prefer showers and avoid baths.
I'm extremely neat / messy.
I stay up late at night.

---

[3] By permission. BASF Corporation.

Learn By Listening 7: Meaningful pauses

One 22" fish   twenty 2" fish

Listen to phrases (a) and (b). Compare the thought groups. The focus words and the pauses change the meaning of the words. Check (✓) the appropriate meaning for each sentence.

Example

a.	the twenty-two-inch goldfish	✓ one fish	___ 22 fish
b.	the twenty two-inch goldfish	___ one fish	✓ 20 fish
1. a.	fifty-one-dollar raffle tickets	___ $1 a ticket	✓ $51 a ticket
b.	fifty one-dollar raffle tickets 50 X	✓ $1 a ticket	___ $51 a ticket
2. a.	fried chicken, potato salad, and a Coke	✓ three things	___ four things
b.	fried chicken, potato, salad, and a Coke	___ three things	✓ four things
3. a.	the computer software and keyboard	✓ two things	___ three things
b.	the computer, software, and keyboard	___ two things	✓ three things
4. a.	a car, phone, and tape deck	___ two things	✓ three things
b.	a car phone and tape deck	✓ two things	___ three things

 n. Partner Practice: More about pauses

1. First listen to sentences (a) and (b). Discuss how the pauses change the meaning.

2. Partner A says either sentence (a) or (b). Partner B gives the appropriate response. Switch roles.

Partner A

Example

   a. WHAT do you THINK / of the TWENty-two-INCH GOLDFISH? /

   b. WHAT do you THINK / of the TWENty / TWO-inch GOLDFISH? /

1. a. Robert is SELLing / FIFty-ONE-DOLlar RAFfle TICKets / for a trip to HaWAii. /
   b. Robert is selling FIFty / ONE-dollar RAFfle TICKets / for a trip to HaWAii./

2. a. I'd like fried CHICKen / with poTAto / SALad / and a COKE. /
   b. I'd like fried CHICKen / with poTAto SALAD/ and a COKE. /

3. a. Jim's new comPUter / SOFTWARE / and KEYBOARD / finally arRIVED. /
   b. Jim's new comPUter software / and KEYBOARD finally arRIVED. /

4. a. I'm planning to buy a new CAR / PHONE / and TAPE DECK. /
   b. I'm planning to buy a new CAR PHONE / and TAPE DECK. /

5. a. "JANE," / said her father, / "is taking piANo lessons." /
   b. Jane said her FAther / is taking piANo lessons. /

6. a. My FRIEND said / "The NURSE / plans to work at a HOSpital / in GuateMAla." /
   b. "My FRIEND," / said the nurse, / "plans to work at a HOSpital in GuateMAla." /

7. a. Robert Louis STEvenson / is an AUthor. /
   b. Robert LOUis, / Steven's SON, / is an AUthor. /

Partner B

It needs a much bigger bowl!

They are very small.

$51 a piece? That's pretty expensive for a raffle ticket.

At $1 a piece, maybe I'll buy five of them.

Do you want butter and sour cream on your potato?

Would you like extra potato salad?

What kind of computer did he buy?

It's too bad he couldn't afford to buy a new computer, too.

What kind of car are you going to buy?

It's too bad you aren't going to buy a new car, too.

How long has Jane been studying the piano?

How long has her father been studying the piano?

Has the nurse worked in Guatemala before?

Has your friend worked in Guatemala before?

He wrote *Treasure Island*.

Really? Steven never mentioned his son.

| pronunciation tip | Pausing in the wrong place can change the meaning and may confuse your listener. |

o. Communicative Activity: Compare the pictures

Partner A looks at the drawing below. Partner B looks at the drawing at the bottom of the page. Exchange information about your pictures. Let your partner know when you are finished with each sentence by falling in pitch. If you use a longer sentence, signal that you have more to say.

Partner A's drawing

Sample Conversation

A: My picture shows **PEO**ple waiting at a **BUS** STOP. There's a **WO**man waiting with a large **BAG**.

B: My picture shows a **BUS** STOP, **TOO**, but there's a **MAN** waiting, and he's carrying a **BRIEF**CASE.

Partner B's drawing

p. Talk: In my opinion . . .

You and your partner will take opposite positions in a discussion in front of the class. Talk about one of the following statements.

- Men should be the primary wage earners in a family while women take most of the responsibility for home and children.
- Divorce could be avoided if more couples lived together before marriage in order to test their relationship.
- The money spent on defense programs and national security would be better spent in the community on homelessness, medical care, and education.
- Although cellular phones are popular and useful, they should not be allowed in cars because they are a safety hazard.

1. To prepare for the discussion, plan a short statement explaining why you agree or disagree with your topic. Use some of the following phrases to express your opinion.

To Express Your Opinion	To Disagree
In my opinion / . . .	I can't agree with that / because . . .
Not everyone will agree, / but I think . . .	I'm not convinced / that . . .
I'm convinced / that . . .	I don't see it that way. / I think . . .
From my point of view / . . .	From a different point of view / . . .
I personally believe / that . . .	I personally do not believe / that . . .
I honestly think / that . . .	I can't go along with that / because . . .

2. Practice with a tape recorder. Use intonation to indicate when you have more to say and when you are finished. Use falling pitch to show confidence.

3. In class, deliver your prepared statement. Use expressions from the list to preface some of your responses and to disagree. After the presentation, respond to two or three questions from the audience.

FINISHING UP

Self-Quiz (Check the answers in the Answer Key.)

Check all the statements in items 1–3 that are true. There may be more than one true statement per item.

1. ____ a. Most English learners need to use more high and low pitches.

   ____ b. Most male English speakers use less pitch variation than women.

   ____ c. People who use more pitch variation sound more friendly, interested, and sincere.

2. Falling intonation can make the speaker sound

   ___ hesitant ___ confident ___ finished

3. ___ a. Abbreviations can be hard to understand unless you stress all the letters.

   ___ b. Abbreviations have both clear vowels and schwa vowels.

   ___ c. The last letter in an abbreviation gets the focus.

4. Underline the focus words in (a), (b), and (c).

   a. Where would you like to go? (basic pattern)

   b. Where would you like to go? (returning a question)

   c. Where would you like to go? (show surprise, seek clarification)

5. Draw pitch lines over the word *go* in the wh-questions above.

Making Your New Pronunciation a Habit

Talk Times in Class: Discussion

1. During Talk Times you will be contacting a music store to inquire about a possible purchase. Prepare for this by interviewing your partner about his or her taste in music. Practice the following interview questions. Monitor end-of-the-sentence intonation. For more natural speech, use these reductions:

- (WHATcher) What is your favorite kind of music? Do you like folk, jazz, Latin, reggae, pop, rock 'n' roll, country/western, classical, alternative, Hawaiian, Irish, or another kind?

- (WHO'Z your) Who is your favorite musical performer or recording artist?

- (WHAT'S the) What is the title of your favorite CD?

- (WHAT'S ONE of your) What is one of your favorite songs?

2. With your partner, make a list of questions to ask when you contact the music store. Discuss the kinds of things you want to find out. What is important to you? What kind of music will you ask about?

Possible topics for questions

- the kind of music the store sells
- discounted tapes or CDs
- the store location and hours
- the store's return policy
- listening to recordings in the store
- availability of favorite recordings

Talk Times in Your Daily Life: Buying music

Call or go to three music stores to inquire about a purchase. Use the questions you wrote with your partner. Ask two or three questions per inquiry. Self-monitor and assess what happened before you make your next call. Target focus words, pitch changes on questions, and end-of-the-sentence intonation.

On Your Own

1. **Audio program.** Practice with the tapes/CDs for chapter 7. Choose one dialogue in this chapter to track until you can say it along with the speakers.

2. **Recorded practice.** Record the following:
   - the dialogue "Trip to Paris?" on page 135.
   - six *wh-* or *yes-no* questions and answers using abbreviations. Monitor for intonation.

   Example When are you going to the ATM? I'm going to the ATM later.

3. **Glossary.** Add words. Then look over your whole glossary list. Use five of your words in conversations this week at school, at work, or in the community.

4. **Mirroring.** Mirror five minutes of a TV program. Review the instructions in "The Talking Mirror" on page 74. Describe your experience in a journal.

UNIT III PROGRESS CHECK

Make a tape to turn in or to review in a scheduled conference with your instructor. Use intonation between phrases to indicate that you have more to say. Before you start, review the tips for recorded practice on page 54.

1. Record the following quotations by famous people. Underline the focus words. Show pitch arrows for the intonation at the end of each thought group and sentence. Monitor for speech melody.

Example

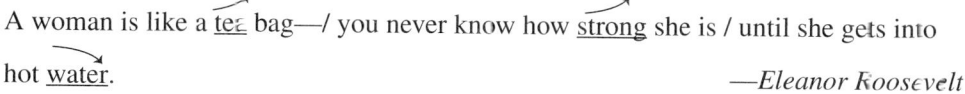

A woman is like a <u>tea</u> bag—/ you never know how <u>strong</u> she is / until she gets into hot <u>water</u>.

—Eleanor Roosevelt

- Anyone who has never made a mistake / has never tried anything new.

   —Albert Einstein

- We do not inherit this land / from our ancestors; / we borrow it / from our children. /

   —Haida Indian

- Even if you are on the right track, /you'll get run over / if you just sit there.

   —Will Rogers

- If you can't feed a hundred people, / then feed just one. /

   —Mother Teresa

- We do not inherit this land / from our ancestors; / we borrow it / from our children. /

  —*Haida Indian*

- Even if you are on the right track, /you'll get run over / if you just sit there.

  —*Will Rogers*

a helpful hint

- If you can't feed a hundred people, / then feed just one. /

  —*Mother Teresa*

2. Talk for 1–2 minutes about one of the quotations. Talk from notes, not a script. Use intonation to make your speech easy to follow and interesting. Re-record until you are satisfied.

Listen to recordings of songs, especially folk songs or songs from Broadway shows. After you listen many times, you will be able to sing or say the words along with the singer. Then try saying the words without the music. Keep the same rhythm.

Web Activities

Go to elt.heinle.com/targetingpron for additional activities related to this chapter.

Unit IV   Sounds: Consonants and Vowels

8

The Speech Pathway—What's Happening Where?

Chapter 8 introduces you to English consonant sounds and how they are made. You will learn how to pronounce challenging consonants and how the pronunciation of some consonants, such as the letters "t" and "r," can vary. In this chapter and the rest of unit IV, you will see how sounds and speech music fit together. They are both important pieces of the pronunciation puzzle.

Follow the Speech Pathway

Talking is so automatic that we usually don't think about how it happens. Babies cry and babble. Eventually they learn to talk. At a young age we listen and learn to repeat the words and intonation of our native language. The sounds we make all start with the air we breathe.

> Explore the pathway for speech that begins at the lungs and ends with the mouth and nose where the breath exits. Walk your finger along the drawing of the head to the various numbered locations as you practice saying the English sounds that you make there. Use a mirror to watch your mouth make the sounds.

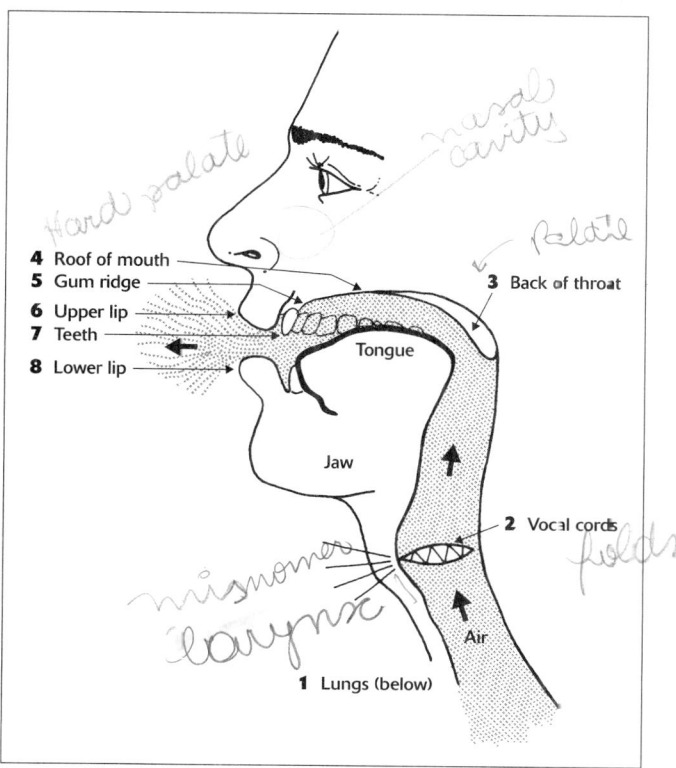

4 Roof of mouth
5 Gum ridge
6 Upper lip
7 Teeth
8 Lower lip
3 Back of throat
Tongue
Jaw
2 Vocal cords
Air
1 Lungs (below)

Lungs: Location 1 on the pathway

Group Practice 1: Breathing for speech

Take in a deep breath (inhale). Say *ah* as you breathe out (exhale). The energy for saying *ah* and all speech comes from the air we breathe. Put your hand near your mouth and say *hat*. Feel the air.

Vocal Cords: Location 2 on the pathway

Group Practice 2: Voicing

What is voicing?

After the air leaves the lungs, it goes through the vocal cords. Sometimes the vocal cords vibrate. The vibration is called *voicing*. Find the vocal cords on the drawing of the speech pathway.

1. Put your hand gently on your throat. Say *aaah*, then *mmm*. Feel the vibration.

2. Say *ssss*. Do you feel any vibration on your throat? Alternate between *ssss* and *zzzz*. The vibration turns on and off. The consonant sounds written in gray boxes with a squiggly underline are voiced. The consonant sounds written in plain gray boxes are voiceless.

Examples   s (voiceless)   z (voiced)   f (voiceless)   v (voiced)

What sounds are voiced?

- All vowels are voiced.
- Some consonants are voiced and some are not.

Stops: The air stops along the speech pathway

To make speech sounds, the air from the lungs either briefly stops along the pathway or continues out without stopping. Look at the picture of the closed window to see the sounds called *stops*. The picture of the open window shows examples of sounds called *continuants*. The air for these sounds continues out the pathway without stopping.

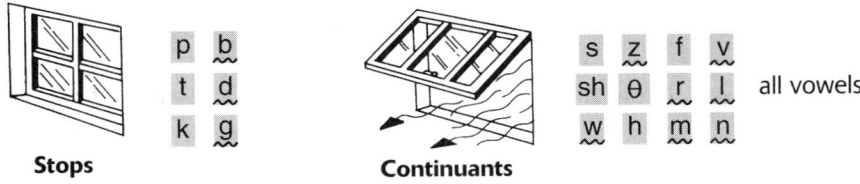

Stops   Continuants

There are three places where you stop the air to make these sounds. Check locations 3 (back of the throat), 5 (gum ridge), and 6 and 8 (lips) on the drawing, page 147.

Back of the Throat: Location 3 on the pathway

Group Practice 3: k and g

k

1. Take a breath and start to say *key*. Squeeze the k sound tightly in the back of your throat to stop the air and build up air pressure. Then release the air and finish saying *key*.

2. Say the words and phrases: kiss   sack   baking   bac**k** away

    ta**ke a** walk   pic**k a** number

3. Write a word starting with k _____ and one ending with k _____. Say each word in a sentence.

g

1. Start to say *go*. Squeeze the g in the back of your throat. Finish saying *go*. Next, slowly run your tongue tip from behind your front teeth along the bony roof of your mouth. Move back toward your throat until you get to the soft part where you stopped the air for k and f.

2. Say the words and phrases: game   big   bigger   bag of gum

    e**gg** and toast   bi**g** apple

3. Write a word starting with g _____ and one ending with g _____. Say each word in a sentence.

4. Put your hand on your throat and say k and g. Which is voiced? _____

    Contrast voicing   **K**ate–**g**ate   **c**ame–**g**ame   a bla**c**k (**c**oat–**g**oat)

    It is (**c**old–**g**old)

Gum Ridge: Location 5 on the pathway

Group Practice 4: t and d

t

1. Lift your tongue to touch the roof of your mouth just behind your top teeth. Take a breath and hold your tongue on your gum ridge. Let the air build up by preventing it from coming out either your mouth or your nose. Whisper t as you release the air in a puff.

2. Say the words and phrases: tiger   bat   attempt   I lost it.

    He kept it all day. Put salt on it.

3. Write a word starting with t _____ and one ending with t _____. Say each word in a sentence.

d

1. Feel the same bony gum ridge behind your top teeth. This gum ridge is an important place for English speech. You put your tongue on your gum ridge when you say the past tense ("ed").

2. Say the words and phrases: **d**ay E**d** rea**d**y re**d** apple Sli**d**e over

   a**dd**e**d** a **d**ollar staye**d** all **d**ay.

3. Write a word starting with **d** _____ and one ending with **d** _____. Say each word in a sentence.

4. Put your hand on your throat and say **t** and **d**. Which is voiced? _____

   Contrast voicing. **t**ie–**d**ie **d**own–**t**own Give me the (**t**ime–**d**ime).

   Let's (**t**ie it–**d**iet.)

Lips: Locations 6 and 8 on the pathway

Group Practice 5: p and b

p

1. Whisper. Take a breath and start to say the word *pop*. Hold your lips closed for the **p**. Let the air build up. Where do you feel the sound? Finish saying *pop*.

2. Say the words and phrases: **p**ay u**p** ha**pp**y Si**p** it slowly.

   Sto**p** it! Ho**p** along.

3. Write a word starting with **p** _____ and one ending with **p** _____. Say each word in a sentence.

b

1. Take a breath and close your lips to stop the air. Then say *baby*. Feel your lips close two times.

2. Say the words and phrases: **b**ee tu**b** ru**bb**er Ru**b** it off. Gra**b** a sweater.

3. Write a word starting with **b** _____ and one ending with **b** _____. Say each word in a sentence.

4. Put your hand on your throat and say **p** and <u>**b**</u>. Which one is voiced? _____

Contrast voicing. **pay–bay**   **pack–back**   Here is the (**pill–bill**).

Do you like (**peas–bees**)?

a. Watch the Air Release: Voiceless stops

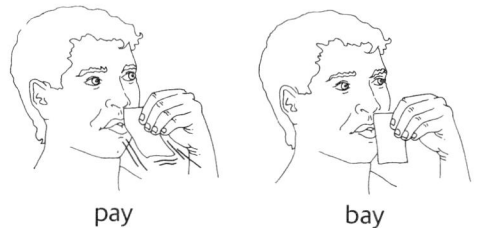

pay   bay

1. With one hand, hold a 1 × 3 inch strip of paper in front of your mouth.

2. Say *pay*. The paper moves as you release the puff. Say *bay*. The paper doesn't move. There are three places along the pathway where the air releases in a puff at the beginning of words. Watch the air blow the strip of paper as you say the voiceless stops.

    p t k   PAUL PAID for TWO CANS of TUna.

3. Tongue exercise for voiceless stops.

    - Slowly whisper *PUH-TUH-KUH* several times. Feel the places in your mouth where the air stops.

    - Say *PUH-tuh-kuh, PUH-tuh-kuh, PUH-tuh-kuh*. See how quickly you can repeat this sequence and still keep up the rhythm.

Group Practice 6: Holding final stops

In casual speech, native speakers of North American English often do not release the air at the end of stop sounds. Practice holding the final stop by leaving your tongue where it is. Let the air build up, but do not release the air in a puff at the end of these sentences: *Turn on the light.   Take a break.*

1. Listen and repeat the following dialogues in unison. Hold your tongue or lips in place and feel the final stop on the underlined word. Underline the place in your mouth where the air stops.

2. Then divide into two groups. Say the dialogues alternating between groups A and B until you sound like a chorus with one voice. Move your hands and lean forward slightly as you stress the focus words. Switch groups.

Example   I tied a **KNOT.**   lips—<u>gum ridge</u>—throat

1. A: Where's the **CAT**?   lips—gum ridge—throat
   B: She's hiding in **BACK.**   lips—gum ridge—throat
2. A: What happened to **BOB**?   lips—gum ridge—throat
   B: He's waiting for **TED.**   lips—gum ridge—throat
3. A: Where's the **MAP**?   lips—gum ridge—throat
   B: It's under the **BAG.**   lips—gum ridge—throat

---

pronunciation tip   When speakers hold the final stop, you can tell the difference between two similar words by the length of the vowel. The vowel before the final voiceless stop sounds shorter.

⟵ (voiceless final stop)   ⟵⟶ (voiced final stop)

mo**p**	mo**b**
rig**t**	ri**de**
pic**k**	pi**g**

Learn By Listening 1: The flap (or tapped "t")

Not all "t's" are the same. Sometimes a "t" sounds similar to a "d." The tongue lightly taps or flaps against the gum ridge without building up or releasing a puff of air, and this is called *a flap*.

Listen to the following examples of a flap. Put your tape recorder on pause after each line and practice.

- Before unstressed "er" or "or": LAter   BETter   WAter   MOTor   TRAITor
- Before "ing" and "ed": SHOUTing   SHOUTed   WAITing   WAITed
- Before an unstressed vowel: CIty   FORty   PAtio   CItizen   PHOtograph
- In linked phrases: right aCROSS   wait aROUND   THOUGHT about it
- In linking past tenses: WASHED it   SLICED it   STOPPED her   inVITed him

b. Communicative Activity: What's happening today?

1. Partner A looks at one of the charts with the pictures of people doing things. Partner B looks at the other chart. Some of the names on both charts are missing pictures. Find out if your partner knows what these people are doing. Take turns asking and answering questions.

2. First, practice the flap. Listen to the names on the charts and the "ing" verbs describing what these people are doing. Repeat what you hear.

   Betty Dotty Eddy Katie Marty Matty Otto Peter Rita Teddy
   batting cutting eating fighting knitting painting
   planting skating voting writing

Sample Conversation

   A: What's happening today? Is Peter batting a baseball?
   B: No, Peter is skating on the lake. What's Rita doing today?
   A: Rita is painting a picture. Do you know what Teddy is doing today?

Partner A's information

Marty	Eddy	Rita	Dotty	Matty
(batting)	(fighting)	(painting)	(knitting)	(writing)
Peter	Betty	Katie	Teddy	Otto

Partner B's information

Marty	Eddy	Rita	Dotty	Matty
Peter	Betty	Katie	Teddy	Otto
(skating)	(eating)	(voting)	(planting)	(cutting)

Learn By Listening 2: Linking

The endings of words in English often provide grammatical information, such as past tenses. You can recognize the past tense when you hear a flap linked to the next word.

1. Listen and repeat the following sentences in unison. Pay attention to the linking.

Present Tense (Linking a Continuant)	**Past Tense (Linking a Flap)**
Let's clean it up.	He cleaned it up.
Don't slam on the brakes.	He slammed on the brakes.
Sew it up.	It's all sewed up.
Puff on the pipe.	He puffed on the pipe.
I have an apple.	I had an apple.
Push it open.	I pushed it open.
She has an idea.	She had an idea.
Breathe easy.	We breathed easy.
Pull over.	I pulled over.

2. Now practice with a partner. Partner A says the present tense linking the continuant and Partner B says the past tense linking the flap.

c. Improve Your Monitoring: Past or present?

1. Listen to either the past or the present tense. Underline the word you hear.

   Example (<u>row</u>–rowed) across the lake

   1. (show–showed) up
   2. (hiked–hike) up the hill
   3. (play–played) the flute
   4. (grab–grabbed) it
   5. (jump–jumped) around
   6. (stay–stayed) all day
   7. (tie–tied) a knot
   8. (move–moved) in October
   9. (share–shared) our dinner
   10. (figure–figured) it out

2. Practice both choices in sentences. Use a flap to link the "ed" ending to the next word.

   Example Let's show up early.   He showed up after lunch.

Learn By Listening 3: Linking the same consonant sound

When you link two sounds that are made in the same place in the mouth, say the sound once, but hold it longer. The symbol : means to hold the sound briefly in place. For example, "Weak: coffee"* should sound different from "we coffee." "Wheat: toast" should sound different from "we toast."

Listen and repeat the following phrases.

| a black: car | stop: pushing | prevent: disease | a wet diaper |
| a fine: night | mile: long | a sick: cat | nine: nations |

Continuants: The air flows out the pathway

All sounds that are not stops are called *continuants*. The air from the lungs continues up the pathway and flows out the mouth or the nose without stopping, until the air is gone.

1. Take a breath and say *ah* for as long as you can. How many times can you tap your finger before you run out of air? Take another breath and say *ssss*. Tap your finger until you run out of air.

2. Look at the window drawings, page 148, to see examples of stops and continuant sounds. How many consonant sounds are stops? _____ How many continuants are shown? _____

Group Practice 7: f and v (locations 7 and 8 on the pathway)

Look at the lips and the teeth in the following picture.

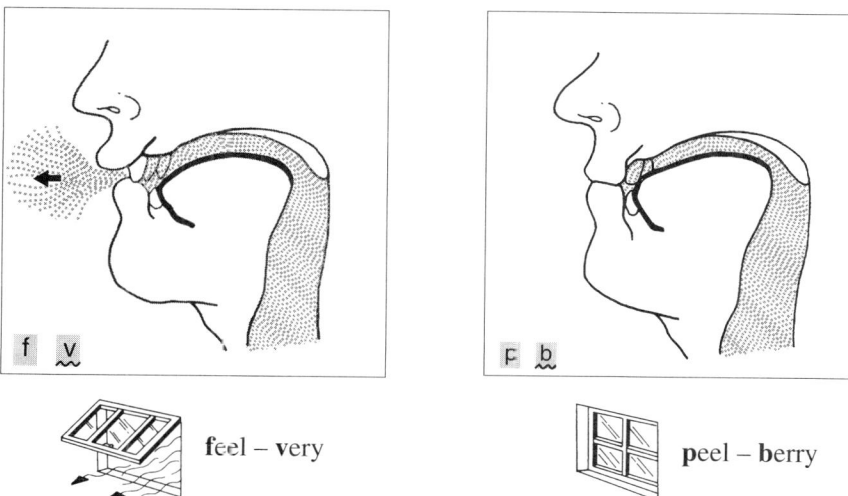

feel – very   peel – berry

*Remember that different letters can have the same sound in English. For example, the "k" and "c" in *weak coffee* sound the same.

1. Say a long slow **f**. Make sure that your top teeth are resting gently inside your lower lip. Keep your lips open and don't stop the air. Say *fan*. Feel the difference as you say *fan–pan–fan–pan*.

2. Put your hand on your throat and say **f**. Then say **v**. Keep your lips open. Which sound is voiced, **f** or **v**? _____

3. Listen and repeat the words and phrases for **f** (voiceless) and **v** (voiced).

   f: fa**c**e forward   loa**f** of bread   hal**f** a muffin   sta**ff** assistant   rou**gh** edges

   v: **v**ery heavy   abo**v**e all   li**v**e alone   ha**v**e everything   microwa**v**e oven

   dri**v**e around

4. Write a word starting with **f** _____ and one ending with **f** _____.

   Write a word starting with **v** _____ and one ending with **v** _____.

   Say each word in a sentence.

d. Partner Practice: Contrast **b** and **v**

1. Practice these word pairs. Both **b** and **v** are voiced. Open your lips for **v**.

   bet–**v**et   **b**an–**v**an   **b**oat–**v**ote   cur**b**–cur**v**e   **b**ail–**v**eil   **b**ase–**v**ase

2. Partner A says either sentence (a) or (b). Hide your mouth with a piece of paper. Partner B answers. Take turns.

Example   a. I chose that **b**et for my horse.   Did your horse win the race?

   b. I chose that **v**et for my horse.   Was your horse sick?

1. a. Tell me about the **b**an.   There's no smoking on airplanes.

    b. Tell me about the **v**an.   It's large and comfortable.

2. a. The president wants my **v**ote.   When is the election?

    b. The president wants my **b**oat.   Your sailboat or your motor boat?

3. a. There's a car near the cur**b**.   Is it parked?

    b. There's a car near the cur**v**e.   Is it coming toward us?

4. a. She needs the **b**ail now.   Who's in jail?

    b. She needs the **v**eil now.   When is the wedding?

5. a. The **b**ase is made of glass.   The top is made of metal.

    b. The **v**ase is made of glass.   It's filled with flowers.

e. Partner Practice: Contrast p and f

1. Practice saying the word pairs. Both sounds are voiceless. Open your lips for f.

    pear–fair   pan–fan   lap–laugh   pace–face   past–fast

2. Partner A says either sentence (a) or (b). Hide your mouth with a piece of paper. Partner B answers. Take turns.

    Example   a. What did you see at the port?   Ships and water.
                    b. What did you see at the fort?   Soldiers and guns.
    1. a. Enjoy the pear.   Is it ripe?
       b. Enjoy the fair.   Is there a merry-go-round?
    2. a. What's the pan for?   Cooking eggs.
       b. What's the fan for?   Keeping cool.
    3. a. How do you spell *lap*?   l-a-p
       b. How do you spell *laugh*?   l-a-u-g-h
    4. a. What do you think of his pace?   He's going too fast.
       b. What do you think of his face?   He's quite handsome.
    5. a. Don't drive past her.   She's waiting at the corner.
       b. Don't drive faster.   I'm driving below the speed limit.

Group Practice 8: w (locations 6 and 8 on the pathway)

1. Round the lips tightly for w and keep the voicing going. Keep your top teeth away from your lower lip. Release your lips quickly. Compare the lips and the teeth in these pictures. Say *wood   water.   Would you like some water?*

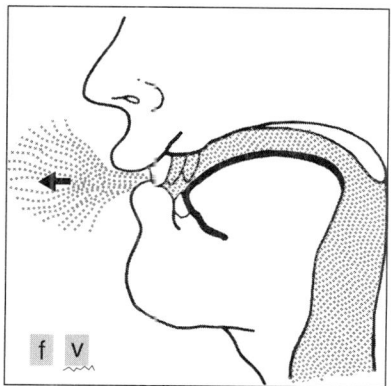
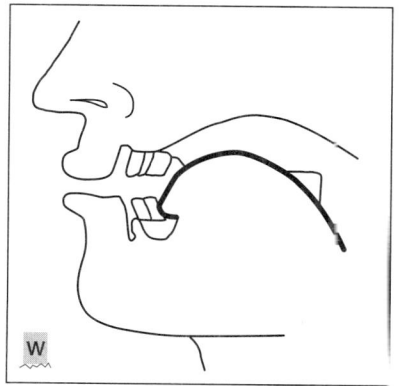

158 UNIT IV Sounds: Consonants and Vowels

2. Practice these phrases: wonderful and wise   a windy winter   a walk in Washington   always aware   words of wisdom

Learn By Listening 4: Contrast w and v (voiced)

1. Listen and repeat the sentences contrasting w and v.

   1. whale–veil   There was a whale in the ocean.   The bride wore a long veil.
   2. wine–vine   People drink white wine with fish. The white vine grew up the wall.
   3. wary–very   We were wary of walking at night. We went for a very long walk.
   4. wet–vet   The streets were wet.   We took our dog to the vet.
   5. worse–verse   The weather got worse.   This is the first verse.

2. Replay the tape. Say each word three times. Then say the sentence.

Example   west–west–west   The sun sets in the west.

vest–vest–vest   The vest is made of silk.

f. Improve Your Monitoring: w and v

1. Listen to each sentence. Decide whether the speaker says the underlined word or substitutes a similar word with a different sound. Check (✓) the word you hear.

   1. My cold has gotten <u>worse</u>.   __✓__ worse   _____ verse
   2. Turn the <u>wheel</u> to the right.   __✓__ wheel   _____ veal
   3. The school is on the <u>west</u> side of the street. __✓__ west _____ vest
   4. We had <u>veal</u> for dinner.   _____ wheel   __✓__ veal
   5. I am <u>very</u> happy to see you.   _____ wary   __✓__ very
   6. The trucks are <u>moving</u> slowly.   _____ mooing   __✓__ moving

2. Practice saying the above sentences correctly. Monitor for w and v.

3. Write three words that start with w and v that you use in your everyday speech. Practice them in sentences. Self-monitor.

Group Practice 9: The voiced and voiceless "th" sounds (location 7 on the pathway)

1. Open your mouth slightly so that your teeth are parted and not touching your lips. Put your tongue gently behind the opening between your teeth, but don't squeeze your tongue against your teeth or bite down. With your tongue inside your mouth, blow air gently over your tongue and whisper *thank*.

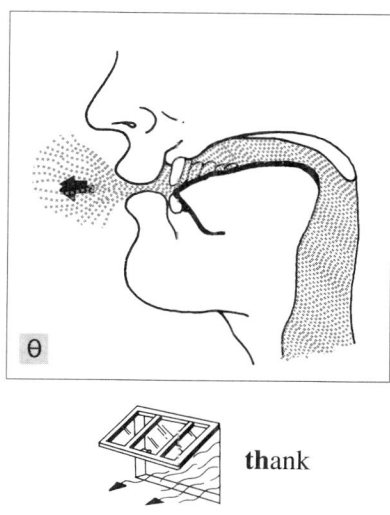

thank

2. Say the words and phrases with "th."

   ð   the   this   father   mother   breathe easy   bathe often   soothe over

   θ   think   nothing   method   fourth of October   Ninth Avenue

   moth-eaten sweater

g. Partner Practice: Contrast th and t

1. Practice saying the word pairs. Both t and θ are voiceless.

   boat–both   thigh–tie   thanks–tanks   thought–taught

   debt–death   boot–booth   mitt–myth

2. Partner A says either sentence (a) or (b). Partner B answers. Take turns.

Example	a. How do you spell *boat*?	b - o - a - t There'<u>s a</u> sailboat.
	b. How do you spell *both*?	b - o - t - h It's for bot<u>h of</u> us.
1. a.	I spilled coffee on my **thi**gh.	Did you get burned?
b.	I spilled coffee on my **ti**e.	Did the coffee stain it?
2. a.	I'm sending you **t**anks.	Are there soldiers driving them?
b.	I'm sending you **th**anks.	You're welcome!
3. a.	I **th**ought about the Civil War.	What did you think?
b.	I **t**aught about the Civil War.	What did your students learn?
4. a.	He's upset about his father's dea**th**.	Did his father die recently?
b.	He's upset about his father's deb**t**.	Did he owe a lot of money?
5. a.	What's in his boo**t**?	His foot.
b.	What's in his boo**th**?	A table, a chair, and some books.
6. a.	Which is your favorite my**th**?	The story of Zeus.
b.	Which is your favorite mi**tt**?	The leather one.

h. Partner Practice: Contrast th and s

1. Practice saying the word pairs. Both θ and s are voiceless.

thank–**s**ank   **th**eme–**s**eam   **th**igh–**s**igh   **th**ick–**s**ick

ten**th**–ten**s**e   mou**th**–mou**s**e   fa**c**e–fai**th**

2. Partner A says either sentence (a) or (b). Partner B answers. Take turns.

Example	a. How do you spell *thank*?	*Thank* is spelled t-h-a-n-k.
	b. How do you spell *sank*?	*Sank* is spelled s-a-n-k.
1. a.	The **th**eme is obvious.	She's a careful writer.
b.	The **s**eam is obvious.	She's not a careful seamstress. (A "seamstress" is a woman who sews.)
2. a.	His **th**igh is painful.	*Thigh* spelled t-h-i-g-h? He pulled a muscle in his thigh.
b.	His **s**igh is painful.	*Sigh* spelled s-i-g-h? He sighed when his girlfriend left him.

CHAPTER 8 The Speech Pathway—What's Happening Where?   **161**

3. a. It's very **th**ick.   *Thick* spelled t-h-i-c-k? It's a **th**ick steak.

    b. It's very **s**ick.   *Sick*, spelled s-i-c-k? It's a **s**ick dog.

4. a. There's a mou**th** in the picture.   Is it open or shut?

    b. There's a mou**se** in the picture.   Can you see the tail?

5. a. Jim is the **t**en**se** person in line.   Is he always this nervous?

    b. Jim is the **t**en**th** person in line.   I thought he was ninth.

6. a. Her fa**ce** is strong.   She looks like her mother.

    b. Her fai**th** is strong.   She is very religious.

2. Look at the window openings. Which sound has the most airflow? Which sound stops the air?

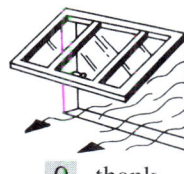 θ thank    s sank    t tank

Group Practice 10: Contrast th and f

Both θ and f are voiceless. For f the upper teeth gently touch the lower lip. For θ the upper teeth do not touch the lower lip. The air flows over the tongue.

 1. Listen and repeat the pairs of sentences in unison. Move your hands and lean forward slightly as you stress the focus words. Then divide into two groups. Say the sentences alternating between groups A and B until you sound like a chorus with one voice. Switch groups. Monitor for θ and f.

Fred–thread   **froze–throws**   **fought–thought**   **free–three**   **fin–thin**

roof–Ruth   **first–thirst**

2. Partner A says either sentence (a) or (b). Partner B says the other sentence. Monitor for f and θ.

1. a. I borrowed it from **F**red.   b. I borrowed the black **th**read.

2. a. He **th**rows the ball.   b. He **f**roze all winter.

3. a. They **f**ought about buying a car.   b. They **th**ought about buying a car.

4. a. The **f**ree people escaped.   b. The **th**ree people escaped.

5. a. Ruth's house has a thick roo**f**.   b. The **f**at **f**ish has a **th**in **f**in.

6. a. My mou**th** is dry from **th**irst.   b. I was asked to speak **f**irst.

i. Dialogue: Happy Birthday to my Brother

 Listen first. Then practice saying the dialogue. Monitor for θ and ð. Switch roles.

1. A: I need a present and a birthday card for my brother. His birthday is tomorrow. What do you think of these cards? Do you like this one or that one?
2. B: Both are nice. But I guess I like this one better than that one.
3. A: My brother mentioned that he needs a sweater. I wonder where the men's clothing is.
4. B: Next to the bathing suits. I think that's on the third floor. There's the escalator.
5. A: Look over there! There are some things on sale on the other side of the escalator.
6. B: That sounds interesting. Let's take a look. Then you'll get the gift for your brother!

j. Communicative Activity: Your family tree

Draw a family tree similar to the one on page 208. Tell your partner about the family members on the tree. Use as many "th" words as possible in your description. For example, you can talk about your mother, father, brothers, grandfathers, mother's brother, father's father, and so on. Monitor for θ and ð.

Group Practice 11: Final nasal sounds "n," "m," and "ng"

The air comes out the nose instead of the mouth for these continuants. Use a mirror to match your mouth to the pictures.

m	n	ŋ
RAM	ran	rang

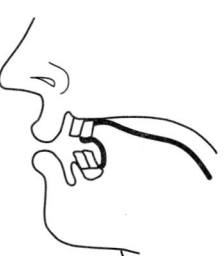

My computer needs more RAM.

The water ran and ran.

The phone rang and rang. It was the wrong number.

k. Partner Practice: Short conversations with final "m", "n", and "ng"

Listen first. Then practice with your partner. Monitor for the final sounds.

1. A: Jim has some news. His son plans to come home soon.
   B: His son? I didn't know Jim had a son. What's his name? Where has he been?
   A: His name is Sam, and he has been living on his own in Japan for some time.
   B: I'll bet Jim is glad that his son is coming home.

2. A: Do you know how to swim?
   B: Yes, but I don't like to swim. I'd rather stay home and play rummy.
   A: Why? Swimming is good exercise. It keeps you trim and strong.
   B: I don't care if I am trim or strong. Rummy is more fun.

3. A: I think I hear the phone ringing.
   B: Hold your tongue![1] Our phone never rings, and we like it that way.
   A: Well, I hear something ringing and ringing.
   B: Perhaps it's Ping Pong, our South American parrot. Poor thing can't sing, so we taught her to ring instead.

l. Partner Practice: Final sounds

Partner A says either sentence (a) or (b). Partner B answers. Monitor for final sounds.

1. a: I'd like to buy a comb.　　　　Do you need a comb AND a brush?
   b: I'd like to buy a cone.　　　　What flavor ice cream cone do you want?

2. a: I need sunglasses today.　　　Me too! The sun is very bright.
   b: I need some glasses today.　　Water glasses or wine glasses?

3. a: The game came as a surprise.　What toy store did it come from?
   b: The gain came as a surprise.　No one expected the economic growth.

4. a: The sun seems high.　　　　　I need some sunscreen.
   b: The sum seems high.　　　　　You can pay it in monthly installments.

5. a: How do you spell *dine*?　　　d-i-n-e　Let's dine at home.
   b: How do you spell *dime*?　　　d-i-m-e　Do you have a dime?

6. a: That is an unusual scream.　　It sounds like an ambulance siren.
   b: That is an unusual screen.　　It is from Japan.

---

[1] **to hold one's tongue:** to remain silent to keep the peace

Are You Ready for "R" and "L"?

Compare the following drawings for r̰ and ḻ. Notice the tongue and the lips.

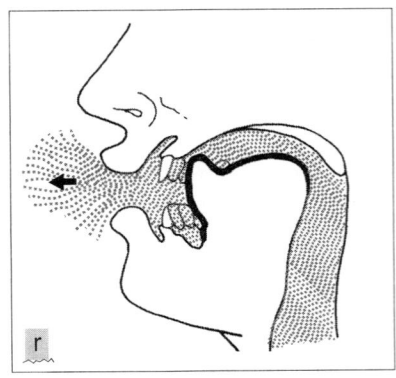 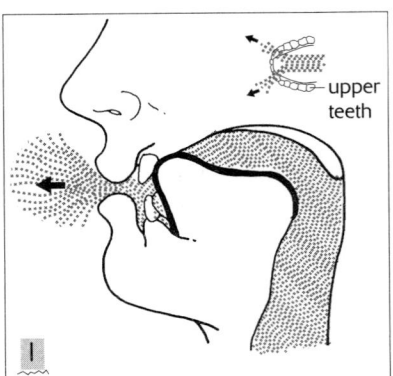

The tongue is not touching the top of the mouth.

The tongue touches the top of the mouth.

Compare the mouth for r̰ and ḻ.

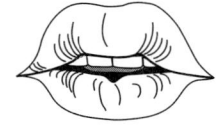 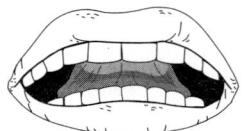

r̰ The lips are slightly rounded.

ḻ The lips are relaxed.

Group Practice 12: How to say r̰

1. Squeeze the sides of your tongue against your upper molars. Tighten and pull the tip of your tongue backward. The tongue tip doesn't touch any part of your mouth. Curl your tongue tighter and round your lips slightly. Say *grrrrr*, like a tiger. Release your tightly rolled tongue into the r̰ words. Say *gray ray*.

2. Use your hand to help say r̰. Make a tight fist with your hands as you tighten your tongue tip. Release your fists and open your palms quickly as your release your tongue and say *gray ray*.

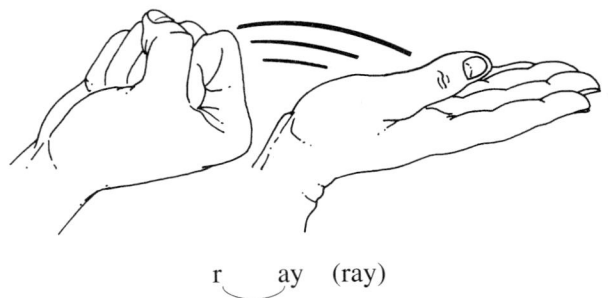

r   ay   (ray)

3. Listen and repeat these words and phrases. Concentrate on what you hear and what it feels like. Use your hand to help.

red   rain   Ron   row   radio   rent

rush around   run around   right reason   ready to rest

---

pronunciation tip for r Use your ears to hear your best r. Sometimes people have an easier time saying r in one word than in another. When you hear a word with your best r, hold the position and concentrate on feeling where your tongue is. Try it again.

Group Practice 13: How to say l

1. Keep your mouth relaxed and only slightly open. An l should be comfortable. The lips are not rounded. Press the front part of your tongue gently up and touch anywhere on the roof of your mouth, either behind your top teeth or further back. Don't point the tip sharply. Keep pressing as you lower your jaw slightly and pull the sides of your tongue down and toward the center so that the air can flow out the sides.

2. Listen and repeat the words and phrases. Find the position for l that works for you.

   lay   lamp   allow   alike   July   fall off   sell everything

   circle around   let's leave   tall and lean   lullaby

---

pronunciation tip for l Find the easiest way to say l. The exact position can change according to the sound that comes before or after it.

m. Partner Practice: Contrast r and l

Partner A says either sentence (a) or (b). Partner B answers. Take turns.

Example	a.	Is the pipe **r**ed?	No, it's black.
	b.	Is the pipe **l**ead?	No, it's copper.
1.	a.	Turn toward the **r**ight.	I'd rather turn left.
	b.	Turn toward the **l**ight.	It's too bright.
2.	a.	I tore my w**r**ist.	Does it hurt a lot?
	b.	I tore my **l**ist.	Can you still read it?
3.	a.	Look at the large c**r**owd.	They're waiting to get in.
	b.	Look at the large c**l**oud.	It's blocking the sun.
4.	a.	How do I **r**ock it?	Push it back and forth.
	b.	How do I **l**ock it?	With a key.
5.	a.	He wants to p**r**ay.	There's a church across the street.
	b.	He wants to p**l**ay.	Baseball or cards?
6.	a.	The river f**r**oze.	Let's go ice skating.
	b.	The river f**l**ows.	Let's go swimming.

Group Practice 14: How to say vowel + r

There are two r sounds in English. One r comes at the beginning of words, such as *right   robin*.

The other r comes after a vowel, in words such as *car   door   pair*.

1. Start by saying the vowel. Your tongue tip rests gently behind your lower front teeth. Squeeze the sides of your tongue against your upper back teeth. Tighten your tongue tip and roll it backward to the r position. The front of your tongue doesn't touch anything in your mouth. Round your lips slightly. Take your time. Slowly whisper *ah-r-r-r-r*. Say *are*.

2. Your tongue has to move and tighten for r. Use your hands to help. Turn up your open palms as you say the vowel before the r. Then curl your fingers to make a fist as you tighten your tongue tip and glide to the r. Say *are*.

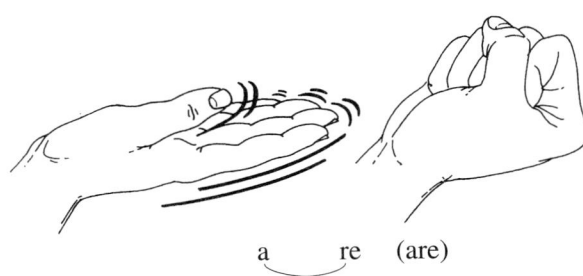

a   re   (are)

3. Listen and repeat the following phrases. Use your hands to help.[2]

near here   four more   bare floor   far star   nearly a year

fair share   warm heart   marry Harry   clear air   glorious morning

See page A-9 for more examples.

Group Practice 15: How to say vowel + l

l has many variations. Some words start with l. In other words the l sound comes after a vowel.

tell   wall   pal   ill   sail   mail-in rebate

1. Start by saying the vowel in *all*. Glide slowly from the vowel to the l. Reminder: You can touch the top of your mouth with any part of your tongue that feels comfortable. Pull the sides of your tongue away from your teeth to let the air escape. Say *a-li*.

2. Listen and repeat the following phrases.

   all around   mail it   pull over   sell everything   full of fun   will he tell him

3. Listen and repeat words that end with a schwa + l. Note the different ways of spelling this ending.

   ANgel   FRAgile   AWful   PUzzle   BIble   LIkable

n. Communicative Activity: Mystery person

1. Practice saying some colors with r and l. Self-monitor.

   red   rust   purple   brown   green   gray   black   blue   yellow   copper

   silver   maroon   orange   violet

---

[2] In some regions, speakers omit many r sounds that follow a vowel. For example, *park* → *pahk*   *market* → *mahket*   and *where* → *wheh*

2. Divide into groups of 6–8. One person from each group will describe someone in the group or room. Use colors to describe the person's hair, eyes, clothes, and possessions. Group members should use the color clues to identify the mystery person.

Example

A: My mystery person has brown hair, blue eyes, and is wearing a red sweater.

B: Is the person Martina?

o. Partner Practice: Figure out the idioms

Work with a partner to match the idiomatic expressions to the definitions. Write the number of the sentence next to the appropriate definition. Say the sentence and monitor for r, l, and ð, one sound at a time.

Idioms

1. She was under the weather last week.
2. Fortunately she's back in the pink.
3. That idea is behind the times.
4. I can't drive because my car is on the blink.
5. The new vice-president is in the loop.
6. You're on track with that solution.
7. Her offer came out of the blue.
8. There's no point fixing it after the fact.

Definitions

___ a. after something happened, when it's too late
___ b. ill, not feeling well
___ c. old-fashioned
___ d. broken
___ e. in good health
___ f. part of the group in charge, informed
___ g. proceeding satisfactorily, reasoning correctly
___ h. unexpected, without warning

More Idioms

1. He paid for the favor under the table.
2. The new employee has a lot on the ball.
3. She kept us in the dark about her background.
4. That guy at the door was off the wall.
5. Let's celebrate out on the town.
6. The business is finally in the black.
7. Let's get to the point right away.
8. Please get off my back about cleaning up.

Definitions

___ a. stop bothering, harassing
___ b. going out and having a good time
___ c. unconventional, eccentric
___ d. in secret, outside the rules or the law
___ e. making a profit
___ f. the main or most important idea
___ g. competent, doing a good job
___ h. in secret, not informed

p. Join the Chorus: "What Did You Say?"

Practice the voiced θ, r, and l in a chant made up of common idioms from Exercise o.

Listen and repeat the chant in unison. Move your hands and lean forward slightly as you stress the focus words. Then divide into two groups. Say the chant alternating between groups A and B until you sound like a chorus with one voice. Switch groups.

A: He's under the **WEA**ther. *sick*

B: She's in the **PINK**. *happy*

A: It's behind the **TIMES**.

B: It went on the **BLINK**. *is not work correctly.*

A: You're out of the **LOOP**.

B: You're on the right **TRACK**. *in the right direction*

A: That's out of the **BLUE**. *no reason*

B: It's after the **FACT**.

A: It's under the **TA**ble. *eligale*

B: He's on the **BALL**. *very fast perfect in the job.*

A: I'm in the **DARK**. *you dont any information.*

B: That's off the **WALL**. *Greasy.*

A: We're out on the **TOWN**. *having a good time*

B: 'Cause we're back in the **BLACK**.

A-B: Get to the **POINT**. And get off my **BACK**!

q. Communicative Activity: Most widely spoken languages in the world

The following charts show the ten languages spoken most frequently by total speakers (native and second language) around the world.[3]

1. Practice the pronunciation of the countries and languages in columns 1 and 2 on both charts.

2. Exchange information with your partner to fill in the chart. Then discuss the information about languages. Monitor for r, l, and θ, one consonant at a time.

Partner A's Information			Partner B's Information		
Language	Country of Origin	Total Speakers	Language	Country of Origin	Total speakers
1. Mandarin	1.	1,075 billion	1.	1. China	X
2.	2. England	514 million	2.	2.	X
3.	3. India	496 million	3. Hindi	3.	X
4.	4.	X	4.	4. Spain	425 million
5.	5. Russia	X	5.	5.	275 million
6.	6. Arabia	X	6. Arabic	6.	256 million
7. Bengali	7.	215 million	7.	7. Bangladesh	X
8. Portuguese	8.	X	8.	8.	194 million
9. Indonesian	9.	X	9.	9. Indonesia	176 million
10.	10.	129 million	10. French	10.	X

FINISHING UP

Self-Quiz (Check the answers in the Answer Key.)

Circle all the correct answers for each item.

1. When air from the lungs passes through the vocal cords, location 2 on the speech pathway, sometimes the cords vibrate to create *voicing*. Which sounds are voiced?

   a. all vowels   b. all continuants   c. v b z d l   d. s f h t p

2. The air stops as it comes up the speech pathway for "b," "p," "t," "d," "k," and "g." These sounds are called *stops*. Which words release a puff of air after the initial stop?

   a. **b**ig   b. **p**ig   c. **t**ime   d. **d**ime   e. **c**oat   f. **g**oat

---

[3] *Sources:* Joseph E. Grimes and Barbara F. Grimes, *Ethnologue,* 13th ed. (Dallas: Summer Institute of Linguistics, 1996), and www.infoplease.com

3. The lips for r are   (a) slightly rounded   (b) relaxed

   The lips for l are   (a) slightly rounded   (b) relaxed

4. The reason the word *thank* can sound like *tank* is that

   a. the tongue is stopping the air from flowing out

   b. the tongue is pressing too hard against the gum ridge

   c. both (a) and (b)

5. Circle the choice that correctly fits in the blank.

   Consonants can vary in the way they are pronounced. One of these variations is called a *flap*. Flaps are important in linking _____ to the next word.

   (a) plurals   (b) past tenses   (c) pronouns   (d) prepositions

Dictation

Write the sentences you hear. You will hear each sentence two times. Replay the tape to check your listening before looking in the Answer Key.

1. _____
2. _____
3. _____
4. _____
5. _____

Making Your New Pronunciation a Habit

Talk Times in Class: Role play

Partner A is considering a trip and calls an airline to gather information about flights. Partner B works for the airline.

1. Write questions to ask the airline representative. You might ask for flight information, the cost, the lowest fare, the available seats, the meals, or the movie. Use departure and arrival cities that start with sounds you find difficult such as r and l. Examples: Montreal, Brasilia, Dallas, Rome, Vancouver, Cleveland. Use θ and ð words such as *the*, *that*, and *thank you*.

2. Underline the focus words, and circle the difficult sounds in your questions.

3. Role-play calling an airline. Monitor for focus words and difficult consonants. Switch roles.

Sample Inquiry

A: I'm going from Vancouver to St. Louis. Do you have any flights on the 20th of the month?

Talk Times in Your Daily Life: Planning a trip

Call an airline for flight information about a possible trip. Use the questions in the role play in the previous exercise as a guide. Add questions of your own. You can make this call on different days to different airlines. Practice your questions before you make the call. Take notes on what happened or tape your part of the conversation so that you can plan your next call. Target difficult sounds. Pay attention to linking final sounds.

On Your Own

1. **Audio program.** Replay the sections about sounds that are difficult for you. Pay attention to the intonation as well as to the sounds when you are repeating phrases and sentences.

2. **Recorded practice**
   - Record any two exercises from the chapter that will help you practice challenging consonant sounds.
   - Record your part of a phone conversation. Keep the tape recorder going in the room as you speak on the phone to a friend or business. You will **not** be recording the other person's part of the conversation. Listen later to discover things about your pronunciation you did not hear when you were talking.

3. **Additional practice.** Use appendix A for more practice with consonant sounds.

4. **Glossary.** Include the names of streets and places in your community. Ask a native speaker how to say them.

5. **Mirroring.** Mirror five minutes of a video. See page 74 for instructions about mirroring. Record your experience in a journal.

---

a good idea — Listen to an interesting book recorded on audiotape. These "books on tape" are often available at a public library. Make sure you are comfortable with the English dialect on the tape you choose. Replay small sections so that you can concentrate on the pronunciation. Listen for specific sounds.

Web Activities

Go to elt.heinle.com/targetingpron for additional activities related to this chapter.

Important Endings

Chapter 9 builds awareness of and provides practice with "ed" and "s" endings. These are critical to English grammar and accurate pronunciation. You will learn about sounds called *sibilants* that affect "s" endings, and you will review the *flap*, the sound often used when linking "ed" endings to the next word. Adding an "ed" or a final "s" to words that link to other words in a thought group can create a cluster of several consonants in a row. Pronouncing these clusters presents a special challenge to many learners of English. The chapter emphasizes listening and self-monitoring for these important endings.

Listen to these examples of "ed" and "s" endings.

Past tenses	PAINTed	WANTed	comPLETed
	I PAINTed it.	They WANTed it.	He comPLETed it.
Plural nouns	PRIces	BOXes	SENtences
	HIGH PRIces	BIG BOXes	LONG SENtences
Verbs	WATCHes	FACes	MISses
	She WATCHes it.	She FACes it.	He MISses it.

PART 1. "ED" ENDINGS

a. Improve Your Monitoring

1. Past or present?

You will hear a sentence in either the present or the past tense. Check (✓) the tense you hear. Replay the tape until you are sure of your answers.

Example   a. It tastes good. ✓ Present   b. It tasted good. ____ Past

1. ✓ Present ____ Past   5. ____ Present ✓ Past
2. ✓ Present ____ Past   6. ✓ Present ____ Past
3. ____ Present ✓ Past   7. ____ Present ✓ Past
4. ____ Present ✓ Past   8. ✓ Present ✓ Past

2. "ǝd" or "ed"?

In some past tenses, the "ed" is an extra syllable with a schwa vowel.
Example ADDǝd
In other past tenses, the "e" is silent.
Example hoped.

Listen to the past tense. Do you hear an extra syllable with a schwa vowel, or is the "e" silent? Check (✓) the correct column.

Examples   painted __✓__ Extra syllable _____ Silent "e"

picked _____ Extra syllable __✓__ Silent "e"

Past Tense	"ǝd"	"ed"
1. rented	✓	
2. rained		✓
3. applied		✓
4. appreciated	✓	
5. used		✓
6. ended	✓	

b. "ED" Endings: What is the rule?

1. The "ed" in these past tenses is an extra syllable. Look at the final sound of the basic verb and write it on the line next to the verb. The final letter may not indicate the final sound.

Example   endǝd   end __d__   skated   skate __t__

1. seated   seat _____   4. wanted   want _____
2. needed   need _____   5. handed   hand _____
3. voted   vote _____   6. wasted   waste _____

2. The past tense of these verbs has a silent "e." Look at the final sound of the basic verb. Write it on the line.

Example   baked   bake __k__

1. stayed   stay _____   5. robbed   rob _____
2. locked   lock _____   6. moved   move _____
3. loaned   loan _____   7. closed   close _____
4. washed   wash _____   8. stopped stop _____

CHAPTER 9 Important Endings

| **figure out the rule** | "ed" sounds like a separate syllable when the regular verb ends with a ___ or ___ sound. All other verbs have a silent "e." |

Learn By Listening 1: Linking "ed"

You can identify the past tense when you hear "ed" linked to the next word. Listen to two ways to link "ed." Then turn off the sound and practice.

1. The flap

Use a flap when linking "ed" to a vowel. Feel your tongue tapping your gum ridge for the flap. (See page 152 to review the flap.)

tired out   laughed at it   used it up

locked her car   walked alone   liked his personality

2. Linking "ed" to a consonant

When linking "ed" to a word starting with a consonant, first hold the final **d** briefly by squeezing your tongue briefly against the gum ridge to stop the air. The symbol : means to hold the sound briefly in place.

moved: twice   listened: to her mother   remembered: to call
worked: together

pushed: the door   skipped: lunch   stopped: quickly
watered: the plants

c. Partner Practice: Past and present

Partner A says either sentence (a) or (b). Partner B says the other sentence. Monitor your own and your partner's pronunciation. Pay attention to the "ed" linking.

Example   Partner A: I dreamed about a trip.

Partner B: I dream about a trip.

1. a. I dream about a trip.   b. I dreamed about a trip.
2. a. They live in a small house.   b. They lived in a small house.
3. a. I love my cat.   b. I loved my cat.
4. a. I want a pound of apples.   b. I wanted a pound of apples.
5. a. We volunteer at the shelter.   b. We volunteered at the shelter.
6. a. I print all the documents.   b. I printed all the documents.
7. a. We exercise at the "Y."   b. We exercised at the "Y."
8. a. I believe it all.   b. I believed it all.

UNIT IV Sounds: Consonants and Vowels

d. Join the Chorus: "The Visitor"

1. Listen and repeat the poem in unison. Move your hands and lean forward slightly as you stress the focus words. Then divide into two groups. Say the poem alternating between groups A and B until you sound like a chorus with one voice. Switch groups.

1. A: I walked up the stairs.
   I stopped at the door.
   B: I pushed on the bell.
   I looked at the floor.

2. A: She peeked through the crack.
   And switched on the light.
   B: She stared at my bag,
   Surprised at the sight.

3. A: I glanced at her face.
   I hoped she could see
   B: That although I had changed
   It really was me.

4. A: She pulled at the knob.
   The door opened wide.
   B: She paused and she smiled,
   And she asked me inside.

5. A: I had dreamed of this moment.
   All regrets vanished fast.
   B: We imagined the future
   Reunited at last.

2. Work with a small group. Prepare one verse to say with your group for the class.

---

pronunciation tip — Self-monitoring by listening is one good way to make sure you say the "ed" ending. Some people benefit as well from feeling their tongue touch their gum ridge behind the top teeth. Which way works the best for you, feeling the tongue or listening?

CHAPTER 9   Important Endings   **177**

e. Improve Your Monitoring: Past or Present?

1. Listen to each sentence. Decide whether the speaker says the underlined past tense or substitutes the present tense without the "ed" ending. Check (✓) the word you hear.

Example   She looked at the book.   ✓ looked   ___ look

1. Yolanda answered all the questions.   ___ answered   ✓ answer
2. My friend reported the accident to the police.   ___ reported   ✓ report
3. The baby bumped his head when he fell.   ✓ bumped   ___ bump
4. Alice finished all her work on time.   ✓ finished   ___ finish
5. Sam improved his grades.   ___ improved   ✓ improve
6. Roberta owned her own house.   ✓ owned   ___ own
7. She managed her mother's affairs.   ___ managed   ✓ manage
8. Yesterday we talked about our plans.   ✓ talked   ___ talk

2. Practice saying the sentences correctly. Self-monitor. Listen for the "ed" ending and the linking.

f. Partner Practice: Idioms

1. Match the definitions with the idioms. Write the number of the sentence with the idiom on the line next to the definition. Discuss your answers.

Idioms

1. She brushed up on her Spanish before she went to Peru.
2. Jane jumped at the chance for an interview.
3. Harry dropped a bombshell when he announced that he was moving to Australia.
4. I wasted my breath when I tried to tell my brother what to do.
5. I washed my hands of the matter when he refused to consult a lawyer.
6. They lived it up after they won the lottery.
7. She changed her mind about getting a dog.
8. We ended up with our first choice.

Definitions

_2_ a. acted quickly on an opportunity
_1_ b. reviewed, refreshed her memory
_5_ c. withdrew from the situation
_6_ d. lived extravagantly
_7_ e. altered her ideas or plans
_3_ f. made an unexpected shocking announcement
_8_ g. final result
_4_ h. spoke without accomplishing anything

2. Take turns saying the sentences. Monitor linking "ed" to the next word.

g. Communicative Activity: Talk about an idiom

Work in groups of five or six. Tell a true story using one or more of the idioms in Exercise f. Tell the details of what you did, where you were, and with whom. Monitor for "ed" and "s" endings.

Example I really lived it up the night after I graduated from . . .

---

pronunciation tip When you talk, pay attention to your own speech to make sure you are saying the "ed" endings.

---

h. Dialogue: "Basket on the Bus"

1. Listen to the dialogue. Monitor for "ed" endings and linking.

1. A: You'll **NE**ver **GUESS** what happened on the **BUS** last week.
2. B: What **HAP**pened?
3. A: The bus driver pulled **O**ver and a little girl carrying a large **BAS**ket hopped on.
4. B: What **KIND** of basket?
5. A: It looked like a **PIC**nic **BAS**ket. A loaf of **BREAD** was wrapped up in a **NAP**kin, and I thought I smelled **COOK**ies.
6. B: She was **PRO**bably headed for[1] a **PIC**nic.
7. A: **MAY**be, but she seemed a little **NER**vous. The bus was **CROWD**ed. She climbed over the other **PAS**sengers and sat next to **ME**.
8. B: Did she **TALK** to you?
9. A: She **START**ed to talk to me, but changed her **MIND**.[2] Suddenly, she jumped **UP**, set the basket on my **LAP**, and hopped off the **BUS**.
10. B: It sounds as if you ended **UP**[3] with a basket of **FOOD**.
11. A: Not e**XAC**tly. I actually ended **UP** with a **PUP**py! He was asleep under the **NAP**kin. The "cookies" were **DOG** **BIS**cuits, and now I'm enrolled in DOG **TRAIN**ing **SCHOOL**.

---

[1] **headed for:** going to, going in the direction of
[2] **changed her mind:** altered her ideas or plans
[3] **ended up:** resulted in, finished

CHAPTER 9 Important Endings   **179**

2. Listen and repeat each line of the dialogue, replaying the tape several times. Look away from your book. Listen for the focus words, compound nouns, and phrasal verbs. (To review, see pages 64–65.)

- List the compound nouns: Stress the first word.

  _____   _____

- List the phrasal verbs: Stress the particle.

  _____   _____   _____

  _____   _____

3. Practice these phrases from the dialogue. Use a flap to link "ed" to the next vowel.

1. what happened on the **BUS**
2. pulled Over
3. carried a large **BAS**ket
4. seemed a little **NER**vous
5. started to **TALK** to me
6. changed her **MIND**
7. ended up with a **PUP**py
8. wrapped up in a **NAP**kin
9. ended up with a basket of **FOOD**
10. enrolled in **DOG TRAIN**ing **SCHOOL**

4. Practice the dialogue. Remember to link the words and say all the important endings. Switch roles.

Learn by Listening 2: Review "ed" endings

1. Look away from your book and listen to a true story about a gorilla. Replay the tape and fill in the missing words with "ed" endings.

Binti, the Heroine

In 1996, a mother gorilla at the Brookfield Zoo in Chicago _rescued_ a three-year-old boy who _tumbled_ into the gorilla pit. As his parents _watched_ in horror, their toddler suddenly _leaned_ into the pit and fell eighteen feet to the concrete below. A mother gorilla named Binti _saved_ him from danger. With her own baby on her back, Binti gently _picked up_ the child and _climbed_ of the pit to safety. She _protected_ the unconscious child from the other gorillas and _delivered_ him to a rescue worker. The boy was _rushed_ immediately to a hospital. He soon _recovered_ from a concussion and some bad bruises, and the gorilla made animal history. Binti was _credited_ with saving the life of a human child.

2. Check your monitoring. Listen to some sentences about Binti. Decide if the speaker says the underlined past tense correctly or if the speaker substitutes the present tense without the "ed" ending. Check (✓) the word you hear.

Example

A mother gorilla <u>rescued</u> a three-year-old boy.   ✓ rescued   ___ rescue

1. A three-year-old boy <u>tumbled</u> into the gorilla pit.   ✓ tumbled   ___ tumble
2. His parents <u>watched</u> in horror.   ___ watched   ✓ watch
3. A mother gorilla <u>saved</u> him from danger.   ✓ saved   ___ save
4. She gently <u>picked up</u> the child in her arms.   ✓ picked   ___ pick
5. Binti <u>climbed out</u> of the pit to safety.   ___ climbed   ✓ climb
6. She <u>protected</u> the child from the other gorillas.   ✓ protected   ___ protect
7. She <u>delivered</u> him to a rescue worker.   ___ delivered   ✓ deliver
8. He soon <u>recovered</u> from a concussion.   ✓ recovered   ___ recover

3. Practice saying the previous sentences in the monitoring exercise correctly. Then replay the paragraph about Binti until you can say it along with the speaker. Look away from the page as much as possible.

4. Retell the story in your own words. Monitor for past tenses, linking, and focus words.

PART 2. "S" ENDINGS

"S" endings are important to English pronunciation and grammar. The following examples show different kinds of "s" endings.

1. My <u>books</u> are due at the library. (plural noun)
2. The library <u>opens</u> at noon today. (third-person verb)
3. My <u>sister's</u> house is near the library. (possessive)
4. <u>It's</u> a good day to visit her. (contraction)

There are different ways of pronouncing "s" endings. The ending can sound like an s , a z , or have an extra syllable with a schwa vowel. The following plural nouns and third-person verbs all end in the letter "s."

CHAPTER 9 Important Endings **181**

🎧 Tap the desk for each syllable as you listen and repeat the words. Pay attention to the ending sound.

s ending	z ending	"es" ending
↓	↓	↓ ↓
tapes	babes	charges
bites	trades	wishes
cakes	bags	beaches
hits	saves	misses

🎧 **Learn By Listening 1: Public Service Announcement (PSA)**

1. Listen to the PSA from the Media Awareness Network at: www.media-awareness.ca.
   Fill in the missing plurals.

   ¹The Internet. ²Over one hundred and fifty million _____users_____ ³Over a billion _____pages_____ of information. _____thousands_____ of new Web _____sites_____ every day. ⁴Open 365 _____days_____ a year, 24 _____hours_____ a day. ⁵Take a minute. ⁶Learn more about where your _____kids_____ are going, who they're talking to, what they're doing online.

2. In line 3, one of the plurals has an extra syllable before the final "s." Write the word here _____pages_____.

3. Track the PSA along with the speakers. Monitor for final "s" and linking final sounds.

🎧 **Learn By Listening 2: s or z?**

1. Listen for the difference between the words with "s" endings. Some of these endings sound like s and others like z.

   These "s" endings sound like s:
   - picks up → pick sup
   - fits in → fit sin
   - Kip's address → Kip saddress
   - puffs on a pipe → puff sonna pipe
   - moths in the closet → moth sin the closet

   These "s" endings sound like z:
   - days are long → day zaar long
   - digs a hole → dig za hole
   - cleans up → clean zup
   - summer's over → summer zover
   - saves his money → save zis money

2. Look at the words in the left column. Underline the sounds that come before the s endings. Are these sounds voiced or voiceless? Example: pic<u>k</u>s up.

182 UNIT IV Sounds: Consonants and Vowels

3. Look at the words in the column on the right. Underline the sounds that come before the z endings. Are these sounds voiced or voiceless? Example: da<u>y</u>s are long.

---

figure out the rule Is it voiced or voiceless? Circle the answer in the parentheses.
A final "s" added to a (voiced voiceless) sound at the end of a word is pronounced s.
A final "s" added to a (voiced voiceless) sound at the end of a word has the z ending.

---

a. Improve Your Monitoring: s and z

Listen to the underlined words with the "s" ending. Decide if you hear s or z linking to the next word. Check (✓) the answer.

		s	z
Example	The <u>boy's</u> arm is broken.	___	✓ z
	She <u>eats</u> everything.	✓ s	___
1.	The <u>dogs</u> are hungry.	___	✓ z
2.	The <u>phone's</u> ringing.	___	✓ z
3.	The <u>cars</u> are honking.	___	✓ z
4.	He <u>drives</u> away.	___	✓ z
5.	She <u>skates</u> very well.	✗ s	___
6.	It<u>'s</u> to the right.	___	✓ z
7.	Yoshi <u>has</u> a new baby.	___	✓ z
8.	Juan <u>is</u> a good teacher.	___	✓ z

Group Practice 1: Pronouncing z

z
zoo

1. To pronounce z, say s. Add voicing and keep it going in your throat.

2. Listen and link the following words ending in z to *a lot*.

   Example has a lot → ha zalot

   Say each phrase ten times. Monitor for voicing.

   has a lot   was a lot   is a lot   does a lot   use a lot   drives a lot

3. Say the following sentences. Monitor for linking of z to "a lot of." Reduce *a lot of* to *alotta*.

   He has a lot of money.   It is a lot of work.   They use a lot of cream.

   It was a lot of fun.   It does a lot of good.   She drives a lot of miles.

b. Two Dialogues

1. Listen and underline the focus words. Mark the thought groups.

2. Circle all the z sounds. Monitor your pronunciation of these words by feeling the vibration in your throat.

3. Practice the dialogues with a partner. Switch roles. Monitor for z.

Dialogue 1: "Noisy Phones"

A: There go all those noisy phones again! Where's Rose?

B: Rose is busy. She's busy on the phones. Rose goes crazy when all the phones are ringing.

Dialogue 2: "Disaster for Roses"

A: This is a disaster. It's thirty degrees below zero in these woods.

B: What about your nose? Doesn't it hurt? Aren't your knees freezing? And what about those toes?

A: Yes it does hurt—my nose, I mean. My knees are no longer freezing because they are already frozen. I don't think I have any toes. They must have frozen along with my nose.

B: Oh, no! I just remembered my prize roses! Everyone knows that below-zero weather is really a disaster for roses.

A: You're worried about your prize roses at a time like this? What good are prize roses to a couple of guys with frozen noses? Can we please go back to Florida on the next plane?

---

pronunciation and spelling tip Many common words that end with the letter "s" are pronounced with a z sound. This is because the sound before the "s" is voiced.

Examples

1. has   was   is   does   goes   there's   these   those   cars   drives

2. rose   raise   praise   choose   use (verb)   close (verb)   pause

3. Rhyming words:

    nose/froze/goes   breeze/sees/these   raise/trays/days/maze

c. Improve Your Monitoring: "ə̆s" or "s"?

In some of the following plural nouns and third-person verbs, the "es" has a silent "e." In others, "es" is a separate syllable with a schwa vowel. Listen and decide which kind of "es" you hear. Check (✓) the appropriate answer.

Example makes (one syllable, silent "e") ___ "ə̆s" ✓ "s"

teaches (two syllables, schwa vowel) ✓ "ə̆s" ___ "s"

	"ə̆s"	"s"
1. shades—shades of gray	___	✗
2. taxes—Pay your taxes.	✗	___
3. judges—ten judges	✗	___
4. dates—Check the dates.	___	✗
5. roses—a dozen roses	✗	___
6. drives—drives a truck	___	✗
7. washes—washes his clothes	✗	___
8. changes—changes the name	✗	___
9. hopes—hopes for rain	___	✗
10. writes—writes a story	___	✗

Group Practice 2: Introducing sibilants

When is final "es" pronounced as a separate syllable with a schwa vowel? The rule has to do with sibilants. Sibilants are sounds in which air flows out through a narrow place in the mouth to make a hissing or a buzzing noise.

1. Sibilants that hiss (voiceless)

Listen and repeat the following words that end with voiceless sibilant sounds. Say the words and sentences in unison.

s	bus	The bus is late.	tʃ	watch	Watch out.
ʃ	rush	Rush around.	ks	box	The box is empty.

2. Sibilants that buzz (voiced)

Listen and repeat the following words that end with voiced sibilant sounds. Monitor for voicing. Put your hand on your throat to check for vibration.

z	does, buzz	Does it buzz?
ʒ	beige	Take the beige umbrella.
dʒ	age	Her age is a secret.

d. "S" Endings: What is the rule?

Write the final sound of the following words on the line next to the word. Remember, the final letter may not indicate the final sound. Say the word in the parentheses. It has an "s" ending. Look for a pattern in the words ending with "əs."

Example dress __s__ (dressəs)   rides __d__ (ridz)

"əs"

excuse ____ (excusəs)
buzz ____ (buzzəs)
wish ____ (wishəs)
box ____ (boxəs)
beach ____ (beachəs)
stage ____ (stagəs)

"es"

give ____ (givz)
hide ____ (hidz)
state ____ (statz)
make ____ (makz)
name ____ (namz)
mile ____ (milz)

---

figure out the rule The "s" ending is a separate syllable with a schwa vowel when it comes after a _____ sound. The "s" ending that comes after all other consonant sounds is not a separate syllable.

---

e. Partner Practice: Voiced and voiceless sibilants

1. Listen to the following pairs of sentences with words that end in sibilant sounds. Sentence (b) has an "s" ending that is pronounced _z_.

2. Partner A says either sentence (a) or (b). Partner B says the other sentence. Link the bolded sibilant to the next word.

Voiceless sibilants

On sentence (a) the linked sibilant is voiceless. For sentence (b), the final "s" sounds like _z_ when linked to the next word. Keep the vibration going in your throat.

1. a. The bu**s** is on time.   b. The buse**s** are late.
2. a. Pu**sh** ahead!   b. She pushe**s** the stroller.
3. a. The mat**ch** is in the box.   b. The matche**s** are gone.
4. a. The bo**x** is heavy.   b. The boxe**s** arrived.

Voiced sibilants

For both sentences (a) and (b), keep the vibration going when linking the sibilants to the next word.

5. a. The prize is $50. b. The prizes are all gone.
6. a. His age is eighteen. b. I waited for ages and ages.
7. a. His badge is crooked. b. All the badges are silver.
8. a. The page is torn. b. The pages are yellow.

---

pronunciation tip When you see a new word that ends with "es," look at the previous sound. If it is not a sibilant, the "e" is silent.
Examples: forgives explodes interferes antelopes promotes.

---

f. Improve Your Monitoring: Final "s" and grammar

1. Listen to the sentences. Decide whether the speaker says the underlined word with the "s" ending or omits the final "s." Check (✓) the word you hear.

Example   I bought two <u>bags</u> of popcorn.   ____ bags   ✓ bag

Plural nouns

1. The <u>charges</u> on my bill are wrong.   ____ charges   ____ charge
2. Steve is twenty <u>years</u> old.   ____ years   ____ year
3. Two of your <u>tires</u> look worn.   ____ tires   ____ tire

Third-person verbs

1. She <u>likes</u> to ride horses.   ____ likes   ____ like
2. Maria always <u>balances</u> her checkbook.   ____ balances   ____ balance
3. Paco <u>leaves</u> for work at eight o'clock.   ____ leaves   ____ leave

Contractions

1. <u>It's</u> very hot today.   ____ It's   ____ It
2. <u>That's</u> to our advantage.   ____ That's   ____ That
3. <u>Where's</u> the entrance?   ____ Where's   ____ Where
4. <u>What's</u> your name?   ____ What's   ____ What

Possessives

1. Someone found <u>George's</u> wallet. ____ George's ____ George
2. I like the <u>clown's</u> costume. ____ clown's ____ clown
3. The <u>plumber's</u> tools are in his truck. ____ plumber's ____ plumber
4. Look at my <u>niece's</u> picture. ____ niece's ____ niece

2. Practice with a partner. Take turns saying the previous sentences with examples of "s" endings. Make sure you say the final "s." Monitor your own and your partner's speech.

g. Join the Chorus: "S's, Messes"

Listen and repeat the chant in unison. Move your hands and lean forward slightly as you stress the focus words. Then divide into two groups. Say the chant alternating between groups A and B until you sound like a chorus with one voice. Switch groups.

A: Catch the buses,

B: Buy some dresses.

A: No excuses,

B: Clean your messes.

A: Fix the boxes,

B: Switch the faxes.

A: The buzzer buzzes,

B: Pay your taxes.

A: Sandy beaches,

B: Forty wishes.

A: Juicy peaches,

B: Wish for riches.

A: Noses, nurses,

B: Vases, matches.

A: Roses, purses,

B: Spaces, patches.

A: Age in stages,

B: Do those stretches.

A: Turn the pages.

B: Time whizzes by.

h. Partner Practice: Challenging plurals

When consonant clusters are hard to say, some learners of English insert a schwa vowel before a plural "s." This can change the meaning. In the following sentences, which word makes sense, (a) or (b)? Use the rule about sibilants and final "es" to decide about the pronunciation of the plurals. Take turns saying each sentence using the correct word. Point to the word you think your partner said, whether or not it fits the meaning. Discuss the pronunciation.

1. I bought some _____ for soup.   a. bones   b. bonus
2. There are _____ growing in the garden. a. ferns   b. furnace
3. I enjoyed visiting with your _____.   a. folks   b. focus
4. Drive by three stop _____ and turn left. a. signs b. sinus
5. They discovered gold in the _____.   a. mines   b. minus
6. He used _____ from Shakespeare.   a. quotes   b. quotas

Group Practice 3: Four more sibilants ʃ, ʒ, tʃ, and dʒ

ʃ
shoe

1. To say ʃ, start by saying s. Continue saying s and round your lips slightly, keeping them relaxed. Now slide your tongue further back on the top of your mouth until you hear ʃ. Sh! Hush! The baby's sleeping.

Spelling tip: ʃ is often spelled with a "sh."

2. Listen and repeat phrases with ʃ. Notice the different ways to spell ʃ.

   washing machine   ocean fishing   fashion show   special permission
   a Haitian family

3. Contrast s and ʃ. Sue–shoe   so–show   see–she   mass–mash

4. Listen and repeat the following sentences in unison many times.

   Shoe Shopping

   They sold my **sh**oes at a **sh**op in **S**idney.

   They're **sh**owing my **sh**oes in a bro**ch**ure from **Sh**anghai.

   She saw my **sh**oes in a fa**sh**ion **sh**ow in **Ch**icago.

   They **sh**ipped my **sh**oes from a **ch**ic **sh**op in San Francisco.[4]

5. Practice *backward build-up*. Say the last word of each sentence. Then say the last two words. Continue adding words until you have built the whole sentence from back to front. Keep up the rhythm.

Example   SIDney.   in SIDney.   SHOP in SIDney.   a SHOP in SIDney.

at a SHOP in SIDney, and so on.

6. Replay the tape and say sentences along with the speaker.

[4] The "ch" in *brochure, Chicago,* and *chic* sound like ʃ.

CHAPTER 9 Important Endings **189**

| ʒ
mea**s**ure | **1.** To say ʒ, find the position for ʃ. Then turn on voicing in your throat. Alternate between saying ʃ and ʒ. Put your hand on your throat to feel the vibration for ʒ. |

Spelling tip: ʒ is spelled a variety of ways, often as "su" and sometimes "ge" or "si."

2. Listen and repeat phrases with ʒ words.

a televi**s**ion set   a mea**s**uring cup   an A**s**ian language   a new re**g**ime

It's a plea**s**ure to meet you.   He's on time as u**s**ual.   She's wearing be**g**e.

| for your
information | ʒ only appears in the middle and at the ends of words. |

Words ending with "sion" sound like ʒən.
Examples: occa**s**ion   televi**s**ion   revi**s**ion

Words ending in "tion" sound like ʃən.
Examples: vaca**t**ion   na**t**ion   ac**t**ion

| tʃ
chip | **1.** To say tʃ start to say "tip." Squeeze the tongue against the gum ridge to stop the air. Hold the t. Round the lips and slide the tongue back and say ʃ. tʃ has two steps: t + ʃ. |

Spelling Tip: tʃ is often spelled with "ch" and sometimes with "tu."

2. Listen and repeat the phrases.

a **ch**eap **ch**air   **ch**ocolate **ch**ip   the fu**tu**re **ch**amp   a for**tu**nate si**tu**ation

3. Contrast ʃ and tʃ.   **sh**ip–**ch**ip   **sh**oe–**ch**ew   di**sh**–di**tch**

mu**sh**–mu**ch**   ma**sh**ing–ma**tch**ing

| dʒ
jump | **1.** To say dʒ, start to say "day." Squeeze your tongue against the gum ridge to stop the air. Hold the d. Round your lips slightly, but keep them relaxed. Push your tongue harder against the gum ridge and slide it back and say "jay." dʒ has two steps: d + ʒ. |

Spelling Tip: dʒ is often spelled with "j," sometimes with a "du," and often with a "ge" at the ends of words.

2. Listen and repeat phrases with dʒ.

jump for **j**oy   **j**am ənd **j**elly   at a **g**ym   a college edu**c**ation

a char**g**e account   a ma**j**or disaster   a ma**g**ic show   avera**g**e income

i. Partner Practice: Contrast ʃ and tʃ

Partner A says (a) or (b). Partner B responds. Take turns.

1. a. Where are the di**sh**es? In the dishwasher.
   b. Where are the di**tch**es? By the side of the road.

2. a. She's busy **sh**opping. What is she buying?
   b. She's busy **ch**opping. Is she making salad?

3. a. I gave him my **sh**are. How much did he get?
   b. I gave him my **ch**air. Did he sit down?

4. a. Please wa**sh** my car. Is it very dirty?
   b. Please wa**tch** my car. When are you coming back?

5. a. The table was **sh**ipped. When will it arrive?
   b. The table was **ch**ipped. Can you repair it?

6. a. Where are the **sh**ips? They are all out at sea.
   b. Where are the **ch**ips? Sorry! We ate them all up.

j. Partner Practice: Contrast dʒ with ʃ and tʃ

Partner A says (a) or (b). Partner B responds. Switch roles.

1. a. How do you spell *jeep*? j-e-e-p   We rode in a jeep.
   b. How do you spell *sheep*? s-h-e-e-p   The sheep provide wool.

2. a. I found the **j**ail. Were there bars on the windows?
   b. I found the **sh**ale.[5] Was there a lot of it?

3. a. The crowd began to **j**eer. They were not happy.
   b. The crowd began to **ch**eer. They were happy.

4. a. How do you spell *Jerry*? J-e-r-r-y   His name is Jerry.
   b. How do you spell *sherry*? s-h-e-r-r-y   Sherry is a type of wine.

5. a. Jim must be **j**oking. Jim is very funny.
   b. Jim must be **ch**oking. Make sure Jim is all right.

[5] **shale:** claylike layers of rock

6. a. Janet brought the **J**ell-O. It is delicious.
   b. Janet brought the **c**ello.[6] I didn't know **J**anet played the **c**ello.

7. a. What do you know about Mar**ge**? She was born in New **J**ersey.
   b. What do you know about Mar**ch**? It is the beginning of spring.

k. Improve Your Monitoring: Sibilants and spelling

Some sibilants have unusual spellings. For example, in *Portugal*, the "tu" sounds like tʃ. Listen to the following words and circle the sibilant sound you hear. Notice the spelling.

Example assumed (s) ʃ

1. permission ʃ tʃ
2. specialized ʃ tʃ
3. sure ʃ t͡ʃ
4. Haitian ʃ t͡ʃ
5. exotic gz ks
6. Asian ʒ tʃ
7. unusual ʃ ʒ
8. schedule dʒ tʃ
9. premonition ʃ t͡ʃ
10. negotiated ʃ t͡ʃ
11. exactly gz ks
12. oranges dʒ t͡ʃ

Group Practice 4: Have fun with tongue twisters

1. Look away from your book. Listen and repeat in unison. Replay the tape several times.

1. **JER**ry **PUT** a **CHER**ry in his **SHER**ry.
2. There's a **CHEAP JEEP** in **BACK** of the **SHEEP**.
3. The **JUDGE** on the **SHIP** WORE a **BADGE** on his **JACK**et.
4. The **MARCH**ing **MAR**tians had a **MILKSHAKE** for **LUNCH**.
5. A **SHOP** in **POR**tugal **SOLD SUE** a **SHELL** in a **FAN**cy **BOX**.

2. Practice *backward build-up*. Say the last word of each tongue twister. Then say the last two words, and so on, until you have completed the tongue twister. Keep up the rhythm.

Example **SHER**ry his **SHER**ry in his **SHER**ry **CHER**ry in his **SHER**ry a **CHER**ry...

3. Replay the tape until you can say the tongue twisters along with the speaker.

4. Divide into groups. Learn one twister with your group to say for the class.

---

[6] *Cello* is pronounced "chello" with a tʃ.

Group Practice 5: y is *not* a sibilant

y is different from d and dʒ. The air does not stop, hiss, or buzz. To say y, rest your tongue tip behind your bottom front teeth. Squeeze the back of the tongue between the molars as you push the middle of the tongue forward.

Listen and repeat in unison with the class. Say these y words and the word pairs contrasting y and dʒ.

yes yam	Yes Iʸ am.	yelled yesterday	Yesterday he yelled at you.
Yale–jail	yam–jam	yolk–joke	yellow–Jell-O

I. Partner Practice: Short dialogues with y

First listen and repeat the dialogues contrasting y and dʒ words. Then practice with a partner. Switch roles.

1. A: Did his father go to jail?
   B: No! His father went to Yale. The convict is in jail.
2. A: What's the difference between jam and yam?
   B: Jam is made out of fruit. A yam is a sweet potato.
3. A: Is the yolk funny?
   B: No! The joke is funny. A yolk is part of an egg and it's yellow.
4. A: What is yell? Is it the same as jell?
   B: No! To yell is to talk very loudly. Jell-O has to jell in the refrigerator.
   A: I like yellow Jell-O! Do you like yellow Jell-O?
   B: Yeah! But orange Jell-O is yucky!

Learn by Listening 3: Story with "ed" and "s" endings

1. Look away from your book and listen to the true story about Jesse Owens from the 1930s. Replay the tape and fill in the missing words with "ed" or "s" endings.

2. Listen to the paragraph until you can say it along with the speaker.
   From the time Jesse Owens was a boy he had ___dreamed___ of becoming an athlete and participating in the Olympic ___games___. This dream came true when he ___enjoyed___ the United States track team and ___competed___ in the 1936 Berlin ___Olympics___. Adolf Hitler had ___wanted___ to use the

___games___ to validate his ___theories___ about the superiority of the Aryan, or white, race. Owens, a 23-year-old black American runner, stole the show by winning four gold ___medals___. It is said that Hitler ___stormed___ out of the stadium in anger. Owens not only ___scored___ a victory against Nazism, but made ___sports___ history by breaking all previous track ___records___.

3. Tell the story in your own words to your partner. Self-monitor for "ed" and "s" endings and linking.

m. Communicative Activity: Magic Johnson

Magic Johnson is a famous and respected basketball player. You and your partner are doing research for a TV documentary about his life. Each of the following charts is missing some of the facts about him.

Cover your partner's information. Take turns asking and answering questions and fill in the missing information on your chart. Monitor for sibilants and "s" and "ed" endings.

Example

A: What happened in 1979?

B: Johnson started playing for the Los Angeles Lakers. What happened in 1991?

Partner A's Information	Partner B's Information
19__ __ Born in Lansing, Michigan, with ____ brothers and sisters.	1959 Born in Lansing, Michigan, with nine brothers and sisters.
1979 Drafted by the Los Angeles Lakers	1979
1980–88	1980–88 Won five basketball championships
1987–90 Named the most valuable player _____ times	1987–90 Named the most valuable player three times
1991 Announced that he was HIV positive and retired from professional basketball	1991
1991 Established the Magic Johnson Foundation to raise funds for AIDS	19__ __ Established the Magic Johnson Foundation to raise funds for AIDS
19__ __ Played on the _____ "Dream Team" and received a ____ medal	1992 Played on the U.S. Olympic "Dream Team" and received a gold medal

continued

Partner A's Information (continued)

1992	Established businesses in the inner-city to help poor communities
1994	Coached the Lakers
1995–96	
2002	Inducted into the Basketball Hall of Fame
_____	Magic Johnson Enterprises released its first feature film, *Brown Sugar*.
By 2003	Became a multi-millionaire through his inner-city investments in _____

Partner B's Information (continued)

19__ __	Established businesses _____
1994	
1995–96	Returned to play 32 games, then officially retired for good
2002	
2002	Magic Johnson Enterprises released its first feature film, _____
By 2003	Became a multi-millionaire through his inner-city investments in theaters, shopping malls, restaurants, and athletic clubs

n. Join the Chorus: From "Through the Looking Glass"

Listen and repeat the poem in unison. Link the words in each thought group and monitor for sibilants. Move your hands and lean forward slightly as you stress the focus words. Then divide into groups of six. Practice with your group and say the poem for the class.

"The time has **COME**," the Walrus **SAID**,

"To talk of many **THINGS**:

Of **SHOES**—and **SHIPS**—and **SEAL**ing **WAX**—

Of **CAB**bages—and **KINGS**—

And why the **SEA** is boiling **HOT**—

And whether **PIGS** have **WINGS**."

—Lewis Carroll

FINISHING UP

Self-Quiz   (Check the answers in the Answer Key.)

1. True or False? The letter "e" in "ed" and "es" endings always sounds like schwa.

2. Finish the rule: "ed" sounds like a separate syllable when the regular verb ends with a __ or __ sound.

3. Circle the sibilant sounds in the following words.

   a. cheese   b. fox   c. nature   d. large   e. quiz

4. Circle the word(s) with a schwa vowel in the "es" ending.

   a. sales   b. chimes   c. taxes   d. brakes

5. Circle the true statements.

   a. "s" endings are important to English pronunciation and grammar.

   b. The letter "s" at the end of many common words such as *is* and *was* is pronounced z.

   c. The letter "x" sounds like "ks." That is why *backs* and *fax* rhyme.

   d. The ʒ sound is sometimes used at the beginning of English words.

Dictation

Write the sentences you hear. You will hear each sentence two times. Replay the tape to check your listening before looking in the Answer Key.

1. _____
2. _____
3. _____
4. _____
5. _____

Making Your New Pronunciation a Habit

Talk Times in Class: Discussion

1. To prepare for Talk Times, write the following information and discuss it with your partner.

- two of your favorite actors
- two of your favorite films
- a type of film you would like to rent (action, drama, comedy, mystery, etc.)
- the name of a video store in your area

2. Make a list of questions you can ask a person who works in a video store. Possible topics are availability of a certain film, names of films with a certain actor or director, rental rates, what day the film has to be returned. Underline the focus words.

Example   Do you have a copy of *Titanic*? I missed *seeing* it / when it was in the theaters. /

3. Draw a dot over the stressed syllables in these words:

   drama   comedy   mystery   foreign   documentary

4. Practice the compound nouns.

   ACtion FILMS   VIdeoTAPES   MOvie STARS   LOVE STOries
   aWARD WINners

5. Practice the descriptive phrases and names.

   SPEcial efFECTS   POpular MOvies   FAvorite diRECtors

   TOM HANKS   JUlia ROBerts   SEAN PENN

Talk Times in Your Daily Life: Renting a video

Call or visit a video store in your community to inquire about renting a video. Prepare sample questions. You do not actually have to rent the film, even if the store has the one you are asking about. Thank them, and either leave or say you have changed your mind. Target "ed" and "s" endings.

On Your Own

1. **Audio program.** Practicing regularly is important to your progress. Repeat the exercises in chapter 9 that are the most challenging.

2. **Recorded practice.** To become independent and able to correct your own errors, follow the tips for recorded practice on page 54. Choose from the following:

- the dialogue "Basket on the Bus," page 178, either with a partner or by yourself
- your story about the idioms, page 178
- a short article from a newspaper or magazine

   Read the article and tell about it in your own words. Use the past tense. Listen to the recording to hear things that you did not hear at first. Monitor for "ed" and final "s." Re-record until you are satisfied.

3. **Glossary.** Underline the parts of your new words that you think are troublesome. Is it the vowel sounds, the consonant sounds, or the word stress?

4. **Mirroring.** Mirror five minutes of a television speaker of your choice. See the directions for "The Talking Mirror" on page 74.

---

pronunciation tip In addition to final sounds, remember to say all the structure words. Although reduced, these small words, like *the* and *to,* build and connect a sentence grammatically. Speaking English with missing structure words can be distracting to listeners who know the language.

10

More about Vowels and Consonants

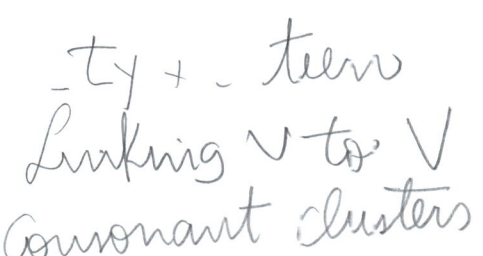

Chapter 10 offers additional guidelines and practice for pronouncing consonants and vowels clearly. It covers some of the lesser-known facts about sounds, including rules about voicing and vowel length, "teen" and "ty" numbers such as sixteen and sixty, the syllabic "n," and the difference between *can* and *can't*. In addition to practice with consonant clusters and challenging consonants such as r, l, there is a song that focuses attention on some key targets for sounds.

More about Vowels

 Group Practice 1: Voicing and vowel length

The vowel before a voiceless consonant sounds shorter than the vowel before a voiced consonant.

1. Listen and repeat the pairs of sentences in unison. Notice the difference in the vowel length of the underlined words.

Voiceless Final Stops	**Voiced Final Stops**
1. a. It's on my <u>lap</u>.	b. I work in a <u>lab</u>.
2. a. I need a new <u>mop</u>.	b. I can hear the <u>mob</u>.
3. a. Let's make a <u>bet</u>.	b. Let's make the <u>bed</u>.
4. a. That's <u>right</u>.	b. Let's go for a <u>ride</u>.
5. a. Put on the <u>boot</u>.	b. The crowd <u>booed</u>.
6. a. What do you <u>think</u>?	b. What is that <u>thing</u>?
7. a. Which film did you <u>pick</u>?	b. Look at the baby <u>pig</u>.

197

Voiceless Final Continuants	**Voiced Final Continuants**
1. a. I can see the <u>bus</u>.	b. I can hear the <u>buzz</u>.
2. a. What's the <u>price</u>?	b. I won the <u>prize</u>.
3. a. Let's hope for <u>peace</u>.	b. They're eating <u>peas</u>.
4. a. She is <u>rich</u>.	b. She is on the <u>ridge</u>.
5. a. Is the money <u>safe</u>?	b. How much did you <u>save</u>?
6. a. I want <u>half</u> of it.	b. I want to <u>have</u> it.
7. a. The <u>carts</u> are over there.	b. The <u>cards</u> are on the table.

a. Partner Practice

Partner A says the underlined word in sentence (a) or (b) in Group Practice 1. Partner B says the sentence. Make sure you and your partner agree about which word was said. Take turns.

Example   Partner A: lab   Partner B: I work in a <u>lab</u>.

b. Partner Practice: Voicing and vowel length

Partner A says either sentence (a) or (b). Partner B says the appropriate answer. Glide or step down in pitch at the end of each sentence. Take turns.

Examples:	a. There's a <u>cap</u> at the corner.	a. I wonder who dropped it.
	b. There's a <u>cab</u> at the corner.	b. Good. I need a ride.
1. a.	He found a <u>buck</u> on the sidewalk.	Did he spend it or save it?
b.	He found a <u>bug</u> on the sidewalk.	Could it fly or crawl?
2. a.	I got a good <u>price</u>.	How much did you pay?
b.	I got a good <u>prize</u>.	What did you win?
3. a.	The <u>seat</u> is hard.	It must be uncomfortable.
b.	The <u>seed</u> is hard.	It's ready to plant.
4. a.	Put the groceries in the <u>back</u>.	In the trunk or the backseat?
b.	Put the groceries in the <u>bag</u>.	Do you want paper or plastic?
5. a.	What does it mean to <u>proof</u> it?	To review it and make corrections.
b.	What does it mean to <u>prove</u> it?	To give logical arguments.

6. a. The people are <u>sinking</u>. Throw them a life raft quickly.
   b. The people are <u>singing</u>. Do you know the song?
7. a. He fell on his <u>knees</u>. I hope they're not sore.
   b. He fell on his <u>niece</u>. I hope she's not hurt.
8. a. Are you planning to <u>write</u> it? Yes, as soon as I find a pen.
   b. Are you planning to <u>ride</u> it? Yes, as soon as I fix the wheels.
9. a. Here is the <u>five</u> I borrowed. Thanks. I need some cash.
   b. Here is the <u>fife</u> I borrowed. Did you play good music with it?
10. a. Look at the <u>white</u> truck. It must get dirty easily.
    b. Look at the <u>wide</u> truck. Will it fit on the narrow bridge?

c. Improve Your Monitoring

1. Listen to each sentence. Decide whether the speaker says the underlined word or another word with a shorter vowel sound. Check (✓) the word you hear. Replay the tape to make sure.

Example: Have you heard the <u>news</u>? ____ news   ✓ noose

1. He is very <u>rude</u>. ____ rude   ____ root
2. The <u>laws</u> are changing. ____ laws   ____ loss
3. She kept her <u>age</u> a secret. ____ age   ____ "H"
4. We try to <u>save</u> money. ____ save   ____ safe
5. I <u>weighed</u> more last year. ____ weighed   ____ wait
6. Did you hear the phone <u>ring</u>? ____ ring   ____ rink
7. Let's go for a <u>ride</u> after lunch. ____ ride   ____ right
8. That's what I <u>said</u>. ____ said   ____ set
9. What do you <u>need</u>? ____ need   ____ neat
10. I wish I <u>had</u> one. ____ had   ____ hat

2. Practice saying each sentence correctly by voicing the final sound and lengthening the vowel in the underlined word. Self-monitor.

Learn By Listening 1: Grammar and vowel length

When nouns, adjectives, and verbs look similar, the part of speech can help you with the pronunciation. The noun or adjective sounds shorter because it ends with a voiceless sound. The verb sounds longer because it ends with a voiced sound. Listen and repeat the following examples.

Examples (noun with final `s`) What's the <u>use</u>?
(verb with final `z`) Can you <u>use</u> it?

Nouns	Verbs	Nouns	Verbs
1. rice	rise	5. proof	prove
2. excuse	excuse	6. half	have
3. loose[1]	lose	7. leaf	leave
4. advice	advise	8. relief	relieve

Learn By Listening 2: Vowels and numbers

To make *sixty* and *sixteen* sound different, pay attention to the vowel in the second syllable.

1. The clear vowel in "teen" is lightly stressed. Remember to say the final "n."

   THIRTEEN   FOURTEEN   FIFTEEN   SIXTEEN

   SIXTEEN <u>DOL</u>lars and FOURTEEN <u>C</u>ENTS.

2. At the end of a sentence "teen" gets more stress. Glide down in pitch.

   I moved here at the age of NINETEEN. She's only THIRTEEN.

3. The "ty" in SIXty dollars is unstressed, short, and low in pitch. Say a flap. Raise the pitch on the stressed syllable.

   THIRty   FORty   FIFty   SIXty   She's only THIRty.   He's turning NINEty.

---

[1] *Loose* is an adjective.

d. Partner Practice: "ty" and "teen"

Take turns dictating sentences to your partner. Choose one of the numbers in the parentheses. Your partner writes the number he or she hears. Monitor for "ty" and "teen." Discuss your answers.

1. Mary is (14–40) years **OLD**.
2. They took the elevator up (13–30) **FLOORS** / to the top of a tall **BUILD**ing.
3. We looked at a **HOUSE** / that was on (216–260) acres of **FARM**LAND.
4. They were selling the **PRO**perty / for (16–60) percent of its market **VAL**ue.
5. The store sold fresh **EGGS** / for (19–90) cents a **PIECE**.
6. The chickens were ($2.19–$2.90) a **POUND**.
7. I saw an ad for roundtrip **TIC**kets / from New York to **PAR**is / for ($680–$618).
8. The agency is closing in (15–50) **MIN**utes.
9. Marco moved here when he was (13–30) / and Aniko came when she was (14–40).

e. Communicative Activity: Discuss the calendar

Partner A looks at the calendar and facts for October. Partner B does the same for November. Ask and answer questions about what happens in your partner's month. Monitor for "ty," "teen," θ and ð.

❧❧❧ OCTOBER ❧❧❧

SUN	MON	TUES	WED	THURS	FRI	SAT
				1	2	3
4	5	6	7	8	9	10
11	12	13	14	15	16	17
18	19	20	21	22	23	24
25	26	27	28	29	30	31

Facts about October:

October has thirty-one days.
The Canadian Thanksgiving is the second Monday.
October 31st is Halloween.
Columbus Day is the 12th (celebrated on the second Monday).

*** NOVEMBER ***

SUN	MON	TUES	WED	THURS	FRI	SAT
	1	2	3	4	5	6
7	8	9	10	11	12	13
14	15	16	17	18	19	20
21	22	23	24	25	26	27
28	29	30				

Facts about November:

November has thirty days.
The U.S. Thanksgiving is the fourth Thursday.
November 11th is Canada's Remembrance Day.
November 11th is the U.S. Veteran's Day.

Sample Topics for Questions

- dates that fall on Thursdays
- days of the week that fall on the 15th, 16th, 17th, etc.
- imaginary or real birthdays (mother's, father's, brother's)
- when the rent is due
- whether or not Friday falls on the 13th
- what day is payday
- other

Learn By Listening 3: Two pronunciations for u^w

1. Listen and compare the difference in the vowels in these pairs of words: booty–beauty, moo–music. In some words, a y is inserted before the u^w.

   Examples   beauty → b^yeauty.   music → m^yusic

2. Listen and repeat more words with the ^yu.

   MEN^yu   F^yUture   H^yUman   conF^yUSE   comP^yUter

3. "Cu" sounds like the name of the letter "q" in these words. Listen and repeat the words, and then use them in sentences.

   c^yute   C^yUba   peC^yUliar   VAc^yuum CLEANer

   CALc^yulate   calc^yuLAtion   CIRc^yulate   circ^yuLAtion

   CHIEF eXEC^yutive OFFicer

Learn By Listening 4: Linking two vowel sounds

You can't always tell from looking at a word with two vowel letters whether the word has one syllable or two.

1. Listen to your instructor say the following words and write the number of syllables you hear.

   ie piece ____   ui suit ____   ea weak ____   ue true ____

   quiet ____   tuition ____   idea ____   fluent ____

2. Listen for the y sound that links the two vowels in the following words.

   appreci^yate   cre^yative   stere^yo   vide^yo   we^yall   the^yend

   To make a y sound, start to say *yes* by pushing your tongue forward. Say *Yes, yam. Yes, I ^yam.*

3. Listen for the w sound that links two vowels in the following words.

   usu^wal   persu^wade   casu^wal   go^win   show^wup   shoe^won

   To make a w, round your lips. Look in a mirror and say: *Win. Go^win.*

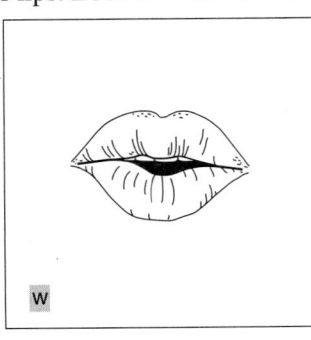

CHAPTER 10 More about Vowels and Consonants

f. Story: "A Cre^yative Ide^ya"

1. Listen and repeat the story line by line in unison. Look away from your book so that you can concentrate on the rhythm and melody. Move your hands and lean forward slightly as you stress the focus words. Link the words connecting two vowel sounds.

¹I had an ide^ya. ²The^y old lady in our apartment building hadn't been feeling so well. ³She seemed lonely, and I thought she'd appreci^yate some attention. ⁴So I persuaded the neighbors to put in a few dollars to buy her a gift. ⁵In the^y end, we^y all decided to have a huge potluck dinner. ⁶We^y all cooked our favorite recipes. ⁷When we went to deliver the dinner, the^y old lady was dressed to go^w out—apparently with a new boyfriend! ⁸So we^y ate the dinner ourselves, and had such a good time that we decided to do^w it again.

2. Practice with a partner, alternating lines. Then tell how you imagine the story ends. Monitor for linking vowels.

g. Join the Chorus: "Timothy Boon"

1. Listen and repeat the poem in unison. Move your hands and lean forward slightly as you stress the focus words.

1. Timothy **BOON**
   Bought a bal**LOON**
   Blue as the **SKY**,
   Round as the **MOON**.
   "Now I will **TRY**
   To make it **FLY**
   UP to the **MOON**,
   Higher than **HIGH**!"
   Timothy **said**,
   Nodding his **head**.

2. Timothy **BOON**
   Sent his bal**LOON**
   Up through the **SKIES**,
   Up to the **MOON**.
   But a strong **BREEZE**
   Stirred in the **TREES**,
   Rocked the bright **MOON**,
   Tossed the great **SEAS**,
   And, with its **MIRTH**,
   Shook the whole **EARTH**.

3. Timothy **BOON**
   And his bal**LOON**,
   Caught by the **BREEZE**
   Flew to the **MOON**;
   Up past the **TREES**,
   Over the **SEAS**,
   Up to the **MOON**—
   Swift as you **PLEASE**!—
   And, ere* I for**GET**,
   They've not come down **YET**!

   —Ivy O. Eastwick

*before (old, poetic usage)

204 UNIT IV Sounds: Consonants and Vowels

2. Write words from the poem with the following vowel sounds. Then say the words.

- ər words. _____ _____ _____

- Complex (long) vowel sounds that sound like the names of letters. See the examples.

    uʷ → "u"   *Boon*   _____ _____ _____
    iʸ → "e"   *breeze* _____ _____ _____ _____
    aʸ → "i"   *fly*   _____ _____ _____ _____ _____

3. Divide into three groups. Work with your group to learn one verse of the poem to say for the class. Practice until you sound like a chorus with one voice. Monitor for focus words and clear vowels. Fall in pitch at the end of each sentence.

More about Consonants

In chapter 2, page 24, you learned that sounds can be clustered, or grouped together, without vowels. It is almost impossible to have a conversation in English without encountering consonant clusters.

h. Building Longer One-Syllable Words

Some syllables are very short: i.de.a (three syllables)
Some syllables are very long: pledged (one syllable)

1. Read the word blocks. Start at the top. The small words get longer as you add consonants.

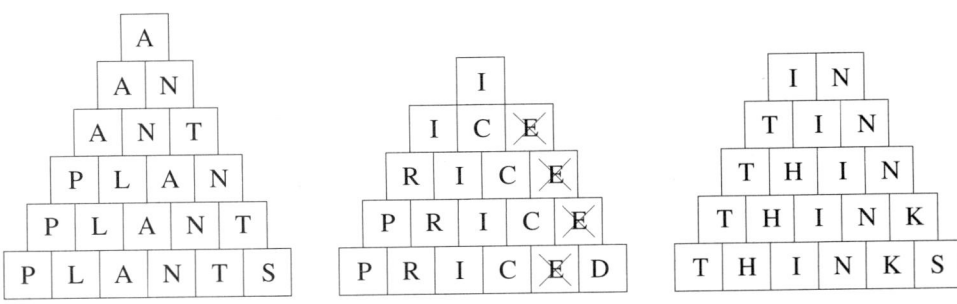

2. Complete the puzzle. Figure out where to add the letters below in order to form new words.[1] Practice saying the words as they get longer. Monitor for consonant clusters.

1. Start with IT. Add s, p, l, and s.
2. Start with AT. Add f, l, and s.
3. Start with TO. Add n, e, and s.
4. Start with AM. Add r, t, s, and p.

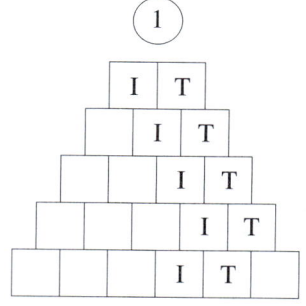

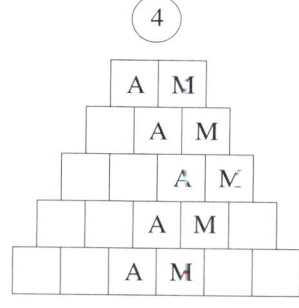

3. Say the words in these phrases: splits in two   four flats of berries
three plants   stamps on the stones

Learn By Listening 5: Clusters across word boundaries

Compound words and words linked in thought groups often blend consonants into unusual clusters that are not found at the beginning or endings of individual words. Listen and repeat the examples. The clusters are written in parentheses.

It looks like new. (ksl)   vine ripened (nr)
What's the problem? (tsth)   stopwatch (pw)
She turned the corner. (ndth)   wastebasket (stb)
It's an expired contract. (rdk)   tax forms (ksf)

i. Partner Practice: Linked clusters

The underlined clusters cross word boundaries. Write the clustered consonant sounds (not letters) on the lines. Remember that the letter "x" represents two sounds, k and s. Compare answers with your partner and take turns pronouncing the phrases.

Example   waves good-bye v z g (The "s" sounds like z in this cluster.)

1. science fiction __ __ __   4. What's new? __ __ __
2. assistant manager __ __   5. vice-president __ __ __
3. saves time __ __ __   6. a Chinese restaurant __ __

[1] Some of the letters may be used more than once.

7. That's probably OK. _ _ _ _   11. tax credit _ _ _ _
8. men's department _ _ _   12. park your car _ _ _
9. plans to quit _ _ _   13. cheap shoes _ _ _
10. an action film _ _   14. tax forms _ _ _

j. Improve Your Monitoring: Final sounds and grammar

1. You will hear one of the sentences in each pair. Listen for the linked final sounds. Check (✓) the sentence you hear.

Example   ✓ I'll pour all the drinks.   (future tense: final _l_ on I'll)
              ___ I poured all the drinks. (past tense: linked flap)

1. ✓ We'll repair all the cracks.   ___ We repaired all the cracks.
2. ___ We'll clear away the trash.   ✓ We cleared away the trash.
3. ___ He'll care about the environment. ✓ He cared about the environment.
4. ✓ We'll order it for next year.   ___ We ordered it for next year.
5. ___ They'll share information.   ✓ They shared information.
6. ___ We'll rehearse every Thursday.   ✓ We rehearsed every Thursday.
7. ✓ She'll compare the answers.   ___ She compared the answers.
8. ✓ He'll contribute his time.   ___ He contributed his time.

2. Compare answers with your partner. Then take turns saying the sentences. Monitor for clusters across word boundaries.

Learn By Listening 6: Linked triple clusters

Even native speakers have difficulty with some triple consonant clusters and simplify them when speaking rapidly. You may hear native speakers dropping the final _t_ and _d_ in some triple clusters that cross word boundaries. However, they will say a flap when the cluster is linked to a vowel.

1. Listen to the examples.

Linked to a Consonant   **Linked to a Vowel**

Will you deduct some of the charges?   Will you deduct a dollar from the bill?
We'll adapt some of the customs.   We'll adapt all the customs.
Jim returned late last night.   Jane was the last of the group to return.
Hand me the salt, please.   Hand over your wallet!

2. Say the three-consonant clusters in words and sentences. Native speakers often drop the middle sound.

Cluster	Word		Sounds Like	Sample Sentences
s t s	tests	→	tes:s	The tests are graded.
	tourists	→	TOURis:s	The tourists are everywhere.
t h s	months	→	mʌns	months and months of work
	tenths	→	tens	nine-tenths of the marbles
s k s	desks	→	des:s	Fourteen desks were moved.
	asks	→	as:s	He asks for his change.
c t s	directs	→	diREX	He directs the traffic.
	facts	→	fax	The facts are obvious

for your information — It's more important to think about including all the consonants than to decide which ones can be left out. In English, most consonant clusters are not simplified, especially when they are part of a grammatical ending such as "ed" or final "s."

Learn By Listening 7: The syllabic n

The unstressed syllables in *MOUNtain* or *PARdon* have a sound called a syllabic "n."

Shake your head to mean *no* and say *nnh-nnh* in your throat. This *no* sound is a syllabic n. Your tongue stays on your gum ridge.

Say the first syllable of *BUTton* and hold your tongue against your gum ridge for the second syllable. Instead of saying *ton*, make a quick sound in your throat. There is no vowel in the second syllable. Say *BUT'n*.

Listen to your instructor and repeat these groups of words with the syllabic n.

Nouns: COTton CARton KITten NEWton DAYton BRItain

Verbs: WRITten forGOTten EAten FATten STRAIGHten

Adjectives and adverbs: CERtain HIDden ROTten SUDdenly CERtainly

Contractions of "not": SHOULDn't DIDn't WOULDn't HADn't COULDn't

Group Practice 2: "A Family Mystery"

1. Listen and underline the words with a syllabic n. See the first sentence as an example. Listen again and repeat the story one line at a time in unison until you sound like a chorus with one voice.

¹Peter <u>Wharton</u> had <u>certainly</u> tried to trace his grandparents. ²His parents had moved from Dayton, Ohio, to Fort Morton, Colorado, east of the Rocky Mountains. ³He knew that one of his grandmothers was from Great Britain, but he hadn't been able to locate her. ⁴Suddenly, when he didn't expect it, a letter arrived from Great Britain. ⁵It was written by a woman named Katie Newton who claimed to be his aunt. ⁶Katie Newton sent a picture that she had found at the bottom of an old carton. ⁷It was taken a long time ago of a little girl that Katie said was her mother. ⁸The girl, wearing a cotton dress with buttons down the front, was holding a kitten. ⁹On the back of the picture was written "Dotty Burton, 1936." ¹⁰Peter had forgotten until now that his grandmother's name was Dotty Burton. ¹¹Apparently the Katie Newton who sent the picture was his mother's sister. ¹²He couldn't believe that he hadn't heard of her before. ¹³Peter Wharton was eager to straighten out the family mystery.

2. Work with a partner. Retell the mystery in your own words. Monitor for the syllabic n.

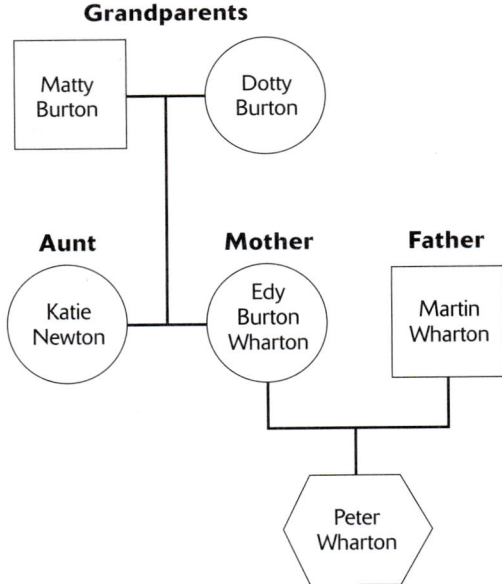

More Practice with "R" and "L"

Review r and l in chapter 8, page 164.

k. Join the Chorus: Limerick

1. Listen and repeat the limerick in unison with the speaker until you sound like a chorus with one voice. Move your hands and lean forward slightly as you stress the focus words.

    There **ONCE** was a **MAN** very **WEIRD**

    Who **SAID**, "It is **JUST** as I **FEARED**!

    "Two **OWLS** and a **HEN**,

    "Four **LARKS** and a **WREN**

    "Have **ALL** built their **NESTS** in my **BEARD**!"

    —Edward Lear

2. If necessary, review *How to Say Vowel* + r on page 166. Practice the vowel + r words below. Use your hands to help.

    weird   feared   four   larks   beard

l. Dialogue with r: "Needs a Ride"

Listen and then say the dialogue. Work with your partner to pronounce the r and l words. Lengthen the focus words and pay attention to the linking.

A: Your friend Ar**LENE** / is on the **PHONE**. /

B: Arlene **RO**per, / my friend from **WORK**? / She's **COM**ing here later. / What does she **WANT**?

A: She needs a **RIDE**. / She's been at the Hare Street **BUS** STOP / for more than an **HOUR**. /

B: Maybe I should **TELL** her / to call a **TA**xi. / They'll come right a**WAY** / and she'll **BE** here / before you **KNOW** it. /

A: I'd rather drive **O**ver / and pick her **UP** / than tell her to call a **TA**xi. /

B: That's **GREAT** / because I don't have a **CAR**. /

m. Role Play: "Ordering from Ron's Barbecue"

Partner A calls to order food by phone. Partner B works at the restaurant.

1. Prepare for the role play by practicing the pronunciation of the name, Ron's Barbecue, and the items on the menu. Target the consonant clusters that cross word boundaries. Pay attention to `r` and `l` and to numbers.

★★★ Ron's Barbecue Take-Out Menu ★★★
"The Price Is Right!"
Main dish price includes two side dishes and buttered French bread.

Main dishes		Any two side dishes	Drinks	
famous "overnight beef"	$6.95	barbecued corn on the cob	club soda	$.99
short ribs	$6.95	fried zucchini sticks	cherry Coke	$.99
marinated chicken wings	$5.50	baked beans	diet Pepsi	$.99
mile long hot dogs	$3.89	french fries	chocolate shake	$2.89
cheeseburgers	$4.79	carrot-raisin salad	**Desserts**	$2.89
mushroom burgers	$4.39	fresh green salad	apricot pie	
		choice of ranch or	chocolate sundae	
		vinaigrette dressing	spice cake	

2. Listen to a sample conversation between a restaurant employee (R) and the customer (C).

R: Ron's Barbecue. May I help you?

C: I want to order food from your take-out menu.

R: OK. What would you like?

C: What's your "overnight beef"?

R: Marinated beef that is slowly roasted overnight.

C: I'll have two orders of the overnight beef, barbecued corn on the cob, and the carrot-raisin salad.

R: Any drinks or dessert?

C: Two diet Pepsis and two pieces of spice cake. How soon will it be ready?

R: You can pick it up in thirty minutes.

3. Make up your own conversation. Switch roles.

Sing Along: "Oh! What a Beautiful Mornin'"

This song by Richard Rodgers and Oscar Hammerstein is from the popular musical *Oklahoma*. The story, set in the early 1900s before Oklahoma became a state, is about cowboys. Some of the vocabulary and language suggest local rural dialects.

1. Listen to the song and fill in the missing focus words. They are listed here in alphabetical order.

> busy   by   day   earth   eye   haze   heads   me   meadow   music   sky   statues   tree   way

1. There's a bright golden **HAZE** / on the _____,

   There's a bright golden _____ / on the **MEA**dow,

   The corn is as **HIGH** / as an elephant's _____,

   An' it looks like it's **CLIMB**in' / clear up to the _____.

   Chorus:

   Oh, what a beautiful **MORN**in'!

   Oh, what a beautiful _____!

   I got a beautiful **FEEL**in',

   Ev'rythin's goin' my _____.

2. All the **CAT**tle / are standin' like **STA**tues,

   All the **CAT**tle / are standin' like _____,

   They don't turn their _____ / as they see me ride _____,

   But a little brown **MAV**'rick[2] / is winkin' her **EYE**.

   Repeat chorus

3. All the sounds of the _____ / are like **MU**sic–

   All the sounds of the **EARTH** / are like _____.

   The breeze is so _____ / it don't[3] miss a _____.

   And a ol' weepin' **WIL**ler[4] / is laughin' at _____.

   Repeat chorus

2. Compare answers with a partner. Replay the song.

3. Discuss the following vocabulary and expressions: haze meadow breeze Everything's going my way

---

[2] **maverick:** a young unbranded colt or range calf

[3] *Don't* instead of *doesn't* in this sentence is a grammatical error common to many rural American dialects. To use correct grammar, you can sing "It won't miss a tree."

[4] Weeping Willow tree. A large, graceful tree with long trailing branches of "weeping" leaves.

n. Partner Practice: Song exercises

1. **Word stress.** Write two- and three-syllable words from the song under the correct stress pattern.

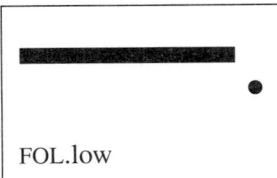

FOL.low

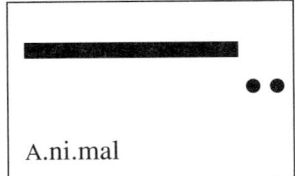

A.ni.mal

2. **Vowel + r.** Write five words from the song with vowel + r. Check with the instructor to make sure you can say the words correctly. Then use them in short sentences.

_____ _____ _____ _____ _____ _____

3. **r.** Write five words from the song with r or r cluster. After you can say the words correctly, use them in short sentences.

_____ _____ _____ _____ _____ _____

4. **Long vowels.** Review pages 109–110 about long vowels. Practice these words from the song, monitoring for the tongue and mouth movements. Feel the glide. Make sure your tongue moves and tightens.

e^y	i^y	a^y	u^w	a^w
day	see	eye	m^{y}usic	sounds
way	tree	ride		
haze	me	high		
	breeze	sky		
	weeping	bright		

5. **Consonant clusters and linking.** Practice these examples from the song of consonants linked to vowels and consonant clusters across word boundaries.

Linking Final "s"

There's a bright golden haze . . .

Ev'rythin'<u>s g</u>oing my way.

head<u>s a</u>s they see me ride by

standing like statue<u>s. A</u>ll the cattle . . .

high as an elephant'<u>s e</u>ye

It looks like it'<u>s c</u>limbing . . .

All the sound<u>s o</u>f the earth

Finishing Words and Linking across Word Boundaries

haze on the meadow

ride by

brown mav'rick

bright golden haze

All the sounds of the earth are like music

6. **Join the chorus.** Divide into three groups. Each group will prepare one verse to present to the class. Practice until your group can sing or say the verse in unison. Monitor for the consonant clusters and final sounds. All groups sing or say the chorus.

FINISHING UP

Self-Quiz Check your answers in the Answer Key.

Circle **all** the true statements in questions 1 and 2.

1. You can tell the difference between the words *fright* and *fried* by the length of the vowel.
    a. *Fried* sounds longer. *Fright* sounds shorter.
    b. The voiced consonant at the end makes the vowel sound longer.
    c. The word with the most letters always sounds longer.

2. In related nouns and verbs such as *rice* and *rise* or *proof* and *prove*, how can you predict the pronunciation?
    a. Look at the part of speech. The vowel length in the nouns is shorter than the vowel in the verbs.
    b. You can't predict the pronunciation. There are no rules for this.
    c. Look at the final consonant. A voiced consonant makes the vowel longer.

3. True or false? The last syllable in *cotton*, *certain*, and *kitten* does not have a vowel sound.

4. Fill in *16* or *60* for each statement.
    a. For _____ unstress the final syllable and lower the pitch a lot.
    b. For _____ stress both syllables. Use clear vowels.

5. Sometimes a consonant is inserted to link two vowels, such as "i" and "e" in the word *quiet*. Fill in the blanks.
    a. Insert the letter _____ to link the vowels in *creative* and *video*.
    b. Insert the letter _____ to link the vowels in *persuade* and *go out*.

Dictation

Write the sentences you hear. You will hear each sentence two times. Replay the tape to check your listening before looking in the Answer Key.

1. _____
2. _____
3. _____
4. _____
5. _____

Making Your New Pronunciation a Habit

Talk Times in Class: Role play

Partner A is expecting out-of-town guests but does not have room for them. To look for accommodations for the visitors, Partner A contacts a hotel or bed-and-breakfast for information. Partner B is the reservations clerk.

1. Make a list of questions to ask the clerk. Possible topics:

   - location (near shopping, transportation, etc.)
   - rates (daily, weekly, weekend specials)
   - description of accommodations (beds, bath, etc.)
   - meals, breakfasts provided
   - availability and cancellation policy

2. Role-play the phone conversation. Partner A must decide whether to make a reservation. Monitor for consonant clusters and for your challenging consonants. Switch roles.

Talk Times in Your Daily Life: Inquiring about hotels

Call or visit several hotels or bed-and-breakfasts in your area. Choose two or three things to ask about during each call, and write down your questions. After you complete each call, take notes so that your next call will be more comfortable and successful. Decide what you will monitor each time.

On Your Own

1. **Audio program.** Try different ways of practicing with the audiotapes. Track an exercise until you can say the selection along with the speaker.

2. **Recorded practice.** Record the following:

   - either the limerick or the dialogue "Needs a Ride" on page 209.
   - three sentences. Make the vowel length differences clear.

     a. He didn't want to pay the price or spend the prize money.

     b. She tried to save time and still drive at a safe speed.

     c. I can provide proof that will prove my argument.

3. **Glossary.** Add new words. Practice using your glossary words in a conversation with a friend.

CHAPTER 10   More about Vowels and Consonants   **215**

4. Mirroring.   Mirror five minutes of a speaker on TV whom you admire. Review the directions for "The Talking Mirror" on page 74. Describe your mirroring experience in a journal.

5. Extra practice.   Check out appendixes A and B for extra practice with consonants and vowels.

---

a good idea   Monitor for specific consonant or vowel sounds when you are watching TV. News and weather reporters usually have clear pronunciation. Make a list of words you hear with your problem sounds and practice them. If you videotaped the program, you can watch it again.

UNIT IV PROGRESS CHECK

Make a tape to turn in or to review in a scheduled conference with your instructor.

Talk for two minutes about your recommendation for either the eye doctor or the plumber on the business cards below, or provide your own card. Tell why you like the person and provide contact information.

1. Start by practicing the information on the cards. Then write out a script and mark your targets, such as focus words and pauses. Monitor for consonant sounds, consonant clusters, and finishing words.

2. Practice using a tape recorder to hear things about your speech that you did not hear at first. Re-record until you are satisfied. Turn in your script along with your tape.

Kathleen Lombardo, M.D.

Eye Physician and Surgeon

Clinical Professor
UCLA Department of Opthalmology
400 UCLA Medical Plaza, Suite 202

Appointments and Messages: 510.849.8205
24-hour emergency number: 510.849.2174

J. F. Gardner Plumbing

Commercial & Residential

Serving all your plumbing needs

repairs ▪ disposals ▪ re-piping ▪ sewer and drain cleaning
remodeling ▪ new construction ▪ water heaters

Family-owned business since 1972
Free estimates. Reasonable rates.

18023 Olympic Blvd. (between Overland and Hill)
24-hour emergency service 818-792-1847

Unit V Putting It All Together

11

More about Conversational Speech

In chapters 2 through 10 you practiced the basic features of American pronunciation. All eight key pronunciation targets introduced on page 2 were covered in these chapters. In chapter 11 you will examine in more depth how English speakers put words together in conversational speech. What you see in print is not what you hear in conversational English. Using authentic speech samples, poetry, and a song you will become more familiar with natural speech patterns. This will improve your pronunciation and your listening comprehension. Target your listening by noticing the features that you want to improve.

Reviewing Reductions and Chunks of Speech

Reductions play a major role in conversational speech rhythm. As you learned in chapter 2, unstressed structure words in everyday speech get *reduced,* or shortened. The more informal the speech, the more reductions you will hear.

- **Linking.** The reduced words can sound like one long word when you hear the words linked together. You might never know this if you learned English from the printed page, where each word is written separately.

    Example   *The cat is hungry* → *theCATizHUNgry*

- **Structure words.** When words are linked, unstressed structure words such as *you* and *or* are not usually pronounced the way they are spelled. Vowels are reduced to schwa. Sometimes consonants are dropped.

    Example   will he → Willy

a. Partner Practice: Reduced phrases

1. Listen to the underlined phrases that, when reduced, sound like other phrases. What you see in print is not what you hear in native speech.

    1. black and blue → blacken blue
    2. day to day → data day
    3. short or tall → shorter tall
    4. off and on → often on
    5. care at home → carrot home
    6. box is full → boxes full
    7. would he → Woody
    8. docked her pay → doctor pay

2. Use the above phrases in these sentences. Fill in the blank by saying what is written in the parentheses.

Example My hip was _____ from the fall. (*blacken blue*)

1. Her eye was _____ after the accident. (*blacken blue*)
2. The weather changes from _____. (*data day*)
3. I don't care if he is _____ as long as he is nice. (*shorter tall*)
4. Why do you keep turning the light _____? (*often on*)
5. My sick father received good _____. (*carrot home*)
6. The _____ and won't hold any more. (*boxes full*)
7. _____ like to come with us? (*Woody*)
8. The company _____ when she stayed home with a sick child. (*doctor pay*)

b. Improve Your Monitoring: Structure words

Listen and fill in the structure words you hear.

1. I'd like _____ borrow _____ book.
2. Janet _____ appointed _____ _____ steering committee.
3. What _____ _____ think _____ _____ outcome?
4. _____ _____ package ready?
5. When _____ _____ call?
6. _____ forgot _____ bring _____ tape.
7. Half _____ _____ pictures _____ missing.
8. _____ dropped _____ off _____ _____ corner.
9. _____ _____ like it now _____ later?
10. He _____ _____ year _____ _____ half more _____ go.

Group Practice 1: Common reductions and parts of speech

Listen and repeat the sentences with reduced words in unison. Then look away from your book. Continue to listen and repeat until you sound like a chorus with one voice.

Pronouns. Linked and reduced pronouns often sound like new words.

1. her   What's her name?   →   WHATser **NAME**?
2. his   When's his appointment?   →   WHENziz ap**POINT**ment?

3.	he	Is he ready?	→	IZZy REAdy?
4.	them	Ask them what they want.	→	ASKum WHAT they WANT.
5.	him	I gave him a ride.	→	I GAVim a RIDE.
6.	you	Do you like it?	→	d'ya LIKE it?
7.	your	Do you have your passport?	→	d'ya HAVE yer PASSport?

Prepositions. The vowels in these reduced prepositions sound like schwa.

1. to — It's next tə the table.
2. of — That's one əf the best.
3. for — Thanks fər the invitation.
4. at — They left ət dawn.

Conjunctions. The vowels in these reduced conjunctions sound like schwa.

1. or — Now ər later?
2. and — The doctors ənd nurses worked late.
3. that — I hope thət ət stops raining.

Articles. The vowels in these articles sound like schwa.

1. the — Please hand me thə pencil.
2. a — I would like ə copy.
3. an — Do yəu have ən extra one?

Helping verbs. The vowels in these helping verbs sound like schwa.

1. have — I should həve left sooner.
2. was — I wəs listening.
3. can — He cən speak Spanish.
4. do — What də yəu think?

---

questions and answers

1. **What is the difference between a reduction and a contraction?**
   A contraction is a reduction that is part of standard written English.

2. **Are reductions ever written?**
   Not usually. Reductions are part of standard spoken English, not standard written English.

   Sometimes common reductions are spelled out in dialogues in plays, novels, or comic strips.

   Occasionally you see reductions in advertising or titles of films or products. For example, "Good 'n' Plenty" is a candy bar. "Pic 'n' Save" is a discount store.

CHAPTER 11 More about Conversational Speech **219**

c. Communicative Activity: Let's talk

With a partner, make up short dialogues (3–4 sentences) that begin with one of the sentences from Group Practice 1. Focus on using reductions. Take turns speaking first.

Example

A: I hope that it stops raining soon.

B: Me too. I want to go out and take a walk.

A: I'll go with you. I need the exercise.

---

just for fun

A: Knock knock.
B: Who's there?
A: Caesar.
B: Caesar who?
A: Now he Caesar, now he doesn't.

Caesar = _____ (See page 106 for more knock-knock jokes.)

Group Practice 2: Review the flap

As you learned in chapter 8, page 152, the flap is commonly used in conversational American English. When a "t" or a "d" comes before an unstressed word, it will sound like a flap, as in *He lost his way. He paid his rent.* Tap your tongue lightly on your gum ridge to make a flap.

Listen and repeat more examples of reductions with a flap. Say the reduced speech until you sound like a chorus with one voice.

1. aLOTta — There's <u>a lot of</u> smog today.
2. THOUGHTa — I already <u>thought of</u> that.
3. OUTta — Let's get <u>out of</u> this lane.
4. STAYta RIGHTta — <u>Stay to</u> the <u>right of</u> the road.
5. GOta — Should we <u>go to</u> the market?
6. MOSta — <u>Most of</u> the time.
7. HAFta — I <u>have to</u> finish by noon.
8. WANna[1] — I <u>want to</u> change jobs.
9. WAYta — That's the <u>way to</u> go.
10. ENDa — I didn't care for the <u>end of</u> the movie.

[1] The in *wanna* is similar to a flap because the tongue taps the gum ridge.

d. Partner Practice: The flap

Practice the previous reductions with your partner. Partner A says the reduction by itself. Partner B makes up a sentence using the reduction. Switch roles.

Example   Partner A: alotta

Partner B: There's <u>a lot of</u> information on the Internet.

e. Partner Practice: Two short conversations

1. Listen to the conversations using reduced speech and the flap. Track the speech until you can say it along with the speaker.

2. Underline the focus words. Circle the flaps in each dialogue.

Conversation 1

A: I'm ready to take a break.

B: Good. I'm ready for a Big Mac and a Coke.

A: I'd rather take a walk than eat.

B: OK. Let's walk over to McDonald's. Then we can walk and eat.

Conversation 2

A: Are you ready to order?

B: In a minute. I have to decide what I want to eat.

A: Do you think we ought to get it for here or to go?[2]

B: We've got to be back in thirty minutes. Maybe we'd better get it to go.

Practice saying the dialogues. Pay attention to the linking and the reductions. Switch roles.

---

[2] Food "to go" is food you take with you to eat later.

more questions and answers

1. Is it OK to reduce sounds when speaking English?
   Yes. Educated native speakers all reduce unstressed words. This is part of English speech rhythm. It's <u>not</u> OK to reduce consonants in most clusters or grammatical endings.

2. Do I have to reduce sounds when speaking English in order to have clear speech?
   No. You need to be able to understand reductions because native speakers use them.

3. If I want to sound more like a native speaker do I have to use reductions?
   Yes.

4. Are the same words always reduced?
   Not always. Reductions can vary with the speaker and the situation. In general, the more informal the conversation, the more reductions you hear.

f. Cartoon: Single Slices

Review compound nouns, phrasal verbs, and thought groups and reductions.

1. Predict the pronunciation of the speaker in the cartoon. In the caption below, draw slashes where you would pause after each thought group. Then underline the stressed word in the compound noun and the phrasal verb.

   "The trouble with dating a soul mate is that even if you break up, the souls mate for life."

 2. Listen to the tape to review your predictions and make any changes.

3. Say the cartoon using conversational speech with reductions.

g. Join the Chorus: "Sneezles"[3]

1. Listen to the poem. The stressed words stand out. You will hear common reductions of structure words such as *him, his, and, at,* and *to.* Then listen and repeat the verses in unison. Move your hands and lean forward slightly as you stress the focus words.

1. Christopher Robin
   Had wheezles and sneezles.
   They bundled him into his bed.
   They gave him what goes
   With a cold in the nose,
   And some more for a cold in the head.

2. They wondered if wheezles
   Could turn into measles,
   If sneezles would turn into mumps.
   They examined his chest
   For a rash and the rest
   Of his body for swellings and lumps.

3. They sent for some doctors
   In sneezles and wheezles
   To tell them what ought to be done.
   All sorts of conditions
   Of famous physicians
   Came hurrying 'round at a run.

4. They all made a note
   Of the state of his throat.
   They asked if he suffered from thirst.
   They asked if the sneezles
   Came after the wheezles,
   Or if the first sneezle came first.

5. Christopher Robin
   Got up in the morning,
   The sneezles had vanished away.
   And the look in his eye
   Seemed to say to the sky,
   "Now, how to amuse them today?"

   —A. A. Milne

[3] Some of the verses are not included here.

2. Divide into five groups. Practice one verse with your group until you sound like a chorus with one voice. Say your verse for the class.

h. Dialogue: "Willpower"

1. Look away from your book and listen to the dialogue. Pay attention to the reductions.

1. A: This is incredible! I can't believe it's not ice cream. It tastes just like real chocolate ice cream.
2. B: Believe it or not, it's not ice cream. It's frozen yogurt—soft frozen yogurt.
3. A: Do you know how many calories it has? I'm on a special diet.
4. B: That depends. Do you want the chocolate or the vanilla? Do you want the nonfat or the regular? What kind do you want?
5. A: I want the good kind. I want it with fat, lots of rich, dark chocolate fat.
6. B: I thought you were worried about calories.
7. A: I am worried about calories. You didn't ask me what kind I should have. You asked me what kind I wanted to have.
8. B: Well, what kind do you want to order?
9. A: I'll have a small dish of vanilla nonfat yogurt, please.
10. B: Now that's what you call "willpower"!

2. Replay the tape and repeat the dialogue, one line at a time. Then practice with a partner. Switch roles. Prepare to perform the dialogue for the class.

Practice with Authentic Speech

Learn By Listening 1: Four public service announcements (PSAs).

Follow these directions for all four PSAs: Listen, chunk, hum, and then track.

1. Listen several times for content. Look away from your book. Pay attention to the focus words.

2. Chunk the thought groups. Listen and draw a slash when you hear a pause. Underline the focus words. The important thing is to hear the stressed places and to feel the rhythm of the speaker.

3. Hum the speech melody. Listen and pay attention to pitch changes. Track the speakers by humming along with the melody.

4. Track the speaker. *Tracking* is like mirroring with no video. Repeat each word along with the speaker. If you miss any words, just hum along. Tracking becomes easier with each repetition. Pay attention to the intonation.

🎧 PSA 1: Paul Newman, movie actor

This skilled actor is reading from a script. It sounds natural, but it has fewer reductions and none of the hesitations and repetitions you will hear in some of the other PSAs.

¹Close your eyes, and imagine you're beside a pure mountain stream—the water cascading over the stones. ²A paradise like this isn't easy to come by, but it does still exist—because **the Nature Conservancy** works locally with people like you to save precious places around the world—forever. ³That way, closing your eyes will never be the only way to get there. ⁴I'm Paul Newman. ⁵Help save the last great places. ⁶Visit The Nature Conservancy at nature dot org.

🎧 PSA 2: Interview at a farmer's market

1. In this informal interview about water, listen for common reductions, and schwa vowels in unstressed words. Both speakers occasionally hesitate and repeat words.

How Many Gallons of Water Does It Take to Grow and Produce Our Food?

And now a water-minute from the Water Education Foundation.

1. A: Here we are at the farmer's market and you're you're holding this big bundle of oranges, an . . . uh . . . Let's look this up. How much water does it take to grow one orange? Here's the answer.
2. B: 14 gallons of water . . .
3. A: How about one ounce of almonds?
4. B: 80 gallons?
5. A: How about 8 ounces of chicken?
6. B: 330 gallons.
7. A: OK, what about 4 ounces of hamburger?
8. B: 616 gallons.
9. A: Now, you want to take a guess on steak?
10. B: I wouldn't have a . . . I don't know. 1232 gallons. I can't believe it! I never realized, honestly.
11. A: Well it takes water to grow and produce all the food we eat.
12. B: I think more people should pay attention to, you know, where water comes from, how precious it is.
13. A: All Californians need plenty of water for home, industry, and food production. But there is only so much water. Use it wisely. Find out more at water education dot org.

2. Remember to listen first, then chunk, hum, and track.

PSA 3: Travis Tritt, country musician

1. This is conversational speech read from a transcript. Listen for reductions. Do you hear any "uh's" or hesitations?

¹You want to know one of the best ways to help kids do better in school? ²Hi, I'm Travis Tritt. ³I visit a lot of schools both at home and when I'm on the road. Unfortunately, I hear from too many students, "ah school's so boring." ⁵And I say to them, "then you haven't taken enough music courses." ⁶You know, exposure to music opens up the mind like nothing else. ⁷It improves something called spatial IQ, which in turn helps students tackle the challenges of other things like math and science. ⁸Some night this week, sit down as a family and play for your kids some music that just really turns you on. ⁹And then listen to what your kids like. Compare notes. ¹⁰ Keep an open mind. Find the common ground.

A Public Service Announcement brought to you by MENC, the National Association for Music Education, Gibson Guitar, Baldwin Piano, and this station. Music, part of a sound education.

2. Remember to listen first, then chunk, hum, and track.

A certain number of hesitations, repetitions, and *fillers,* such as *hmm* or *well uh* or *you know what I mean* or *let's see,* are a natural part of conversational speech. Most people do this as they plan what to say next or search for a lost word.

PSA 4: Alison Krauss, country musician

1. Listen to the speaker hesitate and repeat herself. This does not interfere with the speaker's effectiveness, but it can make it harder to mark the thought groups. When tracking, it is not necessary to track the "uh's" unless this is comfortable for you. The important thing is to move with the speaker and to feel where she puts the stress.

¹What does Alison Krauss remember about music class when she was a kid?

²My finest, uh, memory of music class is kind of, uh, just an overall memory not a specific instance. ³Because, uh, music was something completely different than any other class in school. ⁴It was . . . I remember it as all being fun. ⁵And the reward wasn't, you know, a great test score and it wasn't a higher grade. ⁶It was getting to be a part of an ensemble and singing something at the end where everyone knew their part. ⁷It was all fun and games to me. ⁸And, uh, you made friends, you know. I found that you that you made friends that lasted a really long time. ⁹At least the ones that for me that have lasted the longest are ones that I met in school chorus or music classes and not who I sat next to in math!

2. Now that you have heard all four PSAs, discuss which one was the easiest for you to track and why.

3. Pretend you are making a public service announcement for the public schools, encouraging kids to stay in school. Close your eyes and think back about a school class that you will always remember. Talk about your class for one minute to your partner or a small group about this, as Travis Tritt and Alison Krauss talked about a music class in the PSA. Record your speech. Self-monitor.

i. Role Play: Two invitations

You and your partner receive invitations to different events taking place on June 12. Partner A is invited to a cousin's wedding. Partner B is invited to a retirement dinner for someone important at work. You would like to go together to both events but are not sure it is possible. Role-play a phone conversation in which you tell your partner about your invitation and discuss what to do.

1. First review the pronunciation of the information on the invitations below.

2. In the role play, consider the times and the locations of both events. Decide whether you can attend one event or both and what you will say to each host.

Wedding Bells Are Ringing

Linda Pasternak and Bob Holbrook
request your presence at their wedding
5 o'clock Saturday, June 12

Metropolitan Historical Society Gardens
10292 Riverton Drive, East Lakeville, Ohio
R.S.V.P. by June 1
Reception and dancing following the ceremony

30 YEARS' DEVOTED SERVICE

Our Division Manager, Lewis Anthony, is retiring.

LET'S HONOR LEW

Saturday, June 12, 7 o'clock
Cocktails and Dinner

The Mesquite Grill
258 W. 20th Street • West Lakeville, Ohio
R.S.V.P. by June 5 • Dress: informal

Sing Along: "Leaving on a Jet Plane"

The melody and rhythm of this song follow closely the intonation and stress patterns of spoken English. Listen several times and fill in the structure words that are missing. Compare answers with a partner.

1. All _____ bags _____ packed, _____ ready _____ go.

   _____ standing here outside _____ door.

   _____ hate _____ wake you up _____ say good-bye.

   _____ _____ dawn _____ breaking, _____ early morn.

   _____ taxi's waiting, _____ blowing _____ horn.

   Already _____ _____ lonesome _____ _____ cry.

   Chorus

   _____ kiss _____ _____ smile _____ _____

   Tell _____ that _____ wait _____ _____.

   Hold _____ like _____ never let _____ go.

   _____ _____ leaving _____ _____ jet plane.

   Don't know when _____ _____ back again.

   Oh, babe, _____ hate _____ go.

2. There's _____ many times _____ played around.

   _____ many times _____ let _____ down.

   _____ tell you now, they don't mean _____ thing.

   _____ every place _____ go, _____ think _____ you.

   Every song _____ sing, _____ sing _____ you.

   When _____ come back _____ wear _____ wedding ring.

   Chorus

3. Now _____ time _____ come _____ leave you.

   One more time, _____ let _____ kiss _____.

   _____ close _____ eyes I'll _____ on _____ way.

   _____ _____ dream _____ _____ days _____ come

   When _____ won't _____ _____ leave alone,

   _____ _____ times _____ won't _____ _____ say . . .

   Chorus

   —John Denver

j. Song Exercises

1. Reviewing important endings: Contractions and final "s" and "ed."
Fill in the missing endings. Practice these phrases from the song. Pay attention to the linking.

1. All my bag___ are pack___, I___ ready to go.
2. It___ early morn.
3. The taxi___ waiting.
4. He___ blowing his horn.
5. So many time___ I___ play___ around
6. Dream about the day__ to come

2. Reviewing r. Say these phrases from the song and monitor for r and ər. Look in the song for additional r words to practice. Remember to curl your tongue tightly to say r. Listen for a good sound.

Vowel + r	r and r Clusters
outside y**our** d**oor**	I'm **r**eady to go
I'm standing h**ere**	**br**ing your WEDding **R**ING
early m**orn**	dawn is **br**eaking
tell h**er**	**dr**eam about
one m**ore**	time a**r**ound
blowing his h**orn**	al**r**eady

3. Reviewing stressed words. Divide into three groups. With your group, practice saying one verse as if you are telling a story. Lengthen the stressed words and shorten the unstressed structure words. Tap the desk for the focus words. Say your verse for the class.

1. All my **BAGS** are **PACKED**. / I'm **READy** to **GO**. / I'm **STAND**ing here / outSIDE your **DOOR**. / I **HATE** to **WAKE** you **UP** / to say good-**BYE**. / But the **DAWN** is **BREAK**ing, / it's **EAR**ly **MORN**. / The taxi's **WAIT**ing, / he's **BLOW**ing his **HORN**. / AlREADy I'm so **LONE**some / I could **CRY**. /

2. There're so many **TIMES** / I played a**ROUND**. / So many **TIMES** / I let you **DOWN**. / I **TELL** you **NOW** / they DON'T MEAN a **THING**. / Every **PLACE** I **GO**,/ I **THINK** of you. / EVERY **SONG** I **SING**, / I'll **SING** for you. / When I **COME BACK** / I'll **WEAR** your **WED**ding **RING**. /

3. Now the **TIME** has **COME** to **LEAVE** you. / One more **TIME**, / let me **KISS** you. / Then **CLOSE** your **EYES**, / and I'll **BE** on my **WAY**. / **DREAM** about the **DAYS** to **COME** / when I **WON'T** have to **LEAVE** / a**LONE**, / about the **TIMES** I WON'T have to **SAY** . . . /

All groups: 'Cause I'm **LEAV**ing on a **JET** PLANE. / DON'T **KNOW** / WHEN I'll be **BACK** a**GAIN**. / Oh, **BABE**, / I HATE to **GO**.

FINISHING UP

Self-Quiz (Check the answers in the Answer Key.)

1. When "ed" is linked to a vowel as in *baked a cake*, the "ed" sounds like

    a. t   b. d   c. a flap

2. True or False? In impromptu conversations in English, a confident, interesting speaker will not say "uh" or repeat any words.

3. True or False? You don't have to reduce unstressed words in English to have clear speech.

4. True or False? You do have to reduce unstressed words to have nativelike speech.

5. Circle the answer. To become more comfortable with reductions, it helps if you

    a. move with the rhythm when you watch or listen to native speech

    b. listen and repeat recorded speech one line at a time

    c. track recordings and mirror videos of native speakers

    d. all of the above

Dictation

Write the sentences you hear. You will hear each sentence two times. Replay the tape to check your listening before looking in the Answer Key.

1. _____
2. _____
3. _____
4. _____
5. _____

Making Your New Pronunciation a Habit

Talk Times in Class: Role play

Partner A's car will be in a repair shop for a week. Partner A needs a car to get to work and contacts a car rental agency to ask about renting one. Partner B works for the car rental agency. Both partners need information, and both have information that the other needs.

To prepare for the role play, write two lists of questions that you might ask. For example:

Information the Car Agency Needs

- the kind of car you want to rent
- the date(s) that you need it
- how long you plan to keep the car
- how you will be paying (credit card?)
- the driver's age (over 25, under 25)

Information the Customer Needs

- the cost (daily, weekly)
- any extra charges such as taxes or insurance
- the kinds of cars available
- location of the nearest agency

2. Practice your questions with your partner. Monitor stress and unstress. Make the stressed syllables sound much longer and higher in pitch than the unstressed ones, even if you do not always reduce the vowels to schwa. Use the appropriate intonation for "wh" and "yes–no" questions.

3. In the role play, monitor your own and your partner's speech. Switch roles.

Talk Times in Your Daily Life: Renting a car

Call several car agencies for information. Look for the toll-free phone numbers by searching the Internet for "car rental phone numbers," or by calling information at 800-555-1212. Pick three things to ask about during each call. Monitor your speech for speech rhythm. Lengthen the focus words.

On Your Own

1. **Audio program.** Practice with the tapes/CDs for chapter 11.

2. **Recorded practice.** Record one or more of the following:

   - the dialogues "Two Short Conversations," page 220, or "Willpower," page 223
   - possible responses to the invitations on page 226. Decline one of invitations and give a good reason for being unable to attend. Accept the other invitation. What will you say to give gracious responses to both hosts?
   - a 1–2 minute talk about moving. For example, describe an experience when you moved. How did this affect your life? What were the advantages or disadvantages of moving? Use a conversational style and monitor for speech rhythm.

3. **Song.** Listen to "Leaving on a Jet Plane," and sing along with the singer. Then sing or say the lyrics in the rhythm of the song until they sound natural.

4. **Glossary.** Are you using words that people do not understand or words you want to pronounce more clearly? Write them on your glossary and find out how to pronounce them.

5. **Tracking.** Track the PSAs on pages 223–226 until you can speak along with the speakers. This requires many repetitions. Don't concern yourself with tracking hesitations such as "uh."

12

More about Thought Groups

Now that you have reached chapter 12, your ear is more sensitive to the features of spoken English. You can hear that words are grouped into thought groups, in contrast to written language, where words are grouped into sentences. You are aware of the exaggerated pitch and stress differences that characterize English speech compared to your native language.

In chapter 12 you will review thought groups by listening to both formal and informal speech samples and analyzing a few of the many speech variations you will encounter in everyday life. As you listen to the recordings, think about the speakers that are easy to understand and why. Videos of a few of the speech samples in this chapter can be viewed via Thomson Heinle's ESL website, at elt.heinle.com/targetingpron.

 Learn By Listening 1: Reviewing guidelines for thought groups

Signal a thought group by (1) lengthening the focus word, (2) changing pitch, and (3) pausing. Native speakers do not all choose to pause in the same place for any given sentence. However, they do all make choices within certain guidelines for focus words, such as you learned in chapter 5.

---

guideline 1 Slow speakers use more thought groups than fast speakers. They pause more often and lengthen the focus words more noticeably.

---

guideline 2 Speakers who use more melody, clear focus words, and more pauses are easier to understand.

231

1. Listen to two speakers say this sentence from Ernest Hemingway's short story "A Clean, Well-Lighted Place." Which speaker is easier to understand? Why?

   First speaker: "It was very **LATE** / and everyone had left the **CAFE** / except an old **MAN** / who sat in the **SHA**dow / the leaves of the **TREE** / made against the electric **LIGHT**."

   Second speaker: "It was very **LATE** / and everyone had left the cafe except an old **MAN** / who sat in the shadow the leaves of the **TREE** / made against the electric **LIGHT**."

2. Listen to two speakers say this sentence from Amy Tan's *The Kitchen God's Wife*. Which speaker is easier to understand?

   First speaker: "It was an American **SONG** / about **LOVE**, / and I heard right a**WAY** / that she had a very sweet **VOICE**, / the kind of **VOICE** / that sounded as if her heart had been **BRO**ken / many **TIMES**."/

   Second speaker: "It was an American song about **LOVE**, / and I heard right a**WAY** / that she had a very sweet **VOICE**, / the kind of voice that sounded as if her heart had been broken many **TIMES**."/

3. Look away from your book and listen to two speakers respond to the question, "Where can I find a telephone?" Which speaker is easier to understand? Why?

   First speaker: There's a phone in the next block in front of the **MAR**ket / across the street from that tall stone **BUILD**ing. /

   Second speaker: There's a **PHONE** / in the next **BLOCK** / in front of the **MAR**ket / across the **STREET** / from that tall stone **BUILD**ing. /

a. Partner Practice: Scrambled sentences

Assemble a sentence about celebrations and holidays in English-speaking countries. Start by saying a thought group in column 1. Add a thought group from columns 2 and 3 to complete the sentence. Take turns, and monitor your own and your partner's speech.

Example   Flower shops / sell more flowers in May / because of Mother's Day.

1	2	3
1. Flower shops	a day for remembering someone you love,	and collect candy from their neighbors.
2. In late October,	people celebrate birthdays	is February 14.
3. Valentine's Day,	a national British holiday,	by giving gifts and eating birthday cake.
4. In most English-speaking countries,	children wear costumes on Halloween	originated when wealthy people gave Christmas boxes to the less fortunate.
5. Boxing Day,	sell more flowers in May	because of Mother's Day.

1	2	3
1. Thanksgiving is celebrated	look forward to presents from Santa Claus	with a family gathering and a turkey dinner.
2. Children who celebrate Christmas	people celebrate their country's independence	on Canada Day (July 1) and the Fourth of July.
3. In the United States and Canada,	the whole of Australia unites in celebration	on December 25.
4. On the first Tuesday in November,	by many people in the United States and Canada	surrounding a horse race called the Foster's Melbourne Cup.

Handwritten annotations: "ral to get together", "gather (verb)"

b. Partner Practice: An ad for Delta Air Lines

1. Listen to the ad without looking at your book.

2. Replay the tape. Mark the thought groups with a slash (/) when you hear a pause. Underline the focus words. Notice the pitch changes at the ends of thought groups and the falling pitch at the ends of sentences.

¹We don't need a radar screen,/ or a weather balloon,/ or even the *Farmer's Almanac*. ²But we can forecast with confidence/ that the next time you need to fly overseas,/ the weather inside your big Delta jet/ will be absolutely clear. ³That's because Delta is the only U.S. airline to fly smoke free/ worldwide./ ⁴Delta quit smoking long before most airlines started to,/ shall we say, cut back. ⁵So if you prefer to keep puffy clouds outside the airplane where they belong,/ insist on flying Delta./ ⁶Even our cozy Crown Room Clubs in major airports around the world/ are smoke free. ⁷At Delta, we make one thing perfectly clear—/your next flight.

3. See chapters 3 and 4, pages 46 and 62, to review the intonation of compound nouns and descriptive phrases. Listen to the following phrases and check (✓) the correct column.

Phrases	Compound Noun	Descriptive Phrase
Example radar screen	✓	
1. weather balloon	✓	
2. *Farmer's Almanac*		✓
3. fly overseas		✓
4. absolutely clear		✓
5. quit smoking		✓
6. puffy clouds		✓
7. major airports		✓

4. Listen and repeat the ad one sentence at a time. Put your tape recorder on pause and look away from the book whenever possible.

c. Dialogue: "The Missing Room"

1. Listen and draw slash marks to show thought groups in the following conversation between a customer (C) and a hotel manager (M).

1. C: May I please speak with the **MAN**ager.
2. M: This **IS** the manager. Are you having a **PRO**blem that I can **HELP** you with?
3. C: I think your ho**TEL** is having the problem. I made a reser**VA**tion for five **NIGHTS** in a nonsmoking **ROOM** with a queen-size **BED**. But the reser**VA**tion desk can't **FIND** it.
4. M: Your **NAME**, please.
5. C: My name is Francis **O**liver. I **MADE** the reservation three **MONTHS** ago and have a confir**MA**tion number. It's 9706**3**.
6. M: I am truly **SOR**ry, but we don't have a **RE**cord of this. We are careful to re**CORD** reservations when we **TAKE** them, and yours is not **HERE**. **SOME**how there's been a mis**TAKE**.
7. C: You **TOOK** the reservation over the **PHONE**. Apparently you didn't re**CORD** the reservation. That's the **PRO**blem.
8. M: Let's **SEE** how we can **SOLVE** the problem. We have one room **LEFT** with two double **BEDS** in **SMO**king. Would you **LIKE** it?
9. C: I don't **WANT** a room in "**SMOK**ing." I want **MY** room, the **NON**smoking room, the room I re**SERVED**. I don't **SMOKE**, and I don't **LIKE** smoke. I am an **ACT**or, and smoke irritates my **THROAT**.
10. M: I am terribly **SOR**ry, but that's **ALL** that's a**VAIL**able. You may not **BE** a smoker, but perhaps you can **ACT** like a smoker, and **TAKE** the **ROOM**!

2. Listen again for each of the following targets.

- z : re_s_ervation, zero
- linking final "s"

  fi_ve n_ights in a . . .   It'_s n_ine . . .   three mon_ths_ ago   the_re's b_een a mistake

  tha_t's the_ problem   you_rs is_ not here   two double be_ds in_ smoking

  irritate_s my_ throat   tha_t's all tha_t's available

- word stress: **RE**cord / re**CORD**   reser**VA**tions   **IR**ritates

3. Practice contrastive stress. Fill in the missing sentences from the dialogue. See the first one as an example.

Statement	Response Showing Contrastive Stress
1. C: May I speak with the MANager?	1. M: <u>This IS the manager.</u>
2. M: Are you having a PRoblem . . . ?	2. C: I think your _____
3. C: You TOOK the reservation . . .	3. C: _____
4. C: I don't SMOKE . . .	4. C: _____
5. M: You may not BE a smoker . . .	5. M: but perhaps _____

4. Practice the dialogue with a partner.

5. Create a dialogue with a partner about a situation when you did not receive something you ordered.

Learn By Listening 2: PSAs and thought group signals

Listen to three public service announcements (PSAs) with good thought-group signals and pauses. Which speaker's pauses and thought groups are the easiest for you to mark?

Complete the following directions for all the PSAs in this chapter. Listen, chunk, hum, and then track.

1. **Listen several times for content.** Look away from the book. Pay attention to the focus words.

2. **Chunk the thought groups.** Listen and draw a slash where you hear a pause. Underline the focus words. You may hear other stressed words but only one focus word.

3. **Hum the speech melody.** Listen and pay attention to pitch changes. Track the speakers by humming along with the melody.

4. **Track the speech.** Repeat each word along with the speaker. If you miss words at first, just hum along. Tracking becomes easier with each repetition.

Public service announcement

PSA 1: "Trees for America" (60 seconds)

[1]The Arbor Day Foundation invites you to celebrate life and plant a tree—for the first day of school and the last, to bring songbirds close by, to celebrate a new life beginning, and a life remembered.

[2]Plant a tree to help clear the air, to celebrate two lives coming together, and a new home, to conserve energy, to celebrate a good report card, and a good life. [3]For all those special times, plant a tree. [4]Each tree you plant makes a difference, for a better neighborhood and a better world. [5]Plant a tree and put a smile on the future.

[6]For your free Trees for America brochure, write the National Arbor Day Foundation.

PSA 2: Susan Sarandon, @Your Library (30 seconds)

Your research paper is due tomorrow. You have no idea what to bring to tonight's dinner party, and you could really use some help in deciding about that new car you're thinking of buying. Where do you turn? How about the library? The library is your one stop for everything you're looking for in print and online. Find what you need at your library.

PSA 3: Tim Robbins, @Your Library (30 seconds)

Can you name the one place where you have access to nearly everything on the Web and in print and even have personal assistance to help find what you're looking for? It's right in your backyard. The library. Libraries have always been places for education and self-help. Today they're at the forefront of the information age. Come see what's new at your library.

Reminder: You can watch these three PSA's at http://college.hmco.com/esl/students.

Presenting New Information

Strong thought-group signals will make your speech easier to understand whenever you are presenting new information, for example in oral presentations, casual conversation, or phone messages. Emphasize the focus words. Use a lot of speech melody and pauses. Rephrase new information in different words and define new vocabulary.

Learn By Listening 3: Two PSAs presenting information

1. Follow the same directions for both PSAs. Listen, chunk, hum, and then track. In addition, complete the exercises for compound nouns and descriptive phrases following each PSA.

PSA 4: "Identity Theft" (60 seconds)

[1]The **U.S. Postal Service** wants to remind everyone this year to protect themselves from becoming victims of identity theft. [2]Your personal information is a gold mine for identity thieves. [3]Identity theft involves acquiring key pieces of someone's personal information—such as a name, address, date of birth, or social security number—in order to impersonate them. [4]Often, the identity thief steals mail to get information to apply for credit cards, to order personal checks, or to obtain existing account information. [5]To avoid falling victim to this crime, the Postal Service offers these tips: promptly remove incoming mail from your mailbox; don't deposit outgoing mail from an unsecured mailbox; and don't give out passwords, PIN numbers, or account numbers. [6]Memorize them, and don't write them down where they can be found. [7]For more information, log on to w-w-w-dot-"consumer"-dot-gov-slash-"n-c-p-w."

2. Listen to the paragraph five or six more times. Pay attention to the following two-word combinations and decide whether you hear a compound noun or a descriptive phrase. Check (✓) the answer.

	Compound Nouns	Descriptive Phrases
Postal Service	_____	_____
identity theft	_____	_____
gold mine	_____	_____
identity thieves	_____	_____
personal information	_____	_____
social security number	_____	_____
steals mail	_____	_____
credit cards	_____	_____
mailbox	_____	_____
passwords	_____	_____
PIN numbers	_____	_____
account numbers	_____	_____

PSA 5: "Today's Teens Need to Be a Lot Smarter When It Comes to Money" (60 seconds)

A: [1]Teenagers today are high-tech and media savvy—but are they money smart? [2]Not so, according to Merridy Maynard, vice president at Northwestern Mutual. [3]Spending comes easy to today's teens.

B: [4]That's right, Bob. Each year, kids spend millions of dollars and even more of their parents' money—yet test scores show that they don't understand how money works. [5]More twelfth graders have credit cards than ever before—yet four in ten don't know the benefits of paying more than the minimum balance due on a credit card.

A: [6]How can kids get on the right track?

B: [7]Well, the good news is that two-thirds of teens say they save money and want to know how to invest it. [8]Learning about personal finance and economics can be fun. Parents just need to make it a part of everyday life.

A: [9]But many families find it very hard to talk about money. [10]How can parents bring up the subject?

B: [11]They can go to "the-mint" dot org to find games, calculators, and everyday tips to make managing money fun and easy.

A: [12]I'm Bob Tido for Consumer Radio Network.

1. Listen to the selection five or six more times. Pay attention to the following two-word combinations and decide whether you hear a compound noun or a descriptive phrase. Check (✓) the answer.

	Compound Nouns	Descriptive Phrases
teenagers	___	___
media savvy	___	___
money smart	___	___
parents' money	___	___
minimum balance	___	___
credit card	___	___
save money	___	___
everyday life	___	___
everyday tips	___	___

2. Summarize PSA 4 or 5 in your own words. Tell your partner or the class the main idea and add your own thoughts about the topic. Use focus words to make the information clear.

d. Communicative Activity: An answering-machine ad

1. Look at the ad and listen to the message for a shop called "The Book Bakery." Pay attention to the pauses and the thought groups. Replay the tape several times. You are going to be making a similar answering-machine message.

2. Read the ad for the flower shop and the motorcycle shop below. Write a one-minute answering-machine message for one of these shops. Do not try to tell everything in the ad.

3. Say your phone ad for your partner or the class. Use melody to sound friendly so that people will be interested in visiting your business. Target focus words and pauses to make your message easy to understand.

Thought Groups in Conversational Speech

In conversation, speakers may hesitate, gather their thoughts, rephrase, and start again. Sometimes they use incomplete sentences. The thought group signals in conversational speech may be less clear and harder to mark than in an oral presentation or scripted speech.

Learn By Listening 4: PSAs 6 and 7

The next speakers use informal speech that is not fully scripted. Notice the expressive melody, the reductions and schwa vowels, as well as hesitations and repetitions.

Follow the steps for PSAs on page 235. Listen, chunk, hum, and then track.

PSA 6: "Two Percent of the World's Water Is Drinkable" (60 seconds)

And now a water-minute from the Water Education Foundation.

1. A: Tell us a little about how you use water. What are four or five things you use water for during the day?

2. B: Drinking. Um. Drinking, mostly. Washing dishes. Washing clothes.

3. A: So what you do to . . . um . . .

4. B: Conserve water? Yeah, you know, I mean, you know, full loads of wash, short showers, that kind of stuff.

5. A: Do you buy bottled water?

6. B: Yes.

7. A: What's it going for these days?

8. B: A buck . . . like for what . . . 12 ounces?

9. A: So you're really a fan of pure water. How much of the world's water do you think is drinkable?

10. B: Not much. I have no idea.

11. A: Two percent is drinkable. And we should be conserving that water, don't you think, and taking care of it?

12. B: Yes.

13. A: It's precious.

14. B: Yes.

Water is precious. You know, you can save outside by landscaping with drought tolerant plants and cut off half of your residential use. Find out more at water education dot org.

PSA 7: Richard Marx, rock musician (60 seconds)

The speaker in this PSA hesitates, starts over, and uses incomplete sentences at times.

Rock musician, composer, and producer Richard Marx is not an opera buff. But that doesn't mean he didn't once learn to appreciate it.

When I was in high school, every year we had a an opera, so we had a Gilbert and Sullivan[1] opera. It was the school tradition. And I remember back then begging the music people to please just for once do something different. Let's do *Rocky Horror*.[2] They didn't like that idea. And of course now, I look back on it and I think well, you know, at least they did something. You know what I mean, we had a . . . an opera to do every year and all, the whole school got involved. And so I look back on it now and I applaud them for putting us through that music because I still remember a lot of those shows 'n' and I'm sure maybe some sliver of it affected me, you know, in one of the songs I've written. But I look back on it now and think it was a good thing because there's so much of it missing in schools now.

[1] Gilbert and Sullivan were popular British light opera composers of the late 19th and early 20th centuries.
[2] *Rocky Horror* was a British pop music experimental stage performance and film of the 1970s.

pronunciation reminder	Commas and periods give clues about where to use intonation to end thought groups. However, speakers frequently punctuate speech with thought groups *not* shown by written punctuation.

e. Final Talk: "A Special Celebration"

People everywhere gather to observe significant occasions, such as birthdays, weddings, funerals, and national and religious holidays, very often with special food, dress, or rituals.

> Give a 2–3 minute talk about one specific celebration that you remember and what it meant to you. Bring pictures or objects to help describe the experience. Your talk should have these parts:

- **A brief introduction: A few sentences.** Tell the **main idea** about the history and importance of the celebration. Describe any special foods, rituals, music, clothes, gifts, or other activities.

- **The body of your talk: The biggest part.** Describe in detail a specific celebration that you remember. Where were you living? How old were you? Who was there?

Example One of my earliest <u>memories</u> / was when my grandfather <u>died</u>. / After the service at our (<u>church/synagogue/temple/mosque</u>), / family and friends gathered <u>together</u> / and talked about things we <u>remembered</u> about him.

- **A conclusion: Two or three sentences.**

1. Write sample sentences from your talk including the opening sentence, three or four new ideas, and a conclusion. Underline the focus words and draw slashes to show the thought groups.

Example When I was a <u>little</u>, / I always looked forward to my <u>birthday</u>. / The whole family enjoyed being <u>together</u>, / but I was the center of <u>attention</u>.

2. Make a list of any challenging words from your talk with more than one syllable. Draw a dot over the stressed syllable. Draw the stress pattern.

3. Go to the *Targeting Pronunciation* student website, chapter 12, for additional exercises for preparing your talk.

4. Use a tape recorder to practice and time your talk. Re-record until you are satisfied. Decide the targets you will monitor for, and announce these to the class before you give your talk. Look at the components of an effective talk on the Checklist for Talks on the student website for things to consider as you plan and practice your talk.

a helpful hint If you know you will be making a presentation in a class or at a meeting, allowing enough time to plan ahead and practice can make the difference between a good and a poor presentation. Plan what you will say, but talk from notes made up of key focus words. Make sure the pronunciation of these key words is correct. Use a tape recorder to prepare your talk. Monitor carefully, decide what you want to improve, and make another recording.

f. Join the Chorus: "Pronunciation Rap"

Listen and then sing along. Move your hand or your foot to keep up with the rhythm. Work with a group to learn one verse to chant for the class. Practice with your group until you sound like one voice.

1. If you want to speak English in a way that's cool

    Put it in your body as you learn each rule,

    Tap the rhythm and feel the beat

    Put that language in your feet

Chorus

>   (And) Practice—It's the only way.
>
>   Make small talk—every day.
>
>   (I said) Practice—It's the only way.
>
>   Make small talk—every day.

2. Whether you whisper, whether you shout

    Stress that syllable, stretch it out

    Ice cream in the <u>desert</u> makes a great des<u>sert.</u>

    Pre<u>sent</u> me with a <u>present</u> of a brand new shirt.

3. Reduce those "of's" and reduce those "and's"

    Have a cup o' coffee, Wash your face 'n' hands

    Drop that "h" when you *give 'er a kiss,*

    With all this rhyming, you just can't miss!

Chorus

4. Remember to link those final "s's."

    Add those endings, no more guesses.

    She likes apples while she sits on beaches.

    When <u>he's</u> hungry he goes for peaches.

5. "E-d" endings must be clear.

   Shout them out for all to hear!

   And, when is it *posted,* when is it picked?

   When is it *toasted*, when is it ticked?

Chorus

6. Articulate!—And you'll do great

   You won't say *A* when you mean to say *eight.*

   You won't get *Kay,* when you want to get *cake*

   (See the difference a sound can make!)

7. Put in pauses, where they need to go

   Change those pitches—make 'em high, make 'em low

   Start rapping and tapping, and you'll feel grand

   'cause when you talk, they'll understand!

Chorus

8. Well, that's the way to get things done—

   Ten parts rhythm, and ten parts fun.

   In the shower, and in your bed,

   Practice intonation till it fills your head!

   SISTERS AND BROTHERS, GET INTO THE FLOW—
   INTONATION IS THE WAY TO GO!!
   —Ellen Stein

© Ellen Stein, 1997 DR. GOOSE MUSIC, Inc. Used by permission.

FINISHING UP

Making Your New Pronunciation a Habit

Talk Times in Class

Partner A is shopping by phone, either from a mail-order catalog store or a Web store. Partner B is the sales representative who answers the phone.

1. Select the item that you want to buy. Make a list of possible questions, such as about the availability of an item, colors in stock, accuracy of sizes, the shipping time, how to place an order. Decide what the service rep might ask, such as the credit card number. Look at the sample order page from a catalog.

 2. Listen to the sample conversation. Draw slashes where you hear the end of thought groups. Underline the focus words. See the first sentence in the dialogue as an example.

Ordering a New VCR

A: I'd like to order the VC<u>R</u> / on page 198 of your <u>catalog</u>. / How much does it <u>cost</u>?

B: We're having a special this month on VCRs. That one is one hundred forty-five dollars and ninety-nine cents ($145.99). The shipping is about fifteen dollars ($15), depending on where you are. How would you like to pay for this? By check or credit card?

A: Credit card.

B: I'm going to need your credit card number and a shipping address. May I have the type of card and the card number first, please.

A: Wells Fargo MasterCard number 555**2** 949**1** 216**8** 917**8**.

B: Let me repeat the number. Is it 5532 . . .

A: No. The first four digits are 5552.

B: OK. 5552 9491 2168 9178. What's the expiration date?

A: Uh-oh! I think this card has expired. I'm sorry, but I'll have to call you back later.

Practice saying the dialogue with a partner. Monitor for thought groups and focus words. Switch roles.

Talk Times in Your Daily Life: Shopping by phone

Make several phone calls to the toll-free numbers listed on the backs of the catalogs or on the website that you are shopping from.

1. Write out questions to get information about items you're interested in, such as articles of clothing, things for the house and garden, books, electronic equipment, and so on. It is not necessary to place an order. Explain that you are getting information, thank the person, and say that you will call back later.

2. Use a tape recorder in the room to record your part of each conversation. You will **not** be recording the clerk's voice. Listen to the tape and assess your targets to improve the next call.

On Your Own

1. **Audio program.** Listen to chapter 12.

2. **Recorded practice/glossary.** Make a recording of twenty of your glossary words to turn in to your instructor. Say the word and use it in a short phrase or sentence. Use the correct pronunciation.

3. Track the PSAs in this chapter until you can say them with the speakers.

UNIT V PROGRESS CHECK

1. Prepare your own public service announcement, or PSA, based on information in a newspaper, magazine, or Internet source of your choice. Your PSA should be 45–60 seconds long. The purpose of a PSA is to inform, but a PSA may also try to persuade the listener to take action. In addition to the PSAs in chapters 11 and 12, you can listen to other examples on the *Targeting Pronunciation* website

2. Use thought group signals, a slow speech rate, and melody variation to make the information easy to follow and interesting. Use a tape recorder to prepare and time your announcement. Monitor for any targets you know are important to your speech. Review the list of targets on page 2. Report on the tape which targets you monitored.

3. Submit your tape for review or schedule a review conference with the instructor.

WHAT'S NEXT?

Congratulations! You now have a better understanding of how to pronounce English more clearly. Perhaps you have changed some of the ways you pronounce English and have increased your comfort level when speaking. Examine your progress.

1. Your instructor will administer the *Listening to English* Survey that you took at the beginning of the course and provide the answers so that you can score your survey. Compare your listening scores.

    Pre-course listening score _____   Post-course listening score _____

2. Fill out the following questionnaire to rate your progress and your effort

Assess Your Progress

Circle 1, 2, or 3   1 = Not at all true   2 = Somewhat true   3 = Definitely true

1. I learned a lot about English pronunciation and what it sounds like.	1–2–3
2. I can understand conversations in English more easily.	1–2–3
3. People seem to understand my speech more easily.	1–2–3
4. I have more confidence speaking English and my comfort level has increased.	1–2–3
5. I learned strategies for making my speech easier to understand if I am asked to repeat something in a conversation.	1–2–3
6. I know what my personal pronunciation targets are and which targets I need to improve.	1–2–3
7. I can discover many of my own pronunciation errors when listening to my taped speech.	1–2–3

8. I am better able to monitor my pronunciation when I practice and during conversations. 1–2–3

9. I can communicate more effectively in situations that are difficult for me. 1–2–3

10. I feel that I still have more work to do on my pronunciation, but I can see that I have made progress. 1–2–3

Assess Your Effort

1. I practiced on my own with the tapes almost every day for 10–20 minutes. 1–2–3

2. I made small talk in English frequently. 1–2–3

3. I completed the Talk Times assignments. 1–2–3

4. I attended class regularly and participated in the activities. 1–2–3

5. I looked for native speakers to converse with. 1–2–3

6. I used a tape recorder or video recorder to help improve my pronunciation. 1–2–3

7. I became familiar with the sound of my own voice on tape. 1–2–3

8. I improved my monitoring skills by paying attention to my pronunciation for brief periods every day. 1–2–3

9. I took responsibility for discovering my own errors and correcting them. 1–2–3

10. I remembered to congratulate myself for taking on the challenge of learning new ways to pronounce English. 1–2–3

Keep Working toward Your Speech Goals

Your pronunciation will continue to improve over time. Gradually the changes become automatic. Copy and insert this "to do" list into your daily planner or calendar.

to do
1. Set aside short, regular practice times to review the book and audio program.
2. Keep collecting glossary words and find out how to pronounce them.
3. Continue mirroring TV programs and native speakers. Try "silent" mirroring in your head.
4. Speak English as much as possible and self-monitor for your pronunciation targets.
5. Be patient and have fun.

Appendix A

Consonants

The exercises in this appendix provide extra practice with consonant sounds that many nonnative speakers find challenging. The answers to the exercises are in the Answer Key.

Sound symbols
The sound symbols written inside gray boxes throughout the text stand for sounds. Each boxed symbol always sounds the same, regardless of how the word is spelled. For example, k is the first sound of the words *key* and *cat* and the last sound in the words *hike* and *ache*. s is the first sound of the word *city* and the last sound of the word *mice*. In English, one letter can have different sounds, and different letters can have the same sound.

See the Key to Symbols, page xiii, for the twenty-four *Targeting Pronunciation* sound symbols.

Voicing
There are different ways to describe consonant sounds. One way is to describe where they are made. Another way is to describe whether they are voiced or voiceless. The vocal cords vibrate when you say voiced sounds. See chapter 8 to review voicing and where sounds are made. Voicing is shown by a squiggly line drawn under the boxed sound symbol.

Consonants introduced in chapters 8 and 9 are divided into the following five target groups for additional practice.

Target 1: f and v

a. Improve Your Monitoring: f and p

1. Listen to each sentence. Decide whether the speaker says the underlined word that starts with an f sound or substitutes a similar word with a p sound. Check (✓) the word you hear.

Example They tried to <u>fool</u> us.	____ fool	_✓_ pool
1. The sun <u>feels</u> very hot today.	____ feels	____ peels
2. He works too <u>fast</u>.	____ fast	____ past
3. The <u>fact</u> of the matter is that he can't sing.	____ fact	____ pact
4. She's <u>fine</u> now.	____ fine	____ pine
5. It's a <u>fashion</u> magazine.	____ fashion	____ passion
6. The bus <u>fare</u> went up.	____ fare	____ pear

A-1

2. Practice saying the sentences correctly. Self-monitor. Copy the intonation as well as the sounds.

b. Contrast f and p (voiceless)

p stops the air at the lips. f is a continuant. The air keeps flowing. Review stops and continuants in chapter 8.

1. Listen to the sentences. Then practice saying them. Remember to keep your lips open for f and to close your lips for p.

   1. fool–pool   Jim acted like a <u>f</u>ool. Jim swam in the <u>p</u>ool.
   2. fashion–passion   The actor's clothes are in <u>f</u>ashion. The actor shows a lot of <u>p</u>assion.
   3. fast–past   My watch is a little fast. The time is half-<u>p</u>ast four.
   4. fine–pine   I'm <u>f</u>ine, thank you. Look at the <u>p</u>ine tree.
   5. beef–beep   The <u>b</u>eef is cooking. There's a <u>b</u>eep on the <u>ph</u>one.
   6. leaf–leap   The <u>l</u>eaf is green. Can you <u>l</u>eap across?
   7. laughed–lapped   The boy <u>l</u>aughed at the puppy. The puppy <u>l</u>apped up the water.

2. Write three words that start with f that you use in your everyday speech. Practice them in sentences. Monitor for f.

   _____   _____   _____

c. Contrast b and v (voiced)

1. Listen to the sentences.

   1. berry–very   I like **b**erry pie. I am **v**ery sure.
   2. ban–van   They ordered a **b**an on smoking. Our **v**an broke down.
   3. bet–vet   I **b**et the stores are closed. We took our cat to the **v**et.
   4. bent–vent   The coat hanger got **b**ent. Air conditioning comes through a **v**ent.
   5. boat–vote   The **b**oat left the harbor. I plan to **v**ote in the election.

2. Replay the tape. Repeat each word three times. Then say the sentence.

Example   base–base–base   The **b**ase is made of wood.

              vase–vase–vase   The **v**ase is made of glass.

d. Practice f and v (continuants)

Say the words and phrases. Monitor for f and v.

Verbs	Phrases	Nouns	Phrases
fill	fill the gas tank	fingers	five fingers
fix	fix the flat tire	fame	fame and fortune
forget	forget it	phone	a new phone number
finish	finish the job	favor	do a favor
afford	I can't afford it.	visa	a travel visa
drive	Drive carefully.	divorce	filed for divorce
violate	violate the law	vitamin	Vitamin C
avoid	avoid a penalty	vinegar	vinegar and oil dressing
divide	divide the assets	video	rent a video
prevent	prevent crime	vacancy	Is there a vacancy?

pronunciation tip Unusual spellings for f: **ph**one **phi**losophy geogra**phy** gra**ph** lau**gh**

e. Compare w and v: "Do You Like Westerns?"

1. Before you begin, review the pronunciation and the drawings for w and v on page 157. Listen to the paragraph and fill in the missing words. These are listed below in alphabetical order. Some words appear more than once.

   eventually, evil (2), favorite, save, unwelcome, villain (2), walk, weather, well, Western, Westerns (2), western, when, whoever, why, wins, world's

   The _____ is one of the _____ _____ kinds of film. It is a classic struggle between good and _____ set in a small _____ town in the nineteenth century. The typical town has dirt streets, a cemetery, a saloon, and a general store. Regardless of the _____ a stranger rides into town just in time to _____ its citizens from a cruel, _____ _____. _____, after all kinds of danger and humiliation, the hero confronts the _____ in a "shoot-out." _____ has the fastest draw—that it is to say, whoever pulls his gun most quickly—shoots the other. In _____, after much pain and suffering, the good guy usually _____. That's part of the reason _____ _____ are _____-liked. Good triumphs over _____, and people feel happy _____ they _____ out of the theater.

2. Listen to the paragraph again and underline the focus words. Track the speaker. Say the paragraph monitoring for w and v.

Target 2: Voiced and Voiceless "th"

To review these sounds, see chapter 8. θ and ð are relaxed sounds. The air flows gently over the tongue. If there is too much tension in your tongue when you say "th," it will squeeze the air and sound like an s or z. If your tongue pushes against your gum ridge and the air stops, the "th" becomes a t or a d. If you squeeze your tongue too hard, "the" can sound like "zuh" or "duh." "There" can sound like "zere" or "dare."

f. Stops and Continuants: d and ð

Stop the air at the gum ridge for d. Allow the air to flow out for ð.

1. Practice saying the words and sentences. Contrast d and ð.

1. **day–they**   It was a sunny **d**ay. **Th**ey waited outside.
2. **den–then**   We can meet at the Lion's **D**en. **Th**en we'll have lunch.
3. **doze–those**   Did you **d**oze during **th**e lecture? **Th**ose notes are not complete.
4. **dare–there**   He wouldn't **d**are miss it. **Th**ere he is.
5. **ladder–lather** It is hard to climb up a la**dd**er if your hands are full of la**th**er.

2. Repeat each word five times. Then say the sentence. Remember to keep your mouth relaxed for ð. Feel the difference between the stop and the continuant.

Example   day–day–day–day–day   It was a sunny **d**ay.

they–they–they–they–they   **Th**ey waited outside.

3. Practice these voiced "th" words. Then say them in sentences. Many common ð words are unstressed.

this   **th**e   **th**at   **th**ese   **th**em   **th**ose   Brea**th**e in.   **Th**at was a smooth ride.

g. Contrast θ and s (voiceless)

These sounds are both continuants. The difference is that the air flows out gently for θ. The air squeezes out and makes a hissing sound for s.

1. Listen to the word pairs and sentences several times. Contrast s and θ.

1. **sum–thumb**   The **s**um of 4 and 3 is 7.   She hurt her **th**umb.
2. **sink–think**   I hope the boat won't **s**ink.   I'm trying not to **th**ink about it.

3. worse–worth His flu is much worse. It's not worth it.

4. sank–thank My heart sank when I heard the news. Thank you for your help.

5. sick–thick She's been sick all week. It's a thick book.

2. Replay the tape. Repeat each word five times. Then say the sentence. Feel the difference between the air flowing out gently for θ and the air hissing out for s.

Example sum–sum–sum–sum–sum The sum of 4 and 3 is 7.

thumb–thumb–thumb–thumb–thumb She hurt her thumb.

3. Practice saying the voiceless "th" in ordinal numbers.

the ninth grade   the fourth floor   the seventh day of the week
the tenth of the month

Target 3: Sibilants

The basic hissing and buzzing sounds are s and z. Other sibilants are related to these. Pronunciation problems with sibilants often come from the following:

1. Voicing. Some people switch s and z.

2. Omitting these sounds at the ends of words or when they are part of a consonant cluster.

3. Spelling. Predicting pronunciation from spelling is not easy because letters do not always sound the same in all words. (See the *Targeting Pronunciation* webpage for more tips about spelling.)

s

Practice words with s spelled in different ways.

1. Most common spelling at the beginning of words: **s**

Examples   soup   sip   said   sun

2. Less common spelling at the beginning of words: **c sc**

Examples   cent   century   science

3. At the ends of words: **s ce se ss**

Examples   makes   courteous   peace   house   mess

z

Practice the following examples of different ways to spell z at the ends of words. Lengthen the vowel before all the voiced final z sounds.

Examples   plays   praise   prize

s ze: plays the piano   My toes froze.   the grand prize

se: Did you choose it?   Can you use it?   Did you lose it?   Pause and raise your hand.

h. Paragraph

1. Listen to the paragraph about James. You will hear many common words that are spelled with an "s" but pronounced with a z. Pay attention to the linking.

   James was always a good student. He has a high GPA (grade point average). He's planning to go to graduate school soon. James shows every sign of success. He's friendly and polite, and he does good work. James is a busy guy! He has a daytime job, goes to school at night, raises orchids, and plays in a band.

2. Practice saying the paragraph one line at a time. After you have practiced, say the paragraph looking away from your book. Pretend you are telling someone about James.

ʃ + tʃ and dʒ ("sh", "ch", and "j")

Review how to say these sibilant sounds in chapter 9 on page 188.

ʃ ("sh")

1. Say s and slide your tongue back to say ʃ. Sh! The baby's sleeping. Sh!

2. Listen and repeat the words and phrases.

   Contrast s and ʃ. Sue–shoe same–shame sip–ship

   finish talking   foolish question   Spanish food   Danish pastry

3. Practice saying the following words with ʃ. Lengthen the stressed syllable with the dot over it. These letter combinations can all sound like ʃ ti ci ch ss tion

shortage	shoulder	shiny	shampoo
machine	permission	patient	social
English	Spanish	Swedish	foolish
nation	fiction	aviation	action

tʃ and dʒ ("ch" and "j")

1. Move your tongue from one sound to another to pronounce these combination sounds.

   t + ʃ → tʃ   This sound is often spelled with "ch."

   d + ʒ → dʒ   This sound is often spelled with "j."

2. Listen and repeat the words and phrases.

   ch   choke chain charity watch out catch it reach over
         Which arrived? peach pie

   j   joke Jane Germany joy page eleven wage increase
         MANage MONey badge of honor

i. Improve Your Monitoring: sh and ch

Listen to the words. Check (✓) the sound you hear. Then practice. Use the words in sentences. Monitor for ʃ and tʃ.

Example cash–catch   ✓ sh   ____ ch

1. ship–chip   ____ sh   ____ ch
2. sheer–cheer   ____ sh   ____ ch
3. sheet–cheat   ____ sh   ____ ch
4. dish–ditch   ____ sh   ____ ch
5. wash–watch   ____ sh   ____ ch
6. mush–much   ____ sh   ____ ch

j. Improve Your Monitoring

1. Listen to each of the sentences. Decide whether the speaker says the underlined word or substitutes a similar word with a different sound. Check (✓) the word you hear.

1. Please have a <u>chair</u> while you wait.   ____ share   ____ chair
2. I'd like some <u>chips</u> with my lunch.   ____ ships   ____ chips
3. I'd like to <u>wish</u> you good luck.   ____ wish   ____ witch
4. I <u>watched</u> the basketball game.   ____ washed   ____ watched
5. Can you <u>cash</u> this check?   ____ cash   ____ catch
6. Did you <u>catch</u> a fish?   ____ cash   ____ catch
7. Jane dressed up as a <u>witch</u> for Halloween.   ____ wish   ____ witch
8. The <u>ditch</u> is full of dirt.   ____ dish   ____ ditch

2. Practice saying the sentences correctly. Self-monitor for intonation and for sounds.

Another Sibilant: "x"

1. To say "x" link two sounds. k + s → "x." English words do not start with an "x" sound.

2. Listen and then practice saying "x" in the following words and phrases. Monitor for the k + s combination.

fix   six   tax   trucks   picks   cooks   shakes   explain   extra   exercise

mix up   box of candy   tax deduction   fax modem   "X"-rated movie   backs up

3. "cc" is often pronounced k s. Practice the following examples.

accept   I'm happy to accept your invitation.

accent   I'm learning a new accent.

succeed   You can't succeed without trying.

vaccine   There is a vaccine for many diseases.

accident There was an accident at the corner.

Target 4: r and w

Review w, r, and vowel + r. See pages 157, 164, and 166.

k. Improve Your Monitoring: r and w

1. Listen to the following words contrasting r and w.

   ride–wide   right–white   red–wed   ray–way   raid–weighed

   Listen to sentence (a) or (b). Check (✓) the sentence you hear. Say the sentences.

   Example   ____ It's a long ray.   ✓ It's a long way.

   1. ____ a. Be sure to take the <u>right</u> hat.   ____ b. Be sure to take the <u>white</u> hat.
   2. ____ a. I paid according to the <u>rate</u>.   ____ b. I paid according to the <u>weight</u>.
   3. ____ a. We saw the <u>ray</u> through the window.   ____ b. We saw the <u>way</u> through the window.
   4. ____ a. I didn't like the <u>rage</u>.   ____ b. I didn't like the <u>wage</u>.
   5. ____ a. Let's travel to see the <u>rest</u>.   ____ b. Let's travel to see the <u>West</u>.

l. Improve Your Monitoring: r and l

ride–lied   right–light   red–led   ray–lay   raid–laid

Listen to sentence (a) or (b). Check (✓) the sentence you hear. Say the sentences.

1. ____ a. Did you find the <u>rake</u>?   ____ b. Did you find the <u>lake</u>?
2. ____ a. Take the <u>right</u> backpack.   ____ b. Take the <u>light</u> backpack.
3. ____ a. I finished the <u>race</u> first.   ____ b. I finished the <u>lace</u> first.
4. ____ a. The <u>road</u> was full of bricks.   ____ b. The <u>load</u> was full of bricks.
5. ____ a. I got ink on my <u>wrist</u>.   ____ b. I got ink on my <u>list</u>.

m. Common r and l Words

Practice these words with r and l and use them in sentences. Self-monitor and decide which r and l words are easy or hard for you. Practice the easy ones first.

Plants: flowers   grass   trees   roses   orchids   lilies   tulips   iris

Adjectives: right   real   raw   rusty   long   low   lovely   little

Computer words: monitor   chooser   printer   ruler   hard drive   keyboard   spell check   scroll bar

Verbs: rent   wrap   read   rake   like   leave   laugh   love

Nouns: rope   ring   rug   rose   lamp   life   load   lemon

Names: Randy   Ruth   Robert   Ralph   Laurie   Larry   Lillian   Alice

Fruit: grapes   oranges   tangerines   apricots   lemons   apples   plums   melons

n. Vowel + r

Some r sounds come after vowels. Notice the spelling variations on the following lists

Listen to the first three words in each list. Use the sound of these words to figure out the pronunciation of the rest of the list. Say the words.

1. iʸ + r   2. eʸ + r   3. a + r   4. ɔʷ + r   5. aʸ + r   6. aʷ + r

here	air	far	four	fire	our
ear	fair	heart	pour	hire	sour
fear	there	park	door	dryer	flour
NEARly	VEry	sharp	more	wire	TOWer
EARPHONE	VARious	BARgain	ORder	reTIRE	FOWer
YEARly	MERry	ARgue	STORy	adMIRE	fLOWer
apPEAR	CAREful	PARty	ORganize	reQUIRE	SHOWer

pronunciation tip   Take your time. Glide from the vowel to the r and give yourself time to tighten and curl your tongue when you get to the r. Round your lips.

---

o. Paragraph

Listen to the paragraph and write the missing r and l words. Replay the tape several times and practice one line at a time. Then say the whole paragraph.

Learning to Drive

I first learned to _____ a _____ when I was about _____ or

fourteen _____ old. I was too young to get a _____ license, but my older

brother _____ used to _____ me _____ driving his

_____. We would go over to the _____ in back of the _____

Market after the _____ closed. I would _____ around and _____

in circles. Sometimes we would _____ out to the _____ where the

_____ were deserted, and Larry would _____ me loose.[1] My

_____ never found out about it until _____ later. By then it was too

_____. I already had my driver's license and _____ had graduated from

college and was _____ in California.

[1] Let loose: to set free.

Target 5: Consonant Clusters

Practice pronouncing consonants when they are linked in clusters, either in individual words or across word boundaries. Review chapter 10, page 00.

p. Improve Your Monitoring: r and l clusters

1. Listen to the words contrasting **r** and **l**.

crown–**cl**own   **cr**ime–**cl**imb   **fl**ows–**fr**oze   **cr**owd–**cl**oud   **gr**ass–**gl**ass

2. Listen to sentence (a) or (b). Check (✓) the sentence you hear. Practice saying the sentences.

Example	✓ a. The children **pl**ayed at the church.	___ b. The children **pr**ayed at the church.
1.	___ a. I saw a picture of a **cr**own.	___ b. I saw a picture of a **cl**own.
2.	___ a. It's a major **cr**ime.	___ b. It's a major **cl**imb.
3.	___ a. The river **fl**ows all winter.	___ b. The river **fr**oze all winter.
4.	___ a. There's a **cr**owd in the distance.	___ b. There's a **cl**oud in the distance.
5.	___ a. The **gr**ass is wet.	___ b. The **gl**ass is wet.

q. More r and l Clusters

1. Practice saying the words and sentences. Monitor the clusters and the linking.

fr: **fr**iend **fr**uit **fr**equently	My **fr**iend **fr**equently gives me **fr**esh **fr**uit.
tr: **tr**ue **tr**avel **tr**uck	It's **tr**ue that we **tr**aveled by **tr**uck.
br: **br**ought **br**own **br**iefcase	My **br**other **br**ought his **br**own **br**iefcase.
cr: **cr**ib **cr**azy **cr**edit	We were **cr**azy about the **cr**ib and paid for it with a **cr**edit card.
dr: **dr**op **dr**apes **dr**y cleaners	I **dr**opped off my **dr**apes at the **dr**y cleaners.
thr: **thr**ee **thr**ew **thr**eaten	The pitcher **thr**ew **thr**ee good pitches in a row.
str: **str**eet **str**ipe **str**aight	They painted a **str**aight **str**ipe on the **str**eet.
bl: **bl**ack **bl**ue **bl**ock	Her knee was **bl**ack and **bl**ue after tripping on the **bl**ock.
pl: **pl**an **pl**easant **pl**ay	We **pl**an to see a **pl**easant **pl**ay.
fl: **fl**oated **fl**ash **fl**ood	The car **fl**oated away during the **fl**ash **fl**ood.

2. Practice saying sentences with these words.

Nouns: **cr**eam **dr**ugs **fl**ag **fl**avor **fl**ower

Verbs: t**r**ust **dr**eam **dr**ive **bl**ame **bl**ow

r. Clusters across Word Boundaries

Say the following compound nouns and descriptive phrases along with the speaker on the tape. Then say them in sentences. Make sure that you finish all the words and say all the underlined consonant clusters.

Compound Nouns	**Descriptive Phrases**
BA<u>CK</u>PACK	CHEA<u>P</u> **<u>SH</u>IRT**
CHE<u>CK</u>BOOK	COLleg<u>e</u> **<u>FR</u>ESH**man
COMi<u>c</u> <u>B</u>OOKS	DRU<u>NK</u> **<u>DR</u>IV**er
DA<u>NCE</u> <u>GR</u>OUPS	ecoNOmi<u>c</u> **<u>PR</u>O**gress
HEA<u>LTH</u> <u>C</u>LUB	FINa<u>l</u> **<u>RE</u>**port
HOU<u>SE</u> <u>K</u>EY	HELPi<u>ng</u> **<u>H</u>AND**
inSUR<u>ance</u> <u>C</u>OMpany	HUma<u>n</u> **<u>B</u>E**ing
PAPe<u>r</u> <u>J</u>AM	presiDENtia<u>l</u> **<u>P</u>OL**itics
PRE<u>SS</u> <u>C</u>ARD	PREviou<u>s</u> **<u>B</u>ILL**
rePO<u>RT</u> <u>C</u>ARDS	RI<u>CH</u> **<u>FL</u>AV**ors
SPIde<u>r</u> <u>W</u>EB	ROA<u>D</u> **<u>CL</u>OSED**
SU<u>NSCR</u>een	WELco<u>me</u> **<u>H</u>OME**

Appendix B

Vowels

This appendix provides extra practice with vowel sounds that many learners have difficulty pronouncing. The answers are in the Answer Key.

Introducing Fifteen Vowels: Vowel Chart

The following chart shows the fifteen clear vowel sounds that you hear in stressed syllables. The symbols for the vowel sounds are shown on the chart in gray boxes. You will need blue, orange, and yellow highlighters to complete your vowel chart.

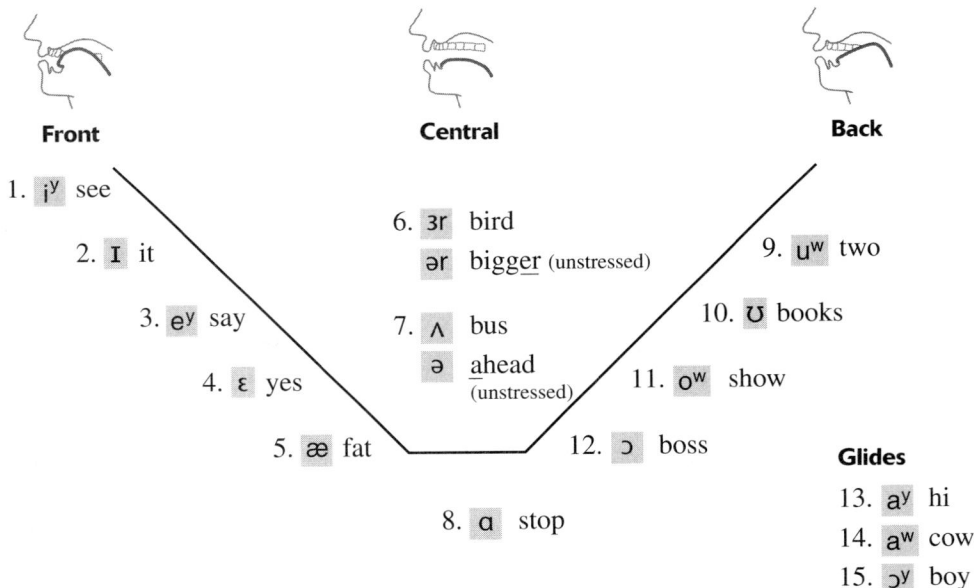

 Cover the box below with a piece of paper. Now listen and repeat fifteen clear vowels in key words and phrases without seeing the words.

1 2	3 4	5 6	7 8	9 10
SEE IT	SAY YES	a FAT BIRD	at a BUS STOP	TWO BOOKS
11	12	13 14 15		
SHOW the BOSS		HI COWBOY		

Long Vowels: Vowels That Glide

Review long vowels on page 109. The drawings there show the gliding movement for these vowels. Take your time when saying a long vowel.

Listen and repeat the word pairs. Contrast the short vowel ʌ in *but* with five long vowel words.

but–bake   but–beak   but–bike   but–boat   but–boot

a. Five Long Vowels: eʸ (say), iʸ (see), aʸ (hi), oʷ (show), uʷ (two)

These five long vowels are easy to recognize because they sound like the names of the alphabet letters "a," "e," "i," "o," and "u."

1. Listen and practice saying words and phrases with five long vowels.

- To say eʸ, start with "eh." Then slowly glide the middle of your tongue forward to start the word "y–es." Feel your tongue glide and tense. Whisper the key word: **SAY**

   Examples   "A"   stay   day   eight   stay all day   a late date   a pay raise

- To say iʸ, rest your tongue tip behind your lower front teeth and push the middle of your tongue forward toward your top teeth and then tense it. Whisper the key word: **SEE**

   Examples   "E"   we   me   tea   green tea   sweet dreams   He seemed pleased to see me.

- To say aʸ, start with ɑ. Then slowly glide the middle of your tongue forward to start to say the word "y–es." Feel it tense. Whisper the key word: **HI**

   Examples   "I"   tie   my   eye   five ties   light in my eyes   The pie was a surprise.

- To say oʷ, pull your tongue toward the back of your mouth. Flatten your tongue and glide it further back. Tense your tongue and round your lips gently. Whisper the key word: **SHOW**

   Examples   "O"   go   note   own   Oh, no!   My toes froze!   So it goes!

- To say uʷ, pull your tongue to the back of your mouth and up. Tense it. Round your lips slightly. Whisper the key word: **TWO**

   Examples   "U"   shoe   blue   moon   Move the new shoes.   Excuse me.   May I have a soup spoon?

2. For this exercise, let your tongue do the work. Rest your tongue tip behind your lower teeth. Push the middle of your tongue forward to whisper iʸ. Then pull it back to whisper oʷ. Alternate between iʸ and oʷ. Feel your tongue glide forward and tense for iʸ and glide back and tense for oʷ, moving your lips as little as possible. Whisper   EʸO   EʸO   EʸO

3. Color the long vowels on the vowel chart (numbers 1, 3, 9, 11, and 13) with a blue highlighter pen. The two symbols for these vowels show where your tongue glides as you say them.

b. Two More Long Vowels: a^w (cow) and $ɔ^y$ (boy)

Vowels 14 and 15 glide a longer distance than the other long vowels. They are often called *diphthongs*. Notice the spelling variations.

1. Listen and repeat words and phrases for two more long vowels.

- To say a^w, start with "ah." Glide to the "w" with your lips rounded. Whisper the key word: **COW**.

Examples   d**ow**nt**ow**n   ar**ou**nd the f**ou**ntain   a l**ou**d s**ou**nd

- To say $ɔ^y$, start with $ɔ$ and glide the beginning of the word "y–es." Tense your tongue. Spread your lips slightly. Whisper the key word: **BOY**

Examples   The b**oy** found his t**oy**.   Av**oi**d sp**oi**led milk.   Destr**oy** the p**oi**son.

2. Color vowels 14 and 15 blue along with the other long vowels.

Short Vowels: Vowels That Don't Glide

Review short vowels on page 111 and the drawings for $ɛ$, $æ$, and $ʊ$ on page 112. Careful listening is the way to improve your vowel pronunciation.

 Listen to the word pairs. Contrast *but* $ʌ$ with seven other words with short vowels.

but–bit   but–bet   but–bat   but–bird   but–top   but–book   but–bought

 c. Six Short Vowels: $ɪ$ (it), $ɛ$ (yes), $æ$ (fat), $ʌ$ (bus), $ɑ$ (stop), $ʊ$ (books), $ɔ$ (boss)

These six vowels take less time to say than the long vowels because they don't glide. For this reason, they are called *short vowels*.

1. Listen and repeat the phrases. The words with short vowels are underlined.

SEE <u>IT</u>   SAY <u>YES</u>   a <u>FAT</u> BIRD   at a <u>BUS</u> <u>STOP</u>   TWO <u>BOOKS</u>   SHOW the <u>BOSS</u>   HI COWBOY

2. On the vowel chart, color the six short vowels—numbers 2, 4, 5, 8, 10, and 12—with an orange highlighter. You have now colored eleven of the fifteen vowels. The long vowels are blue. The short vowels are orange.

d. Contrast Short Vowels

Listen and repeat the words and sentences for the following short vowels. Then practice on your own. Monitor your speech carefully and make sure you are matching the speaker.

ʌ BUS and ɔ BOSS (Vowels 7 and 12)

1. cuff–cough   He has a <u>cuff</u> on his slacks.   He has a bad <u>cough</u>.
2. bus–boss   The <u>bus</u> is late again.   The <u>boss</u> is late again, too.
3. cut–caught   She <u>cut</u> it (her hand).   She <u>caught</u> it (the ball).
4. lung–long   They took an x-ray of her <u>lung</u>.   It took a <u>long</u> time.
5. gun–gone   The soldier has a <u>gun</u>.   The soldier is <u>gone</u>.

ʌ BUS and ʊ BOOKS (Vowels 7 and 10)

1. buck–book   He found a <u>buck</u> in his pocket.   He bought a <u>book</u>.
2. luck–look   Take a good <u>look</u>.   Lots of good <u>luck</u>.
3. tuck–took   <u>Tuck</u> in your tummy.   Are you sure you <u>took</u> it?

e. Improve Your Monitoring: ɛ (yes) and æ (fat) for vowels 4 and 5

1. First listen to the word pairs for vowels 4 and 5. Then listen to either sentence (a) or (b) below and check (✓) the sentence you hear.

mess–mass send–sand bend–band men–man pest–past kept–capped left–laughed guesses–gases

1. _____ a. There's a <u>mess</u> in the church.   _____ b. There's a <u>mass</u> in the church.
2. _____ a. Please <u>send</u> the table.   _____ b. Please <u>sand</u> the table.
3. _____ a. I'm waiting in line for <u>bread</u>.   _____ b. I'm waiting in line for <u>Brad</u>.
4. _____ a. The <u>men</u> waited for a cab.   _____ b. The <u>man</u> waited for a cab.
5. _____ a. The <u>pest</u> is gone forever.   _____ b. The <u>past</u> is gone forever.
6. _____ a. She <u>kept</u> the jar of jelly.   _____ b. She <u>capped</u> the jar of jelly.
7. _____ a. Everyone <u>left</u> after dinner.   _____ b. Everyone <u>laughed</u> after dinner.
8. _____ a. The chemist made some new <u>guesses</u>.   _____ b. The chemist made some new <u>gases</u>.

2. Say both sentences (a) and (b). Monitor for æ and ɛ.

3. Listen and repeat phrases with ɛ and æ.

ɛ : send a letter   best friend   confiDENtial MESsage   less ENergy

æ : have a match   PLAStic WRAPper   flat tax   a bad HABit   a fanTAStic chance

ɛ YES, æ FAT, and ɑ STOP. (Vowels 4, 5, and 8)

First listen and repeat the words contrasting ɑ, æ, and ɛ, then the sentences. Write the number of the vowel over the underlined words. Open your mouth more for ɑ than for the other vowels.

```
 4  5  8      4   5   8      4 5 8     4   5   8      4  5   8
pet–pat–pot  wreck–rack–rock "x"–ax–ox  den–Dan–Don  Ed–add–odd
```

1. <u>Pat</u> my <u>pet</u> dog and give him a <u>snack</u>.   There is <u>not</u> a <u>lot left</u> in the <u>pot</u>.
2. The <u>rocks wrecked</u> my car.   They put it on a <u>rack</u> to see the <u>damage</u>.
3. <u>Don</u> carved an <u>"x"</u> on the <u>ax hand</u>le.   <u>Tom watched</u> the <u>ox</u>.
4. <u>John</u> and <u>Sam sat</u> in the <u>den</u>.   <u>Sam asked John</u> about his <u>rock band</u>.
5. <u>Ed added</u> the <u>odd</u> numbers.   <u>Don</u> and <u>John added</u> the even ones.

Contrasts with Vowel + r

f. Contrast ɜr (bird) with ʌ (bus)

Short vowels 6 and 7 are called *central vowels* because the tongue stays in a neutral position without pushing forward (as for ɛ) or backward (as for ʊ). Vowel 8, ɑ, is also a central vowel.

- ɜr. Review how to say r in chapter 8, page 164. Curl and tense your tongue tip. This r comes after the ʌ vowel.

- ʌ is made like a schwa, but is stressed. Keep your tongue very relaxed. Open your lips slightly. Say "uh" without moving or tensing any part of your mouth.

1. Listen and repeat the word pairs and then the sentences.

bun–burn hut–hurt such–search shut–shirt ton–turn fun–fern gull–girl bud–bird

1. I'd like a hot dog on a <u>bun</u>.   Don't let the hot dog <u>burn</u>.
2. He lives in a <u>hut</u>.   He got <u>hurt</u>.
3. <u>Such</u> an interesting day!   <u>Search</u> the Internet.
4. <u>Button</u> it <u>shut</u>.   <u>Button</u> the <u>shirt</u>.
5. I have a <u>ton</u> of homework.   I have to <u>turn</u> it in tomorrow.

6. I have <u>fun</u> in my garden.		I have a <u>fern</u> in my garden.
7. The <u>gull</u> flew over the sand.		The <u>girl</u> sat on the sand.
8. Put the <u>bud</u> in a vase.		Put the <u>bird</u> in its nest.

2. Say the word pairs and the sentences. Monitor your speech.

3. Color the central vowels a different color.

g. Improve Your Monitoring

1. Listen and check (✓) the word you hear. Replay the tape to make sure.

Example	The business was <u>hurt</u> by a recession.	____ hurt	✓ hut
	The business was <u>hurt</u> by a recession.	✓ hurt	____ hut
1.	The <u>fern</u> was tall and green.	____ fern	____ fun
2.	The <u>search</u> party found the missing hiker.	____ search	____ such
3.	Don't <u>burn</u> the soup.	____ burn	____ bun
4.	Let's give everyone a <u>turn</u>.	____ turn	____ ton
5.	The <u>girl</u> decided to study Russian.	____ girl	____ gull

2. Practice saying the sentences correctly. Self-monitor for intonation as well as for sounds.

h. Learn about Shirley

1. Listen to the paragraph. The **3r** words are underlined. The bold type shows focus.

There is a <u>**GIRL**</u> named <u>**SHIR**</u>ley, and she's in the <u>third</u> **GRADE**. Her <u>personality</u> is quiet and re<u>**SERVED**</u>. <u>S</u>hirley's **MO**ther <u>works</u> as a <u>**NURSE**</u>, and <u>her</u> father <u>works</u> as an at<u>**TOR**ney</u>. They're often in a <u>**HUR**ry</u>, and they <u>worry</u> about <u>**SHIR**</u>ley. Shirley spends a lot of **TIME** with her pet <u>**GER**bil</u>.[1]

2. Practice saying the paragraph. Then answer the questions, looking away from the book.

Example   Who is <u>Shirley</u>?   <u>Shirley</u> is a <u>girl</u> with a pet <u>gerbil</u>.

1. What is the girl's name and what grade is she in?
2. What kind of personality does Shirley have?
3. What kind of work do her parents do?
4. What else do you know about Shirley's parents?
5. How does Shirley spend a lot of her time?

---

[1] **gerbil**: Pronounced JERbel. A small rodent similar to a mouse that is often kept as a pet.

i. Spelling Variations for ɝ

The following words have the same vowel sound although they are spelled with different letters. Listen to the first example for each spelling. Then say the words and monitor for ɝ.

"er"	"ir"	"ur"	"or"	"our"	"ear"
were	sir	turn	WORry	COURage	earth
PERfect	THIRsty	SURface	work	JOURnal	EARly
NERvous	CIRcle	HURry	word	JOURnalism	earn
eMERgency	THIRty	URgent	worse	adJOURN	heard
inTERpret	DIRty	ocCUR	WORKing	FLOURish	LEARNing

j. Other vowels + r

Although ɝ is the most common vowel + r combination, any clear vowel can be followed by an r.

Listen to the first three vowel + r words in each list. Use the sound of these words to figure out the pronunciation of the rest of the list. Note the spelling variations. Practice the words on each list by saying them in sentences.

1. i^y + r	2. e^y + r	3. a + r	4. o^w + r	5. a^y + r	6. a^w + r
here	air	far	four	fire	our
ear	fair	heart	pour	hire	sour
fear	there	park	door	dryer	flour
NEARly	VEry	sharp	more	wire	TOwer
EARPHONE	VARious	BARgain	ORder	reTIRE	POwer
YEARly	MERry	ARgue	SORT	adMIRE	FLOwer
apPEAR	CAREful	SORry	ORganize	reQUIRE	SHOwer

k. The Unstressed ɜr

Stressed and unstressed ɜr sounds vary with different English dialects. Some speakers curl their tongues very little and say an ɜr that is closer to a schwa.

Examples   BIGger ⟶ BIGgə   EASTern ⟶ EASTən

The majority of North American speakers, however, curl and tighten their tongues for this sound.

Listen and practice some examples.

Comparatives	BIGger	SMALler	HIGHer	LOWer
Jobs	SINGer	LAWyer	ACtor	inVENtor
Directions	EASTern	WESTern	NORTHern	SOUTHern
Nouns	MUStard	PEPper	RAzor	YOgurt
Family members	MOther	FAther	BROther	SISter

Long and Short Vowel Contrasts

l. Contrasting Word Pairs

Listen and repeat the words and sentences. Take your time and feel your tongue tighten for the long vowel. Even when you say long vowels quickly, you need to glide and tense your tongue.

1. ɪ rich   iʸ reach: Is the man <u>rich</u>? Can you <u>reach</u> the top?

    Don't say: Can you "rich" the top?

2. ɛ pen   eʸ pain: I have a <u>pen</u> on my desk. I have a <u>pain</u> in my foot.

    Don't say: I have a "pen" in my foot.

3. æ cat   aʸ kite: Sarah is petting her <u>cat</u>. Sarah is flying a <u>kite</u>.

    Don't say: Sarah is flying a "cat."

4. ɔ fawn   oʷ phone: The <u>fawn</u> is near its mother. The <u>phone</u> is ringing.

    Don't say: The "fawn" is ringing.

5. ʊ pull   uʷ pool: The hotel has a swimming <u>pool</u>. Can your car <u>pull</u> a trailer?

    Don't say: The hotel has a swimming "pull."

m. Contrasting iʸ (see) and ɪ (it) (Vowels 1 and 2)

To say both iʸ and ɪ, push the middle of your tongue toward the front of the mouth. For iʸ push your tongue further forward and then tense it. ɪ is a short vowel and does not glide or tense.

1. Listen and practice saying the words and phrases.

iʸ	reach the ceiling	easy teacher	season the pizza	the recent peace
ɪ	fix dinner	the kitchen window	finish the mystery quickly	busy women

2. Listen and repeat the rhyming words. Then say the phrases and add your own.

1.	seek	seek help		6.	sick	sick and tired
2.	peek	peek out of the window		7.	pick	pick the apples
3.	leak	leak in the roof		8.	wick	the burning candle wick
4.	week	_____		9.	Dick	_____
5.	meek	_____		10.	stick	_____

n. Improve Your Monitoring: iʸ and ɪ

1. Listen to either sentence (a) or (b). Check (✓) the appropriate response.

Example	a.	Don't <u>sleep</u> on the wet floor.	✓	Don't worry. I prefer my bed.
	b.	Don't <u>slip</u> on the wet floor.	____	Don't worry. I'll be careful.
1.	a.	She took the <u>lead</u>.	____	I hope she knows the way.
	b.	She took the <u>lid</u>.	____	I hope it fits the pot.
2.	a.	The <u>peach</u> is good.	____	Let's save it for lunch.
	b.	The <u>pitch</u> is good.	____	It sounds too high to me.
3.	a.	The dog <u>beat</u> him.	____	Dogs can run fast.
	b.	The dog <u>bit</u> him.	____	Dogs have sharp teeth.
4.	a.	Are you planning to <u>leave</u> here?	____	Yes. I'm taking the next plane.
	b.	Are you planning to <u>live</u> here?	____	Yes. I'm looking for an apartment.
5.	a.	What does <u>reach</u> mean?	____	You can touch it.
	b.	What does <u>rich</u> mean?	____	You've got a lot of money.

2. Practice saying the sentences correctly. Make iʸ and ɪ words sound different.

o. Improve Your Monitoring: Short and long vowels

1. Listen and repeat the word pairs.

men–main pills–peels pepper–paper Tom–time live–leave fawn–phone

2. Listen to each sentence. Check (✓) the word you hear, not the word you expect to hear. Then practice saying the sentences correctly.

1. The book's <u>main</u> idea was clever. _____ main _____ men
2. I bought some vitamin <u>pills</u>. _____ peels _____ pills
3. I put the pills in a <u>paper</u> bag. _____ paper _____ pepper
4. What <u>time</u> is it? _____ time _____ Tom
5. Andrew wants to <u>leave</u> the country. _____ leave _____ live
6. Please answer the <u>phone</u>. _____ phone _____ fawn

p. Improve Your Monitoring: e^y (say) and ε (yes)

1. Listen and repeat the word pairs contrasting vowels 3 and 4.

pepper–paper debt–date test–taste letter–later edge–age less–lace

2. Listen to either sentence (a) or (b). Check (✓) the sentence you hear. Then say both sentences (a) and (b). Make them sound different. Monitor your speech for e^y and ε.

Example a. I have a big <u>pen</u>. b. I have a big <u>pain</u>.

1. _____ a. Please pass the <u>pepper</u>.   _____ b. Please pass the <u>paper</u>.
2. _____ a. We discussed the <u>debt</u>.   _____ b. We discussed the <u>date</u>.
3. _____ a. I didn't like the <u>test</u>.   _____ b. I didn't like the <u>taste</u>.
4. _____ a. She's approaching the <u>edge</u>.   _____ b. She's approaching the <u>age</u>.
5. _____ a. I'd like <u>less</u> on the tablecloth.   _____ b. I'd like <u>lace</u> on the tablecloth.

q. Contrast u^w (two) and υ (books) and o^w (show) and $\mathrm{\mathfrak{o}}$ (boss)

1. Many languages have only two vowels that are similar to these four English vowels. Listen and repeat the words and phrases for each of the sounds below.

- To say u^w, vowel 9, pull your tongue back and tense it. Let your tongue do most of the work. Your lips will round gently. When speaking English, keep your face relaxed.

Examples Do it Tuesday beautiful music the new moon a cool June a loose shoe

- To say o^w, vowel 11, pull your tongue back and down. Tense it and take the time to make your tongue glide.

Examples my own coat   go on a boat   no smoking   totally broke   wrote a note   remote control

- To say ʊ, vowel 10, relax your tongue a little after saying uʷ and relax your lips even more.

Examples couldn't   shouldn't   wouldn't   took a look   push and pull   a sugar cookie

- To say ɔ, vowel 12, pull your tongue down and back. Tense it slightly, but don't glide. Some native speakers pronounce this short vowel closer to an ɑ.

Examples call   author   because   across the mall   bought some coffee   a small loss

2. Find ʊ and ɔ the vowel chart. Make sure they are colored orange along with the other short vowels.

r. Contrast uʷ (two) and ʊ (books)

Listen carefully because the spelling of these vowel sounds can be confusing. Replay the tape and practice saying the words and sentences. Tense and tighten your tongue and lips for the long uʷ, vowel 9. The lips are much more relaxed for ʊ, vowel 10.

1. look–Luke   Take a <u>look</u>. His name is <u>Luke</u>.
2. cook–kook   He's a good <u>cook</u>. He's a real <u>kook</u>.
3. full–fool   The committee is <u>full</u>. The head of the committee is a <u>fool</u>.
4. could–cooed   I would if I <u>could</u>. The baby gurgled and <u>cooed</u>.
5. pull–pool   <u>Pull</u> the door open. The <u>pool</u> door is open.
6. should–shooed   I <u>should</u> fly. I <u>shooed</u> away the fly.

s. Vowel Practice: The Beatles

1. Listen to the paragraph, underline the focus words, and track the pronunciation until you can speak along with the speaker. Monitor, first for long vowels, then for short vowels.

[1]Ever since the Beatles crossed the Atlantic in the early 1960s America has experienced varying degrees of Beatlemania. [2]The anniversary of their arrival in the United States is still celebrated by devoted followers. [3]Long after John, Paul, Ringo, and George went their separate ways, the Beatles have remained the world's most famous rock group. [4]The country still mourns the tragic death of John Lennon, who was shot in 1980 on the streets of Manhattan near where he lived. [5]Beatles' songs are still requested on the radio and used in films. [6]Old recordings are re-released and sold in record numbers. [7]People are eager to pay cash for original recordings. [8]The Beatles seem to be a permanent part of American popular culture.

2. Write the following symbols in four columns on a separate piece of paper:

   iʸ see   ɪ it   æ fat   ɑ stop

   Now listen to the following words. Write each word under the symbol that matches its stressed vowel.

   AtLANtic, BEAtles, cash, deGREES, EAger, films, FOLlowers, John, lived, oRIGinal, PEOple, POPular, RINgo, re-reLEASED, rock, TRAgic, seem, since, shot, streets, still

 t. Vowel Practice: "Pets Are Big Business"

1. Listen to the paragraph, underline the focus words, and track the pronunciation until you can speak along with the tape. Monitor, first for long vowels, then for short vowels.

   ¹It is estimated that about 60 percent of all U.S. households have an animal as a companion to the family. ²Pet pampering has gone beyond buying manicures, jeweled collars, and hand-knit sweaters for toy poodles. ³Mail-order catalogs, pet hotels, day care, and transportation services are just a beginning. ⁴There are also personal trainers for the home, pet psychiatrists, and an array of specialized food products. ⁵Pet superstores are changing things for customers, retailers, suppliers, and investors. ⁶More than 500 discount giants sell foods, toys, clothes, and furniture for pets at lower prices. ⁷Superstores that provide special services are especially popular. ⁸These may offer bathing and grooming, obedience training, basic health treatment, and in some cases animal adoption. ⁹It is clear that pets are big business.

Index of Topics

Abbreviations, 131, 132
Adverbs, 84
Answering machines, 32–33
Assessment
  speech-effectiveness level, 4
  listening, 5–8
  making a speech tape, 9–11
-*ate* endings, 115–116
Audio program
  Making the most of the text audio program 13, 33
  Making the most of recorded practice, 54

/b/, 155
/b/ and /v/ contrast, 156

Can and *can't*, 104–106
Clear vowels, 108, 114
Compound nouns
  creating consonant clusters, 50
  focus to show contrast in, 91
  intonation for, 46–49, 64
  spelling of, 47
Consonant clusters
  compound nouns creating, 50
  explanation of, 2, 24, 173, 204–205, 206
  practice with, 24–25, A-10–A-11
  across word boundaries, 205–206
Consonant sounds
  in dictionaries, 57
  linking same, 155
  linking -ed to, 175
  practice with, *See* Appendix A, A-1–A-11
  pronunciation of, 2, 147–151
  /v/ and /w/ contrast, 158
  voicing of, 148
Content words *See also* Sentence Stress
  explanation of, 2, 25, 76–77, 80, 96
  stress in, 2, 25, 76, 81, 83–84
Continuants, 148, 155
Contractions, 180
Contrastive stress, *See* Focus, changes in
Conversational speech. *See also* Small talk
  Hesitations and fillers in, 225
  melody in, 124
  reductions in, 216
  showing emotion in, 134
  strategies for improving, 99
  thought groups in, 238
  Conversation Strategies, 99

Descriptive phrases, 62–64
Dictionaries and pronunciation, 56–58

-ed endings, 22, 45, 173–178
-es endings, 184–188

/f/, 155–156, 161
Falling intonation, 25
Final sounds, 2, 20–22, 163
Flap
  explanation of, 152–153, 173
  in common reductions with "t" or "d," 219
  in conversations 220
  when linking -ed to vowel, 175
Focus, changes in, 89–95
  new information-old information, 20, 89, 93–94
  disagreement, 90
  to emphasize agreement, 90
  to show contrast, 90
  to return a question, 90
Focus words
  explanation of, 2, 19, 83, 96
  listening for, 19, 20, 26, 28–29
  in poetry, 176, 209
  in songs, 29–30, 69–70, 136-7, 211, 227
  stress in, 25, 76, 83
  in thought groups, 84, 231, 235

Glides, *see* Steps and Glides
Glossaries, 34
Gum ridge, 147, 149–150

Intonation, *See also* Melody
  in abbreviations, 131
  in compound nouns, 46–49, 64
  connection to speech rhythm, 25
  at end of sentences, 25–27, 45, 135
  explanation of, 2, 16
  falling, 25
  guidelines for, 125
  different messages for, 126
  patterns in longer sentences, 136–139
  to show emotion, 134, 136
  in longer sentences, 136–139
  in stressed syllables, 26
  in *wh*-questions, 127, 129, 130, 135
  in *yes-no* questions, 127, 135

Jaw movements, 17
Journals. *See* Reflection journals

/k/ and /g/, 149

/l/, 164–167
Linking
  when saying addresses, 23–24
  in consonant clusters, 205–207
  in conversational speech, 216
  explanation of, 2, 22–23
  with numbers, 23
  with past tense, 154
  with same consonant sound, 155
Lips, 17, 147, 168
Look-alike words, 38, 40, 115
Lungs, 147, 148

/m/, 162
Melody, *See also* Intonation
  conversation with, 124
  culture and use of, 123
  four pitch levels of English speech, 123–124
Mirroring, 74–75
Mouth movements
  for English, 17
  for long vowels, 110
  for short vowels, 111–112
  for "r" and "l," 164
  using a mirror to see, 17,

/n/, 162, 163
Nasal sounds, 162
Nouns
  compound, 46–47
  plural, 173, 180
  pronunciation of, 200
  stress on two-syllable, 37
Numbers
  linking with, 23
  -teen and -ty and stress, 200

/p/ and /b/, 150
/p/ and /f/ contrast, 157
Past tenses. *Also see* "ed endings" 22, 154, 173, 174
Pauses. *See also* Thought groups
  Listening for, 18–19
  changing the meaning with, 140–142
Phone meetings, 15
Phrasal verbs, 64–67
Phrases, descriptive, 62–64
Phrases for practicing vowels, 108, A-12
Pitch patterns, *See* Intonation; Melody
Plural
  nouns, 173, 180
  "s" and "es" endings, 184–186

Poetry. *See also* Index of Activities, Join the Chorus
  focus words in, 176, 209
  past tenses in, 176
  plurals in, 187
  reductions in, 222
  thought groups in, 18
Possessives, 180, 187
Prefixes, 59
Presentations, hint for, 242
Pronunciation improvement
  assessing your priorities for, 5–11
  Conversation Strategies for, 99
  methods for, 11–14, 32, 34, 54, 98, 142
  plan of action for, 14
  setting goals for, 1–4
  targets for, 1–2
  using a mirror for, 17

Questions
  answering with rising pitch line, 131
  asking for clarification 129, 130
  choice, 94–95
  using focus to respond to, 89, 91,
  using focus to return, 90
  intonation in, 127, 135
  with rising intonation, 129, 130,
  yes-no, 127, 128

/r/, 164–167, 209
Reductions
  chant with, 27–28
  contractions vs., 218
  in conversational speech, 216, 220, 231
  in dialogues, 221
  explanation of, 27, 104, 218, 221
  monitoring for, 103
  schwa vowels and, 102
  structure words and, 102–103
Reflection journals, 14
Rhythm. *See* Speech rhythm

/s/, 160–161
Schwa vowels, *See also* reductions
  in dictionaries, 57
  explanation of, 37–38, 100, 116
  reductions and, 102–104
  -s endings and, 180, 188
  unstressed syllables with, 114
Secondary stress, 57
Self-monitoring, 11
-s endings 180–194
  pronunciation of, 180–183, 186
  schwas and, 180, 188
  sibilants and, 184, 186, 188, 189, 191, 192
Sentences. *See also* Sentence stress.
  intonation at end of, 25–27, 45, 135
  intonation patterns in longer, 136
Sentence stress. *See also* Content words; Structure words; Focus;
  chart for predicting, 80
  levels of, 76–77

Short vowels, 111
Sibilants 173, 184, 186, 188, 189, 191,
Small talk, 11–15, 34. *See also* Conversational speech
Songs *See* Index of Activities, Sing Along; and Focus words.
Sounds *See* Consonant sounds; Final sounds; Speech pathway
Speech
  chunks of, 27
  defining effective, 4
  elements of easy-to-understand, 19
  evaluating your, 4–5
  reductions in, 27 (*See also* Reductions)
Speech pathway
  air flows out of, 155
  explanation and drawing of, 147–148
  stops along, 148, 151, 152
  continuants, 155
Speech rhythm, *See also* Content words; Focus words; Structure words
  in conversational speech, 216
  explanation of, 2, 25, 83
  listening to, 25–26
  in content words, 2, 76, 83, 84
  in structure words, 76, 81
Spelling
  of compound nouns, 47
  tips for vowel, 114
  of sibilants, 191
Steps and glides, 25–26
Stops
  explanation of 148
  final, 151–152, 197
  voiced, 197
  voiceless, 151, 198
Stress, *See* Word Stress; Sentence Stress
Strong stress. *See* Focus words
Structure words. *See also* Unstressed words
  in conversational speech, 216
  end-of-sentence, 84
  importance of saying, 196
  stress in, 76, 81
Suffixes
  "er" and "or," 39
  word patterns with specific, 58–59
Syllabic "n," 207
Syllables
  dropping middle, 57
  rules for stressed and unstressed vowels in 116
  shortening vowels in weak, 100
  stress in words with four, 41–42
  stress in words with three, 41
  stress in words with two, 36–38, 40
  unstressed, 37–38, 57, 114
  using dictionaries to identify stressed, 56–58

/t/, 150, 152
"th," 159–161

Thought groups
  in conversational speech, 239
  explanation of, 2, 18, 136
  focus words in, 84, 231, 235
  listening and identifying, 18–19
  pitch in, 125
  in poetry, 18
  punctuation and, 241
  speaker speed and, 231
Throat, 147–148
Tongue movements. *See* Mouth movements
Tongue twisters, 191
Tracking, 74, 223, 230, 235.

Unclear vowels, 100
Unstressed syllables
  with clear vowels, 114–115
  in dictionaries, 57
  explanation of, 37–38
  suffixes with, 39
  pitch and shortening of, 104
  vowels in, 100
Unstressed words. *See also* Structure words
  at end-of-sentence, 84
  explanation of, 76–77
  listen and fill in the, 81

/uw/, 202

/v/, 155–156, 158
Verbs, 48,
  -ed endings for, 173–175
  ending in -ate, 115–116
  phrasal, 64–66
  -s endings for, 180
Vocal cords, 147–148
Voiced consonants, 149–152, 184–186, 197, 198
Voiceless consonants, 149–152, 184–186, 197, 198,
Voicing,
  explanation of, 148
  and vowel length, 197–199
  grammar, vowel length, and, 200
Vowels, *see also* Appendix B
  clear, 108, 109, 111, 114
  in dictionaries, sounds, 57
  before voiceless, voiced final stops, 152
  + /l/ 167
  length of, before voiced consonants, 197–199
  long, 110, 114
  in numbers, 200
  phrases for practicing, 108, A-12
  + /r/, 166–167
  reduced, 101–103
  rules for stressed and unstressed vowels, 116
  schwa, 100–103
  short, 111–114
  two pronunciations, for /uw/, 202

unclear, 100
unstressed, 100, 116
before voiceless consonants, 197–199
voicing of, 148
words linking two, 202

/w/, 157–158
What's next?, 245
Wh-questions, 84, 127–131
Word Stress
   charts to predict, 80
   in descriptive phrases, 62–64
   explanation of, 2, 35–37
   in compound nouns, 46–49, 64
   in four-syllable words, 41–42
   in look-alike words, 38, 40
   in names, 67–68
   in nouns, 37
   in phrasal verbs, 65, 66
   in prefixes, 59
   in suffixes, 39, 59
   in three-syllable words, 41
   in two-syllable words, 36
   in related words, 60
   secondary, 57
   using dictionaries to learn about, 56–58
Yes-no questions and intonation, 127

Index of Activities

Cartoon
Drabble, 66
Single Slices, 221

Communicative Activity
An answering-machine ad, 239
Compare the pictures, 142
Countries and names, 101–102
Discuss the calendar, 201
Interview, 39, 68–69
Let's talk, 219
Magic Johnson, 193–194
Making appointments, 105
Most widely spoken languages in the world, 170
Mystery person, 167–168
Planning a party, 88
Talk about an idiom, 178
Talk about where you live, 68
Talk about yourself, 139
What's happening today?, 153
Your family tree, 162
Your ideal weekend, 67

Dialogue
"A Great Weekend," 71–72
"Basket on the Bus," 178–179
"Disaster for Roses," 183
"Fix the Roof," 85
"Happy Birthday to my Brother," 162
"The Missing Room," 234
"Needs a Ride," 209
"Noisy Phones," 183
"Not My Bag," 135
"The Optical Shop," 118
"Phone Confusion," 106
"Trip to Paris," 135
"Willpower," 223

Dictation 32, 121, 171, 195, 213, 229

Group Practice
k and g, 149
Breathing for Speech, 148
Common reductions and parts of speech, 217–218
Contrast th and f, 161
Conversation with melody, 124
Dialogue with movement, 44
The Echo Game, 42–44
f and v (locations 7 and 8 on the pathway), 155–156
"A Family Mystery," 208
Final nasal sounds n and m and ng, 162
Finishing numbers and linking, 23
Four more sibilants, 188
t and d, 149
Have fun with tongue twisters, 191
Holding final steps, 151–152
How to say l, 165
How to say r, 164–165
How to say vowel + l, 167
How to say vowel + r, 166–167
Identifying stressed words, 81
Introducing sibilants, 184
k and g, 149
p and b, 150–151
Pronouncing z, 182
Reductions and chunks of speech, 27
Review the flap, 219
t and d, 149
Tap the rhythm, 78
Unstressed syllables and schwa vowels, 37–38
The voiced and the voiceless "th" sounds (location 7 on the pathway), 159
Voicing (location 2 on the pathway), 148
Voicing and vowel length, 197–198
w (locations 6 and 8 on the pathway), 157–158
Walking the rhythm, 82
"Where's Bob?", 78–79
y is *not* a sibilant, 192

Improve Your Monitoring
Confident or hesitant?, 127
"Ed" endings, 177
"es' or "es"?, 184
/E/ (yes) and /æ/ (fat) for vowels 4 and 5, A-15–A-16
/ey/ (say)and /E/ (yes) (Vowels 3 and 4), A-21
f and p, A-1–A-2
Final "s" and grammar, 186–187
Final sounds and grammar, 206
Finished or unfinished?, 126
/iy/ and /I/, A-20
Listening for reductions, 103
Missing "ed," 22
Missing sounds, 21–22
Past or present?, 154, 173
r and l, A-8
r and l clusters, A-10–A-11
r and w, A-8
s and z, 182
Schwa or clear vowel?, 114–115
sh and ch, A-7
Short and long vowels, A-21
Sibilants and spelling, 191
Steps and glides, 26
Structure words, 217
Two-word combinations, 62
Vowel length, 199
w and v, 158
Words and sentences, 45

Join the Chorus
"Get to the Airport Early," 132–133
"It's Missing, It's Gone," 50–51
Limerick, 46, 209
"Pronunciation Rap," 242–243
"Sneezles," 222–223
"S's, Messes," 187
From "Through the Looking Glass," 194
"Timothy Boon," 203–204
Two poems, 85
"The Visitor," 176
Whaddya WANT?, 27–28
"What Did You Say?", 169
"What's Happening?", 86–87
"Wishes," 66

Learn By Listening
Abbreviations, 131
Answering questions with a slightly rising pitch line, 131
"ate" verbs and related words, 116
Beyond the words, 136
Clusters across word boundaries, 205
Compound noun intonation, 46–47
Contrast phrasal verbs and compound nouns, 65
Contrast w and v (voiced), 158
Descriptive phrases, 62
Different messages for intonation, 126
End-of-the-sentence intonation, 25–26
The flap (or tapped "t"), 152
Focus words, 19
Focus words (level 1) and content words (level 2), 77
Four-syllable words, 41–42
Grammar and vowel length, 200
Guidelines for focus words, 83–84
Guidelines for shifting the focus, 89–91
Knock-knock jokes, 106
Linked triple clusters, 206–207
Linking, 154
Linking "ed," 175

INDEX OF ACTIVITIES

Linking the same consonant sound, 155
Linking two vowel sounds, 202
Listen to a teacher talking, 12
Long vowels, 109
Meaningful pauses, 140
More compound words, 48
More emotion, 134
Names and descriptive phrases, 67
Nouns, 37
Overview of American English vowels, 108
"Owl and the Pussy-cat" by Edward Lear, 18
Prefixes and suffixes, 58–59
Public speaker, Dwight D. Eisenhower, 18–19
Reducing structure words, 102–103
Related words, 60
Review "ed" endings, 179–180
Reviewing guidelines for thought groups, 231–232
Rhymes, 79
Short vowels, 111
s or z?, 181
Story with "ed" and "s" endings, 192–193
The syllabic n, 207
Three-syllable words, 41
Two-part sentences, 138
Two pronunciations for uw, 202
Two-syllable words, 36–37, 100–101
Unstress: Structure words (level 3), 77
Unstressed syllables with clear vowels, 114
Vowels and numbers, 200
The weather report, 87
What's the difference between can and can't?, 104
Word pairs, 35–36
Words and phrases, 22–23

Partner Practice
An ad for BASF, 139
An ad for Delta Air Lines, 233
Can and can't, 105
Challenging plurals, 188
Compare clear vowels and reduced vowels, 101
Comparing Dictionaries, 57–58
Compound nouns, 47–48
Compound nouns and descriptive phrases, 63–64
Consonant clusters, 24–25
Contrast b and v, 156
Contrast dzh with sh and ch, 190–191
Contrast sh and ch 190
Contrast /p/ and /f, /157
Contrast /r/ and l,/ 166
Contrast "th" and /f,/ 161
Contrast "th" and/ s,/ 160–161
Contrast "th" and/ t,/ 159
Contrast the basic pattern with changes in focus, 93
Conversations at the office, 134–135
Conversation with names, 67
Dialogues with wh- questions, 129
Dictating information, 23–24
End-of-the sentence intonation, 128-129
Figure out the idioms, 168
Finish the descriptive phrases, 63
Finish the link, 20–21
Finish the sentences, 108
The flap, 220
Focus words, 85
Giving a choice, 94–95
How many syllables?, 107
Idioms, 177–178
Linked clusters, 205
Linking, 23
Look-alikes, 38, 115
Match the rhythm, 80
More about pauses, 140–141
More to say, 137–138
New information - old information, 20
Past and present, 175
Phrasal verbs and compound nouns, 65
Predict and pronounce "look-alikes," 40
Predict the stress, 60
Reduced phrases, 216–217
Rising and falling wh- questions, 130
Scrambled proverbs, 118
Scrambled sentences, 232
Short conversations, 48–49, 91–92
Short conversations with final "m", "n," and "ng," 163
Short dialogues with /y,/ 192
Small talk plan, 12
Structure words, 81
Two dialogues, 28–29, 94
Two-part sentences, 138
Two short conversations, 220
"ty" and "teen," 201
Using abbreviations, 132
Voiced and voiceless sibilants, 185–186
Voicing and vowel length, 198
Vowels 7 and 8, 113
"What am I?", 39

Public Service Announcements
Alison Krauss, country musician, 225–226
Identity Theft, 237
Media Awareness Network, 181
Nature Conservancy, Paul Newman, 224
Richard Marx, rock musician, 240
Teenagers and Money, 238
Travis Tritt, country musician, 225
Trees for America, 236
Water Education Foundation, 224, 239–240,
@ Your Library, Susan Sarandon, Tim Robbins, 236

Role Play, See also Talk Times in Class
"Ordering from Ron's Barbecue," 210
Tuesday night at the planetarium, 61
TV weather reporter, 88
Two invitations, 226
Visitor with a shopping list, 49–50

Sing Along
"Getting to Know You," 29–30
"Home on the Range," 136
"Leaving on a Jet Plane," 227
"Oh! What a Beautiful Mornin'," 211
"This Land Is Your Land," 69–70

Story
Binti, the Heroine, 179
"Breakfast Conversation," 117
"A Creative Idea," 203
Jesse Owens, 192–193

Talk
Getting to know your partner, 31
In my opinion, 143
A proverb and a personal experience, 120
"A Special Celebration," 241
You're the expert, 95–96

Talk Times
Buying music, 144
Calling about moving, 121
Choosing a health club, 74
Choosing a restaurant, 98
Inquiring about hotels, 214
The message machine. 33
Planning a trip,   172
Renting a car, 230,
Renting a video, 196
Shopping at a store, 54
Shopping by Phone, 244

Talk Times in Class
Buying music, Discussion 144
Calling about moving, Role play, 121
Choosing a health club, Role play, 73
Choosing a restaurant, Role play, 97
Inquiring about hotels, Role play, 214
The message machine. Write a message, 32–33
Planning a trip, Role play, 171
Renting a car, Role play, 229–230,
Renting a video, Discussion, 195
Shopping at a store, Role play, 53
Shopping by Phone, Sample conversation, 243–244